d 17-80

Power, Efficiency and Institutions

Power, Efficiency and Institutions

A critical appraisal of the 'markets and hierarchies' paradigm

Edited by
Arthur Francis, Jeremy Turk and
Paul Willman

 HEINEMANN EDUCATIONAL BOOKS · LONDON

Heinemann Educational Books Ltd
22 Bedford Square
London WC1B 3HH

LONDON   EDINBURGH   MELBOURNE   AUCKLAND
HONG KONG   SINGAPORE   KUALA LUMPUR   NEW DELHI
IBADAN   NAIROBI   JOHANNESBURG
EXETER (NH)   KINGSTON   PORT OF SPAIN

British Library Cataloguing in Publication Data

Power, efficiency and institutions.
   1. Industrial organization
   2. Industrial sociology
   I. Francis, Arthur   II. Turk, Jeremy
   III. Willman, Paul
   306.36   HD6955

ISBN 0-435-82315-9

Acknowledgements

The conference on Markets and Hierarchies at which these papers were presented was held in December 1980 at Imperial College, London. It was sponsored by the European Group for Organisational Studies, with financial assistance from the Social Science Research Council. We would like to express our appreciation for this support and its contribution to the present work. In preparing the papers for press we received valuable secretarial assistance from Angela Hallett, Patricia Burge and Joan Wright. The bibliography was prepared by Brian Price.

Arthur Francis
Jeremy Turk
Paul Willman

Typeset by Inforum Ltd, Portsmouth
Printed and bound in Great Britain by
Biddles Ltd, Guildford and King's Lynn

Contents

List of Contributors

Michael Bauer, Centre de Sociologie de l'Innovation, Ecole des Mines de Paris, France

Asger Braendgaard, Institute of Production, University of Alborg, Denmark

Richard Butler, Management Centre, University of Bradford, UK

Elie Cohen, Centre de Sociologie de l'Innovation, Ecole des Mines de Paris, France

Herman Daems, Institut Européen de Recherches et d'Etudes Supérieures en Management, Brussels, Belgium

Arthur Francis, Department of Social and Economic Studies, Imperial College, London, UK

Tony McGuinness, Department of Economics, University of Sheffield, UK

William G. Ouchi, Graduate School of Management, University of California, Los Angeles, USA

Otto H. Poensgen, Department of Economics, Universität des Saarlandes, Federal Republic of Germany

Jeremy Turk, Department of Social and Economic Studies, Imperial College, London, UK

Oliver Williamson, Department of Economics, University of Pennsylvania, USA

Paul Willman, Department of Social and Economic Studies, Imperial College, London, UK

Introduction

Once again economists are invading the territory of those who work in other theoretical traditions. The 'economic theory of democracy' (Downs 1957; Buchanan and Tullock 1962) and the 'economic approach to human behaviour' (Becker 1976) have already shown the remarkable – but always controversial – ability of the model of Man as an individual maximiser to penetrate the rationale and results of human conduct, and extend the domain of economics by providing temptingly logical pointers to the resolution of problems previously thought about in much less formal terms.

On this occasion, it is the economic institution of the firm which is under scrutiny, and industrial sociology and organisation theory which are the questioned approaches. The institutional economics of Oliver Williamson is the catalyst (Williamson 1975; 1979b; Chapter 2 of this book). It provides an explanation in broadly neoclassical terms for the size, shape and texture of the firm and its associated labour 'market'. Previously, most economists had been scarcely interested in the firm as an institution, and were content to think of it as a 'point decision-maker' or a 'black box', leaving its internal structure to be examined by sociologists and organisational theorists without direct encounter with economic theory. It was interest in the ramifications of Williamson's explanation of the differential comparative advantages of markets and hierarchies as forms of economic organisation which drew about fifty academic economists, sociologists and organisation and industrial relations theorists together at Imperial College, London, in January 1980, under the aegis of the European Group for Organisational Studies (EGOS), to develop and assess the implications of the 'markets and hierarchies world view' for their own specialisms. The outcome was lively discussion and criticism of Williamson's most fundamental ideas, as well as their extension to further areas of institutional study. Perhaps there was an accent on criticism, but this was as it should have been, since Williamson's work represents a very serious challenge to a great deal of the theoretical analysis and empirical investigation which has become the core of institutional study. The tendency of economics to engulf less hardy disciplines can be a very strong one. Nine of the papers presented at the Conference are reproduced, sometimes in a considerably revised form, in this volume, which aims to examine, in both a critical and a constructive way, the prospects for the Markets and Hierarchies Research Programme which is outlined by Williamson and Ouchi in the first contribution.

Economists, when dealing with the individual firm or organisation, have most often been interested in production; that is, outputs in relation to inputs, normally taken to be the result of the technology and proportion of factors of production used. This has left a large area of the organisation of the firm to other disciplines, which have been free to fill in the gaps according to their own traditions. Of course, the economist has always assumed that the firm is efficient, and regarded these other disciplines as specifying the features of economic organisations which lie behind, or are related to, the conditions of productive efficiency, whether this involves human relations, motivational analysis, authority hierarchies, or whatever. But there is so much which appears un-explained to economists who take this uncompromising view. The physical continuity of production is no problem, since it is fairly clear that this is dictated by the cost conditions of the best practice tech-nology as, for example, in the case of the integrated steel mill. However, the continuity of the social organisation of production is altogether more mysterious. There is nothing contained within the production-based model itself, nor in the assumptions explicitly made in setting up the model, to show why a steel mill should be under common ownership, or why the workforce which turned up today should be substantially the same people who turned up yesterday. Two extra factors are needed to make economic sense of the firm as a social institution, a consideration of skill and a recognition of the non-pro-duction aspects of the organisation of the firm. The 'human capital' interpretation of skill initiated by Gary Becker (1964) is a natural adjunct to the Williamson model, and has been incorporated with the transaction costs explanation of the social and economic organisation of the firm which was being examined at the EGOS Conference.

The key to an analysis of the firm as an economic institution is to be found in allowing the relationships within it to be more than a merely technically efficient means towards production by recognising the reflection of a broader context of economic behaviour in its contractual structure. It is in this way that Williamson has formulated a convincing explanation of the existence and structure of the firm and its internal labour 'market' which remains typically economic in its concentration on individual rational behaviour in the face of well-defined costs. But his approach is still novel and interesting to all economists because it uses a fairly sophisticated concept of rationality – bounded rationality (Simon 1957); a new assumption about behaviour – opportunism; and concentrates on the role of uncertainty in creating previously unrecog-nised transaction costs. Williamson has been able both to work out an intrinsically interesting treatment of the 'human factors' in institutional design and to use the modified rationality which this yields to overcome the difficulty in explaining the existence of economic institutions. In several further articles, he has argued that this kind of analysis is not only essential for the study of institutions themselves, but cannot be ignored in tackling some problems for which the 'black box' view of the firm was once thought to be all that was necessary (Wachter and Williamson 1978; Williamson 1979b). To economists, Williamson's work is both in the mainstream and in many respects radical: it opens up an area of the subject previously neglected in a way which poses little threat to fundamental economic concepts such as real resource costs, efficiency and competition – indeed, it is founded upon them.

In order to uncover those costs which are of crucial importance in explaining the character of economic institutions, Williamson draws upon one of the most prominent of the old school of American institutional economists, John R. Commons. Commons argued that the transaction is the basic unit of economic activity, and that it is not just a physical exchange of goods or services. It involves a change of ownership, and hence a social relationship between the people who are parties to it (Commons 1934, 1950). Commons, in building on this foundation a proper description of the role of 'custom and practice' in economic life, was on the whole little impressed by the abstractions of law-finding, and evolved a pragmatic theory which concentrated on an essentially idiographic analysis of the firm as a 'going concern'. Williamson's approach has developed on very different lines.

Williamson sees the socio-legal aspects of the transaction as the source of a special and previously neglected kind of *cost*. First, the assumption of 'Opportunist Economic Man', who may act strategically and with guile, gives rise to potential costs resulting from the enforcement (or breach) of agreements and contracts. Secondly, the existence of specific (especially human) capital investments gives rise to exchange relationships in which the individual identity of the participants matters, and in which each is committed to some form of continuity for that relationship. It is under these circumstances (called by Williamson 'idiosyncratic exchange') that the market is unable to neutralise opportunism because there cannot exist the large number of bidders necessary to render any attempts at strategic behaviour unimportant. Thirdly, the limited calculative and linguistic capacities of the human mind mean that only a restricted number of options can ever be considered so that complex problems can never be solved and implemented by preparing a completely specified set of contracts in advance. The possibility that different forms of economic organisation may be associated with different 'contractual' or 'transactions' costs is clearly an important one. The problem of economic organisation, and by the same token that of the existence of economic institutions, is then one of cost minimisation. The two paradigmatic forms of economic organisation are 'impersonal' control by means of the market, and hierarchical 'authority relations' in firms and internal labour 'markets'. The different cost structures of these two institutions under different transactional conditions are the essential features required to explain why markets and hierarchies dominate distinct regions of the matrix of economic transactions. Transactions costs are the pivotal element in determining when hierarchies will supersede markets on efficiency grounds. Such organisational hierarchies are assimilated into broader markets for products and factors which are competitive in the long run and, therefore, serve to enforce, by the normal process of economic selection, the criteria for organisational efficiency which minimum real resource costs dictate.

Renewed interest, amongst economists, in the 'internal' working of the firm, and its concentration on rational cost-minimising solutions to old problems of economic organisation defined in new ways, could hardly fail to have had a perceptible effect on disciplines that have had considerable freedom to colonise those areas of study formerly left beyond the domain of economics. On the one hand, the markets and hierarchies approach has brought a new awareness of the economic constraints within which all organisations must perforce operate, and on the other, the level of detail of Williamson's economics is sufficient to challenge many concrete components of non-economic organisation theory.

Organisational theory, as a discipline, has hitherto tended to regard the object of its study as given, both in terms of the limits of the individual institution and in terms of the economic relationships operating within that institution. So it is not surprising that the work of Williamson is interesting as a possible stimulus to the extension of the scope of organisational studies. But, more importantly, the Williamson approach tends to shrink the domain open to some typically 'organisation behaviour' types of explanation, namely those which derive from the Weberian model of institutional rationality and give little weight to environmental influences. Like most economic theory, the new institutional economics postulates competitive processes which somewhat alarmingly limit the freedom of action of individual participants and hence the feasible set of institutions. On the other hand, it offers the opportunity to study the evolution of a population of firms in a particular environment not only in terms of the characteristics of successful individual organisations, but also in terms of the extent to which hierarchical organisations as an institutional form have survival capability. As an economist, Williamson naturally started from the assumption that 'in the beginning there were markets' (Williamson

1975, p. 20), whereas specialists in organisational theory have equally understandably taken the existence of hierarchies as given. Consequently, the Markets and Hierarchies Research Programme, which takes the existence as well as the form of an organisation as 'resource dependent', implies a challenge to some of the detailed work of the 'resource dependency school' in organisational theory, but certainly not to its spirit (Aldrich 1979). The new institutional economics is a serious threat to some methods of organisation analysis, but is at the same time a means of setting the subject in a complete and rigorous economic context.

The position of industrial relations is somewhat different. As a problem based study, industrial relations gains life from its concern with the detail of industrial structure and behavior, and is less concerned with general theory. The concentration of the markets and hierarchies approach on contractual relations has an especial appeal. Its conflict with industrial relations lies primarily in the difficulty that what industrial relations practitioners see as important independent elements, Williamson sees as heavily constrained, especially where conflicts between the various participants in the economic game are concerned. Social theorists are even more alive to this particular difference in orientation. They frequently respond by arguing that the assumptions and simplifications which Williamson makes in introducing the 'human factors' are based on a far too selective sample of sociological writing, and are unsustainable, usually amounting to an elision of just those issues which the sociologist sees as his central concern.

In discussing the contribution of the markets and hierarchies paradigm to work in their own specialisms, industrial sociologists and organisational behaviour theorists often link the writings of Williamson with those of Albert Hirschman (1970). While Williamson is primarily concerned with the structures that result from transaction costs, Hirschman concentrates on the processes that operate within these structures – the mechanisms by which efficiency is achieved rather than the conditions for the achievement of efficiency. In his book *Exit, Voice and Loyalty*, Hirschman argues that there are, in general, two mechanisms through which institutions may respond to declines in efficiency: voice – the expression of protest and the desire for change from within the institution; and exit – the withdrawal from association with that institution (either as a purchaser of its product or as a supplier of a factor of production) in the traditional economic manner. Exit is the process most closely associated with the market, while voice is more frequently asserted within an organisational hierarchy. This is not the place to debate in any detail the Hirschman thesis, but just to note that it attempts to deal with problems of institutional efficiency by the definition of processes that are congruent with Williamson's treatment of the structural issues (Williamson *et al.* 1976c).

How far have the ideas of Williamson been embraced by those working in other disciplines which have received a cold shower of economic formalism? Some more economically-minded organisational theorists seem ready to accept the new institutional economics as a useful tool for the reworking of old problems. The more general reaction – at least as far as it was represented by the participants at the Conference – is to argue that the simplifications made by Williamson are to a degree inadmissible, and then to consider to what extent they can be ignored, modified or limited in their reach. Few are wholly negative.

At this point, it is perhaps worth drawing out from the economic analysis of the markets and hierarchies paradigm those aspects that are most novel to economists and that are having most influence outside the discipline. Firstly, Williamson has extended the idea of economic exchange to encompass the transaction, a concept which includes both the material and the contractual aspects of the exchange. His conception of the transaction does not, however, go as far as the generalised concept of social exchange, and could not, because of his material conception of efficiency. Secondly, Williamson utilises an idea of rationality which is bounded by Man's limitations of calculation and language. But it is still an instrumental conception of rationality. Thirdly, Williamson extends the model of Economic Man to the model of Opportunistic Economic Man. But it is a model of Man which does not include any aspects of altruism or commitment (nor, indeed, downright malevolence or dishonesty). Fourthly, Williamson postulates that a relevant class of transaction costs arises from uncertainties about interpersonal behaviour. These costs are well-defined real resource costs despite the fact that they arise from strategic considerations in complex economic games. The concept of 'atmosphere' is introduced to cover less-easily specified, but still essentially cost-based, differences between firms. Fifthly, power in the Williamson model is diffused, as would be expected in any fundamentally competitive model, and is most important at the micro level, where 'information impactedness' and idiosyncratic investments give rise to elements of monopoly. Sixthly, competition in markets which approach perfection in the long run places the pressure on institutions: this ensures that the need for efficiency dominates any sectional interests that may lie below the surface.

From these aspects of the economic debate arise the major themes of the interdisciplinary debate. Taken together, they help us to understand the sense in which Williamson can claim that he is concerned only with the relatively value-neutral issue of economic efficiency, and that such efficiency concepts must, in the long run, prove superior in explanatory power. In particular, he believes that the approach to economic organisation through the requirements of economic efficiency will be more likely to bear fruit than that through the idea of power, which Williamson thinks is far less easy to pin down in 'operational' terms. Power reflects or expresses, rather than moulds, economic forces.

The debate over the relative attractiveness of efficiency and power as the fundamental concepts in economic organisation dominated the discussions at the Conference. It recurs constantly in the chapters that follow. It is an expression of the divergence in 'world view' between the majority of economists and the majority of sociologists, the former arguing that it is efficiency which provides all the predictive possibilities, and the latter that the economists' concept of efficiency masks structures of power and normative preconceptions which they are almost wilfully reluctant to recognise. But other important debates also polarised opinion. The formalist/substantivist controversy in economic anthropology (Sahlins 1972) occasionally broke the surface; participants differed over whether real resource costs are in some way irreducibly given, or whether all costs are negotiable. Whether markets and hierarchies are the only equilibrium institutional forms, or whether other institutions such as communes and co-operatives can be justified as efficient economic institutions is explored in several of the papers that follow. And, of course, the dialogue between 'liberal' and 'radical' philosophies arose at every turn.

The contributions to the debate represented in the subsequent chapters touch on all these problems.

Part I is reserved for the exposition of the Markets and Hierarchies Research Programme offered as the keynote for the Conference by Williamson and Ouchi. Williamson and Ouchi identify the crucial features of the markets and hierarchies model. They argue that its theoretical constructs can be made operational in terms of significantly differing transaction costs in three principle dimensions – frequency, uncertainty, and transaction-specific investments – and potential organisational arrangements which show distinct comparative advantages in relation to these costs. Williamson and Ouchi make their position in the efficiency/power debate very clear. They believe that in the long run, say ten years or so, competition in both factor and product markets will ensure that efficiency considerations dominate. Power phenomena within firms are largely transient, and represent the working out of competitive forces towards internal efficiency: in other words, a capability for efficiency confers power, where power is observed, primarily in the internecine struggles of the firms' managers. It is perhaps worth pointing out that two important issues in subsequent papers are not explicitly discussed here: the strategic use of power to achieve efficiency at the expense of the workforce (presumably on the grounds that competition in the factor markets will make this impossible to any great degree) and the characteristics of the efficient set of entrepreneurs (since there is no discussion of the rules of competition 'agreed' implicitly by society). Taken as a whole, the transactions costs theory of economic institutions is considered to be worthy of systematic further development, and an agenda of urgent problems is put forward.

Part II is devoted to papers about applications of the markets and hierarchies approach, and which thus form part of the Research Programme. Daems develops the Williamson thesis by postulating a threefold division of industrial organisation: 'market', 'federated', and 'hierarchy'. Federations are more or less loose combinations of firms which allow the internalisation of externalities. Daems is thus clearly on the side of those who see a wide range of possible institutional forms. Market constraints in conjunction with cost minimising responses, both to problems of information exchange and to the enforcement of compliance, are the principal determinants of a particular selection from that range.

In Chapter 3, Poensgen examines in considerable detail the spectrum of economic organisation in West Germany, and considers the thesis that the major force stimulating the achievement of a cost-minimising structure of industry has been the discipline of competition, which has become increasingly strict in recent years. But Poensgen differs from Daems in believing that this increase in competition has tended to polarise institutional structure, with movements being towards either traditional markets populated by simple firms or towards fully articulated complex hierarchies – in his terms, the centre cannot hold.

Part III comprises three conceptual critiques of the work of Williamson (and also to a lesser degee of Hirschman) on general sociological grounds. Bauer and Cohen present the Research Programme with a challenge on the most fundamental level. They argue that it is based on just another variety of liberal, structural-functionalist, equilibrium social theory, and so suffers from all the well-rehearsed defects of such theorising: it thus diminishes the introduction of social relations into the analysis of the economic organisation. Bauer and Cohen then argue for the abandonment of the competitive model and its replacement by a framework that can handle much richer conceptions of power and domination than Williamson's austere and self-regulating model will allow. They thus go outside his belief that in the long run the forces of competition will reduce the scope of economic institutions to a very restricted feasible set, and hold that such phenomena as vertical integration and internal labour markets arise not so much from economising on transactions costs as from an active manipulation of institutional 'atmosphere' and form in directions that facilitate dominance: the initial distribution of resources is crucial in determining which directions these tendencies will take.

Francis, like Bauer and Cohen, argues that hierarchy is chosen as a preferred method of organisation not necessarily because it is more efficient, but because it allows one party to dominate, override or suppress the interests of others. He claims that monopoly and asymmetrical market power relations are much more important than allegedly neutral considerations of efficiency in understanding the emergence of the factory system and the development of vertical integration (Marglin 1975; Chandler 1977). Clearly, one of the most interesting theoretical issues is the relationship between dominance and monopoly, whether of markets or of information. Following Weber, Francis remarks that dominance can arise either from monopoly or from authority. The empirical arguments that Francis has examined tend to favour dominance by monopoly, but authority can enforce the implementation of asymmetrical bargains which he sees as being so influential in the development of hierarchical organisations. In this case, the economist cannot handle the problem entirely by himself and must be prepared to accept a sociological analysis of legitimation. The implication is that systems interests should not be assumed, but that the issue should be fully argued out from individual and group interest conflicts and resources.

Lastly, in this section, a rather more sympathetic paper by Willman seeks to uncover the sociological assumptions inherent in Williamson's treatment of economic relationships within organisations, especially in the case of the employment relationship. Willman contends that although in theory opportunism and bounded rationality are universal human characteristics, in practice Williamson assumes that it is workers alone who are liable to opportunism, an opportunism which must be controlled by managers subject to bounded rationality. Many of the normative issues are thereby obscured. Similarly, the content of 'atmosphere' is vague, and the idea behind it is more usefully developed by Alan Fox's analysis of trust (Fox 1974). Willman exploits the latent symmetry of these concepts to argue that Marglin's well-known article (Marglin 1975) describes a case in which workers are the system agents and capitalists the opportunists. Is there really any competitive process which allows Williamson to argue that it is impossible for capitalists to maintain an exploitive advantage in the long run? In short, opportunism and atmosphere are neologisms which obscure the sociological content of the Williamson model and suppress its normative implications.

The essays in Part IV seek to make conceptual extensions to the markets and hierarchies framework. In doing so, they highlight critical points already made, raise new problems, and make clearer the eventual limits of the range of the approach. Butler argues that the two standard economic forms of market and hierarchy should be supplemented by a further form, the commune. Each form of organisation has its own associated model of Man – bureaucratically calculative and rule-following in the hierarchy, selfish and narrowly materialist in the market, and altruistic and committed in the commune. Each has its own particular form of social control to limit recalcitrance, which has efficiency implications as well as intrinsic qualities. Communes are needed to control transactions when vagueness as to the aims of the institution is added to the problems of uncertainty and interdependence. It is then necessary to nurture gregariousness and caring commitment in order that the institution may survive to fulfil its original purpose. The implications of 'efficiency' are, therefore, capable of a generalisation which allows for a considerably wider range of institutional forms.

In the next paper, Braendgaard considers two issues neglected by Williamson, exploitation and international competition. The very conditions – micro-bilateral monopolies – which give rise to transaction costs in the Williamson model are also those which are most liable to give rise to exploitation within the firm. Who gains from exploitive strategies will depend primarily on the possibilities for exit. As well as exploitation within the firm, Braendgaard considers exploitation at the international level, by arguing that, now that business is internationally mobile, increased opportunities for exit from unfavourable labour markets are available to the firm. (This arises implicitly in Braendgaard's argument from a contention that originates at least with J.S. Mill; namely, that the rules of competition are set by the morally least reputable participant.) Braendgaard's paper is particularly useful in making clear the importance of mobility in determining the incidence and degree of manipulation of transaction costs, and the importance of the rules of the market place in defining the practical meaning of efficiency.

With the paper by McGuinness, we return to the concerns of economists, but concerns informed by the realisation that the normative implications of Williamson's positive analysis, even within the confines of a broadly competitive capitalist society, are far less simple than would appear at first sight. McGuinness argues that Williamson's thesis is based on a far too narrow conception of competition and efficiency. He prefers to concentrate on a wider conception of efficiency, one not associated merely with material costs and rewards, which he calls 'psychic efficiency'. This is related to, though not identical with, Williamson's poorly-articulated idea of atmosphere.

Institutions may be merely 'materially efficient' or 'psychically efficient', the difference being essentially in the distribution of non-monetary advantages. McGuinness contends that this opens up new possibilities for the consideration of distributional issues within the firm by examining whether organisational changes always lead to both improvements in 'material efficiency' and in Pareto improvements for the workforce when 'psychic efficiency' is taken into account. McGuinness believes that they need not, but in a sense his extension merely shifts the analysis of the competitive enforcement of efficiency from the product market to the labour market, since 'psychic efficiency' can always be made compatible with 'material efficiency' when we can be sure that a firm's employees can freely trade material reward for psychic gains. In markets where some participants are interested only in material gains, only firms which are 'materially efficient' and 'psychically efficient' can survive. But can a capitalist economy supply a wide enough variety of economic institutions to satisfy everybody's tastes for 'atmosphere' and at the same time supply everyone's subsistance material needs? McGuinness's paper raises extremely important questions about whose plans lie behind organisational changes: are organisations as they are because of efficiency considerations or for distributional reasons, even if one accepts the liberal's disposition to take the structure of an institution largely at its face value?

Despite the criticisms levelled by many writers of papers in this volume, the Research Programme outlined by Williamson and Ouchi is likely to flourish: and, indeed, many of the issues raised in these papers point towards a broadening of the Programme beyond the range that most economists working in this area have so far explored.

We cannot pretend that the Conference reached any kind of consensus view on the controversies that form the main themes of the papers and discussions. Perhaps sociologists discovered even more clearly the power of economic processes to prove determining and to restrict drastically individual and group freedom. Perhaps economists became more aware of the normative assumptions and preconceptions that underly their modelling. But there has been no resolution of the power/efficiency debate. Williamson's model, in making central use of idiosyncratic exchange, is exceptionally useful in pinpointing the sources of power in a microeconomic context, but is less adept at handling the wider issues of the structural sources of power: to all intents and purposes it assumes from the start that power shows a tendency to be widely diffused. And not all aspects of power can be captured in elements of monopoly.

If Williamson's belief that his conception of efficiency is relatively value-neutral is unlikely to be widely accepted outside the economics profession, then his positive arguments that, in a broadly competitive capitalism, efficiency will be an explanatory concept of very consider-able predictive ability, might usefully be given more credence in industrial sociology, industrial relations and organisation theory. There are important ways in which the range of economic explanation can effectively restrict the feasible set of institutions, even in dimensions that are not ostensibly economic. And this may well be the more true where wages are insufficiently sensitive to non-monetary advantages and disadvantages.

On the other hand, application of Williamson's transactional economics to organisational theory has stimulated a critique which is essentially sociological. In so far as this critique has successfully countered some of Williamson's claims for the dominance of economic efficiency, the economic analysis of institutions in general cannot remain unmodified. Chapter 10 takes up the contradistinction between 'power' and 'efficiency', as a touchstone of the differences between the two disciplines and considers the 'third side' as the triangular debate among sociologists, organisation theorists and economists, in an attempt to define more closely the relationship between economic and sociological concepts. It attempts to argue that the 'power versus efficiency' debate cannot be resolved within economics, partly because of the often ignored complexity of the idea of economic efficiency, and partly because the notion of 'economic power' does not encompass the full range of the sociologists' concern with power. Economic and sociological approaches to institutions must therefore coexist. The paper then seeks to delineate the domains of economic and sociological explanation, concluding that the sociological critique of Williamson's work in organisation theory reveals that differences in the treatment of 'preferences' and 'rationality' are at least two ways in which fundamental divergences exist, and which may lead to disputes about which method of analysis is appropriate to any particular problem. The lesson for economists is not only that the subject should be less ambitious in its annexation of other discipline's traditional territory, but also that some aspects of the core of economics itself need re-assessment.

Williamson has made a number of very civilising innovations in economic theory, even if they may not go far enough to satisfy those outside the discipline. A small degree of convergence may be discernible, but the debate clearly has a good deal of life left in it yet. The economists' territorial gains may in the end prove to have been no more than indefensible bridgeheads.

1 The Markets and Hierarchies Programme of Research: origins, implications, prospects*
O.E. Williamson and W.G. Ouchi

Although organisation theory has its origins in sociology and is principally identified with that field, the subject matter is inter-disciplinary to an unusual degree, and is incompletely informed by exclusive reliance on any single social science. We contend that organisation theory is seriously underdeveloped with respect to its economic content, and argue that it needs greater appeal to economics, though economics of a non-traditional kind. Specifically, we suggest that organisation theory in general and organisational design and assessment in particular need to be more sensitive to transaction costs and to the importance of economising on those.

But economics and organisation theory have a reciprocal relation (Ouchi and Van de Ven 1980). Economics stands to benefit by drawing upon organisation theory. This applies both to the refurbishing of its behavioural assumptions, which tend to be stark and sometimes implausible, and to the level of analysis, which in economics tends to be rather aggregative. The Markets and Hierarchies (M & H) programme of research is based precisely on such a strategy. Thus it draws on organisation theory to enrich its behavioural assumptions, and it regards the transaction, rather than the firm or market, as the basic unit of analysis.[1] Joining these behavioural assumptions and microanalytic focus with the economising concepts and systems orientation characteristic of economics yields new and deeper insights into economic and social organisation. This chapter reviews the origins and applications of the Markets and Hierarchies approach with special emphasis on its organisation theory aspects. It develops the ramifications for organisational design, and addresses research agenda issues of special interest to organisation theory specialists.

Origins
It is rarely possible to do justice to earlier work on which subsequent

* Reprinted, by permission, from Perspectives on Organisation Design and Behaviour, ed. by Andrew Van de Ven and William Joyce. Copyright © 1981 by John Wiley & Sons, Inc.

research relies; nevertheless the following brief statement indicates the origins and background of our research.

Where to begin is somewhat arbitrary, but one decisive contribution to the evolution of the M & H approach was the interdisciplinary programme of research and teaching at Carnegie Tech (now Carnegie-Mellon) in the early 1960s. The central figures at Carnegie were Richard Cyert, James March, and Herbert Simon. Williamson was a student in the economics programme at Carnegie during this period and was greatly influenced by the prevailing interdisciplinary research atmosphere. The strategy of using organisation theory to inform economics in the study of firm and market structures is evident in his work on managerial discretion and in other early papers (see Williamson 1964, 1965, 1967).

It was not until later that the possibility of accomplishing a genuine synthesis between economics[2] and organisation theory became evident. Two papers were of special significance. The first of these was 'The Vertical Integration of Production: Market Failure Considerations' (Williamson 1971), which was an effort to assess the question of make-or-buy in a fully symmetrical way. Ronald Coase, in a remarkably insightful paper, had posed this issue in 1937 and recognised that transaction costs were central to its resolution. Coase observed that vertical integration permitted the firm to economise on the 'cost of negotiating and concluding' many separate intermediate product market contracts by substituting a flexible employment agreement (Coase 1952, p. 336). But because the factors that were responsible for differential transaction costs in the intermediate product market were not identified, the argument lacked testable implications. Why not use a flexible employment agreement to organise all transactions rather than just some? Until such time as the transaction cost argument was able to explain the organisation of transactions in a discriminating way, it remained rather tautological (Alchian and Demsetz 1972). Coase's observation, some thirty-five years later, that his 1937 article was 'much cited and little used' (Coase 1972) is presumably explained by the failure to make the issues operational over that interval.

If, as Coase asserted, differential transaction costs were responsible for decisions to organise some activities one way and some another, a level of analysis that was sensitive to transaction cost differences was evidently needed. Williamson accomplished this by (i) making the transaction the basic unit of analysis, (ii) expressly identifying alternative market and internal modes of 'contracting', (iii) identifying the critical dimensions with respect to which transactions differed, (iv) tracing out the transaction cost ramifications, and (v) matching modes of transactions in a discriminating way. Once the vertical integration problem had been made operational in this way, a variety of related

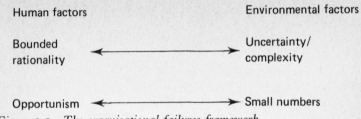

Figure 1.1   The organisational failures framework

applications followed. In this sense, the puzzle of vertical integration was a paradigm problem that, once solved, provided a research strategy that could be repeated. Any problem that could be posed, directly or indirectly, as a contracting problem could be assessed in terms of the identical conceptual apparatus.

These paradigm features were not entirely evident, however, until the paper 'Markets and Hierarchies: Some Elementary Considerations' took shape (Williamson 1973). This paper had its origins in a class discussion of market failures, with special emphasis on Arrow's classic statement of the problem (Arrow 1969). For each type of market failure that was identified (public goods problem, appropriability problem, information asymmetry, small numbers exchange, etc.), the object was to move the explanation for the condition back to a statement of primitives. The same basic human and environmental conditions that arose in assessing vertical integration kept reappearing. *Bounded rationality* and *opportunism* were the recurring human factors. The environmental factors were *uncertainty-complexity* and *small numbers exchange*. The patterned way in which these human and environmental factors were paired is shown in Figure 1.1.

Conceptual Framework
The rudiments of the conceptual framework upon which the Markets and Hierarchies programme of research relies have now been identified. What follows is an elaboration on these.

Behavioural assumptions
Bounded rationality and *opportunism* are the key behavioural assumptions. These assumptions about the characteristics of human actors are joined with the assertion that viable modes of organisation (market, quasi market, or internal) are ones that serve to *economise* on transaction costs. While organisation theory specialists relate easily to the concept of bounded rationality, many economists resist it. By contrast, economising is a much more congenial notion to economists than it is to organisation theorists. Opportunism is a concept of which both are wary.

Arrow has characterised an economist as one who 'by training thinks of himself as the guardian of rationality, the ascriber of rationality to others, and the prescriber of rationality to the social world' (Arrow 1974, p. 16). Given this commitment, any assumption that appears to be at variance with rationality is apt to be dismissed out of hand. If it is not rational, it must be non-rational or irrational, and these are matters for other social sciences to grapple with.

As Herbert Simon has pointed out, however, economists exaggerate the extent to which non-rationality is emphasised by other social sciences. Although economists are the only social scientists who invoke hyperrationality assumptions, rationality is nevertheless a common theme throughout all of the social sciences (Simon 1978, p. 2–4). The issue thus is not whether human agents are rational or not. Rather the question is whether the assumption of hyperrationality is needed or if weaker rationality assumptions will suffice.

Partly this is a matter of taste in choosing between strong and weak assumptions where both yield the same implications (Simon 1978, p. 8). But there is more to it than tastes. Conceptualising a problem one way rather than another can have a profound effect on the follow-up research agenda. Thus organisation structure is of little import and hence can be disregarded if hyperrationality assumptions are maintained, which explains why the neoclassical theory of the firm describes the organisation as a production function rather than a complex hierarchy. The opposite assumption, that human agents are so overwhelmed by complexity that they are incapable of planning, likewise reduces the study of organisational design to insignificance. This appears to be close to the view of March and Olsen (1976) and Mintzberg (1973).

The Markets and Hierarchies approach avoids both of these extremes. An intermediate degree of bounded rationality is attributed to human agents. Organisational design takes on economic significance precisely because the productive utilisation of this intermediate capability is of crucial importance. But there is more to organisational design than economising on bounded rationality. Issues of opportunism also arise and need to be addressed.

Opportunism extends the usual motivational assumptions of self-interest seeking to include self-interest seeking with guile. Thus, whereas bounded rationality suggests decision-making less complex than the usual assumption of hyperrationality, opportunism suggests calculating behaviour more sophisticated than the usual assumption of simple self-interest. Opportunism refers to 'making false or empty, that is, self-disbelieved threats or promises', cutting corners for undisclosed personal advantage, covering up tracks, and the like. Although it is a central behavioural assumption, it is not essential that all economic agents behave this way. What is crucial is that *some* agents behave in this fashion and that it is costly to sort out those who are opportunistic from those who are not.

Faced with bounded rationality on the one hand and the proclivity for some human agents to behave opportunistically on the other, the basic organisational design issue essentially reduces to this: organise transactions in such a way as to economise on bounded rationality while simultaneously safeguarding those transactions against the hazards of opportunism.

The governance of contractual relations

The governance of contractual relations warrants careful attention in the degree to which economic agents are subject to bounded rationality *and* are given to opportunism. In the absence of either, the ubiquitous contracting model goes through.

Thus suppose the absence of bounded rationality among opportunistic agents. Mind-boggling though it is to contemplate, such agents will engage in 'a single gigantic once-for-all forward "higgle-haggle" in which all contingent goods and services (i.e., all goods and services at each possible time-cum-environmental condition) are bought and sold once and for all now for money payments made now' (Meade 1971, p. 166). Propensities to behave opportunistically will simply be of no account.

Suppose alternatively that agents are subject to bounded rationality but are free of opportunism. Autonomous contracting again applies, though the reasons here are different. Since each party can depend on his or her opposite to honour the spirit as well as the letter of an agreement, successive adaptations can and will be implemented as contingencies unfold. Bridges are thus crossed when they arise, whereas the unbounded rationality model stipulates bridge crossings exhaustively in advance. Adaptive, sequential decision-making by non-opportunistic parties will nevertheless reach the same joint profit-optimising result.

The fact is, however, that human agents are neither unboundedly rational nor reliably free of opportunism. Interesting transaction cost issues thereby arise, and organisational design is a relevant concern precisely for this reason. But a predictive theory of efficient organisational structure requires more than an acknowledgment that human actors are subject to bounded rationality and given to opportunism. A schema for framing the dimensions of transactions is needed and must be joined with a description of alternative modes for organising transactions. In addition, a strategy for matching organising modes (governance structures) to transactions needs to be devised.

The rudiments of such an approach have been set out elsewhere

(Williamson 1979b). The critical dimensions for describing trans-actions are (i) uncertainty, (ii) the frequency with which transactions recur, and (iii) the degree to which durable transaction-specific invest-ments are required to realise least-cost supply. The main governance modes to which transactions need to be matched are: (i) markets (with varying degrees of adjudicatory support); (ii) internal organisation; and (iii) an intermediate form of bilateral exchange referred to as 'obli-gational market contracting'.

Our principal interest here is internal organisation. Internal organ-isation is well-suited to transactions that involve recurrent exchange in the face of a non-trivial degree of uncertainty and that incur trans-action-specific investments. Since internal organisation requires the development of specialised governance structure, the cost of which must be amortised across the transactions assigned to it, it is rarely economical to organise occasional transactions internally. Likewise, transactions for which uncertainty is low require little adaptation, hence little governance, and thus can be organised by market contract-ing. Except, however, as transaction-specific investments are involved, neither frequency nor uncertainty – individually or in combination – justifies the creation of internal organisation (with its associated trans-action-specific governance structure).

Considering the importance that we attach to transaction-specific investments, some explication is needed. The crucial issue is the degree to which durable, non-marketable expenses are incurred. Items that are unspecialised among users pose few hazards, since buyers in these circumstances can easily turn to alternative sources, and suppliers can sell output intended for one buyer to other buyers without difficulty. (The argument also turns on the degree to which inputs can be diverted from one use to another without loss of productivity.) Non-market-ability problems arise when the *specific identity* of the parties has important cost-bearing consequences. Transactions of this kind will be referred to as idiosyncratic.

Occasionally the identity of the parties is important from the outset, as when a buyer induces a supplier to invest in specialised physical capital of a transaction-specific buyer. Inasmuch as the value of this capital in other uses is by definition much smaller than the specialised use for which it has been intended, the supplier is effectively 'locked into' the transaction to a significant degree. This is symmetrical, moreover, in that the buyer cannot turn to alternative sources of supply and obtain the item on favourable terms, since the cost of supply from unspecialised capital is presumably great.[3] The buyer is thus com-mitted to the transaction as well.

Ordinarily, however, there is more to idiosyncratic exchange than specialised physical capital. Human-capital investments that are transaction-specific commonly occur as well. Specialised training and learning-by-doing economies in production operations are illustrations. Except when these investments are transferable to alternative suppliers at low cost, which is rare, the benefits of the set-up costs can be realised only so long as the relationship between the buyer and seller of the intermediate product is maintained.

Additional transaction-specific savings can accrue at the interface between supplier and buyer as contracts are successively adapted to unfolding events, and as periodic contract-renewal agreements are reached. Familiarity here permits communication economies to be realised: specialised language develops as experience accumulates and nuances are signalled and received in a sensitive way. Both institutional and personal trust relations evolve.

In consideration of the value placed upon economies of these kinds, agents who engage in recurring, uncertain, idiosyncratic transactions have a strong interest in preserving the exchange relation. Autonomous contracting modes give way to internal organisation as the value associated with exchange continuity increases. The continuity advantages of internal organisation over markets in these circumstances are attributable to its more sensitive governance characteristics and its stronger joint profit-maximising features.

Applications

A theory is judged to be more fruitful the 'more precise the prediction, the wider the area within which the theory yields predictions, and the more additional lines of future research it suggests' (Friedman 1953, p. 10). The basic exchange paradigm that was originally worked up to address the issue of vertical integration across successive manufacturing stages has proved to be remarkably robust. Although this was not evident at the outset, it quickly became apparent that any organisational relation that can be reformulated as a contracting problem can be addressed in substantially identical terms. Applications of the exchange paradigm include: assessments of the employment relation (Williamson, Wachter, and Harris 1975; Hashimoto and Yu 1980); franchise bidding for natural monopolies (Williamson 1976a); the efficacy of capital markets (Williamson 1975: Chapter 9); oligopoly (Posner 1969; Williamson 1975: Chapter 12); vertical market restrictions (Williamson 1979a); and aspects of inflation (Wachter and Williamson 1978).

Other applications include a restatement of contract law in transaction cost terms (Williamson 1979b, pp. 235–54); the uses of transaction cost reasoning by market specialists (Carman 1979); possible applications to the study of comparative economic systems (Campbell

1978); and uses of the exchange paradigm to examine non-economic phenomena – family law being an example (Williamson 1979b, p. 258). Of special interest here are the applications of the Markets and Hierarchies approach to matters of internal organisation. These design issues are developed in the following section.

Empirical tests of three kinds have been used to assess predictions of the Markets and Hierarchies approach: cross-sectional studies, experimental studies, and case studies. The cross-sectional studies that have been performed test what is referred to as the multidivisional form hypothesis (Williamson 1975, p. 150):

The organisation and operation of the large enterprise along the lines of the M-form favours goal pursuit and least-cost behaviour more nearly associated with the neoclassical profit-maximisation hypothesis than does the U-form organisational alternative.

Three studies have been done in which organisation form is used as an explanatory variable in studies of business performance. The studies by Peter Steer and John Cable (1978) of British firms and by Henry Armour and David Teece (1978) of U.S. petroleum corporations both confirm the importance of organisation form. Teece has since extended the analysis from petroleum firms to assess the ramifications of organisation form differences among the principal firms in fifteen industries and obtains results that confirm the hypothesis (Teece 1979).

Richard Burton and Borge Obel (1980) have tested the M-form hypothesis by examining the ramifications of organisational design for profitability in the context of a linear programming model of the firm in which the Danzig-Wolf decomposition algorithm was used. Two different technologies, one more decomposable than the other, were studied. The M-form hypothesis is confirmed for both technologies, the profit difference being greater for the more decomposable technology – which is also an implication of the theory.

Case studies of several kinds have been performed. The most complete of these involves an assessment of franchise bidding for natural monopolies. Demsetz (1968), Posner (1972), and Stigler (1968, pp. 18–19) have argued that franchise bidding in an attractive alternative to rate-of-return regulation in dealing with natural monopolies. An abstract assessment of the contracting ramifications of franchise bidding discloses, however, that the purported benefits of franchise bidding are suspect where market and technological uncertainty are great and incumbent suppliers invest in specialised, long-lived equipment and acquire idiosyncratic skills (Williamson 1976a). A case study of franchise bidding for CATV in Oakland, California, confirmed this. Not only were general ramifications of the contracting approach borne out by the study, but the study corroborated contracting details as well.

Organisational Design

Consistent with the general thrust of the Markets and Hierarchies approach, organisation design is addressed as a transaction cost issue, and economising purposes are emphasised. The general argument is this: except when there are perversities associated with the funding process, or when strategically situated members of an organisation are unable to participate in the prospective gains, unrealised efficiency opportunities always offer an incentive to reorganise.

Inasmuch as these perversities are more common in non-commercial than in commercial enterprises, the argument has stronger predictive force for the latter. Indeed our attention in this section is restricted entirely to the commercial sector. We nevertheless believe that the spirit of the analysis carries over to non-profit enterprises and government bureaux, which we include in our discussion of the research agenda.

Although the main organisational design 'action' entails economising on transaction costs, this is not to say that technology is irrelevant. But technology by itself rarely has determinative organisational consequences for more than a small group of highly interdependent workers. Indeed, except when the transaction costs of adapting interfaces between technologically separable work stations are great, markets will be the governance mode by which the exchange of intermediate product is accomplished. Internal organisation not only has little to offer in these circumstances but incurs unneeded costs.

However, in circumstances in which autonomous contracting is costly and hazardous, governance structures of an internal organisational kind arise. Three applications of this general argument follow, after which we summarise the implications and go on briefly to consider other organisational design traditions and contrast them with the approach favoured here.

Vertical integration[4]

The recent monograph by Alfred Chandler, Jr. (1977), describing marketing developments during the late nineteenth century, provides strong support for the proposition that transaction costs are sufficiently significant to affect the structure of industries, sometimes motivating firms to integrate forward from manufacturing into the distribution stage.

Chandler's findings Chandler's description of forward integration into distribution by American manufacturers distinguishes between the developments of infrastructure and the induced distributional response. The appearance of the railroads and the telegraph and the telephone systems in the latter part of the nineteenth century permitted wider geographic areas to be served in a reliable and timely way. The 'reliability and speed of the new transportation and communication' permitted greater economies of scale to be realised in factory organisation (Chandler 1977, p. 245). These economies of scale at the factory level were latent, in the sense that the technology was there waiting to be exploited. Because it is not manufacturing cost but delivered cost that matters, however, it became profitable to realise these scale economies only when a low-cost distribution system appeared. That is, so long as transportation expenses were great, the most efficient way to serve markets was by dispersing factories.

Once the new transportation and communication infrastructure was in place, the stage was set for the distributional response. A crucial question was how to devise a co-ordinated manufacturing–distribution response. In principle, both stages could have remained autonomous: manufacturers could have remained specialised and built larger-scale plants while specialised distributors could have responded simultaneously, either on their own initiative or by contract, by assembling the requisite distribution network. In many industries, however, 'existing marketers were unable to sell and distribute products in the volume they were produced. . . . Once the inadequacies of existing marketers became clear, manufacturers integrated forward into marketing' (Chandler 1977, p. 287). An administrative override was evidently needed.

Not all industries integrated forward, however, and when they did it was not to the same extent. Some industries linked manufacturing only with advertising and wholesaling; retail integration was not attempted. Non-durable industries that had recently adopted continuous process machinery – cigarettes, matches, cereals, and canned goods are examples – were in this category (Chandler 1977, p. 287). More ambitious and interesting were producer and consumer durables that required 'specialised marketing services – demonstration, installation, consumer credit, after-sales service and repair', services that existing middlemen 'had neither the interest nor facilities to provide' (Chandler 1977, p. 288). Examples here included sewing machines, farm machinery, office machines, and heavy electrical equipment.

A transaction cost interpretation   The new transportation and communication infrastructure permitted manufacturers to serve larger markets in a low-cost way. The effects of these infrastructural developments on plant size are displayed in Figure 1.1. (On the motivation for this, see Scherer, Beckenstein, Kaufer, and Murphy 1975).

The *APC* curve shows the average cost of production as plant size increases. These average costs decrease over a wide range due to

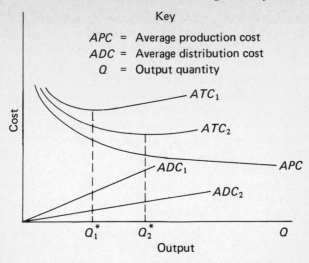

Figure 1.2   Effects of average distribution cost on average total cost

assumed economies of scale. The curve ADC_1 shows the original average distribution cost of delivering products from a plant. This curve increases throughout because greater sales require marketing to a larger geographic region. The curve ADC_2 shows the average distribution cost after the new infrastructure is put in place. It is consistently lower than ADC_1 but also rises throughout. ATC_1 and ATC_2 are average total cost curves that are given by the vertical summation of APC with ADC_1 and ADC_2, respectively. Average total costs reach a minimum at $Q_1{}^*$ and $Q_2{}^*$, where $Q_2{}^*$ is necessarily larger than $Q_1{}^*$, given the stipulated shift in average distribution costs. An increase in plant scale and the extension of service to larger geographic markets are thus indicated.

Problems of implementation, however, are not addressed by this cost curve apparatus. How are the linkages between manufacturing and distribution to be forged? They are not created automatically. If existing middlemen respond in a slow and faltering way to the opportunities that the new transportation and communication infrastructures afford, the stage is set for someone, in this instance the manufacturers, to experiment with new organisational structures.

The issues here are of a transaction cost rather than of a production cost kind. Although a definitive analysis of the 'inadequacies of existing marketers' reported by Chandler (1977, p. 287) would require further research, we conjecture that these distributional difficulties are due to goal incongruence coupled with the hazards posed by small numbers supply relations between autonomous parties. It was difficult for marketers who were accustomed to operating in a local market regime to perceive the opportunities that awaited them. And there was no obvious way to signal these opportunities by relying upon decentralised pricing (Malmgren, 1961). Moreover, even if manufacturers and distributors both perceived the opportunities that the new transport-ation and communication infrastructure afforded, and if each re-sponded independently in reliance upon the other, problems of divergence would arise if each recorded or interpreted the data differently. Such goal incongruence would exist, moreover, at both an aggregate and a disaggregate level.

In principle, manufacturers could have taken the initiative and effected goal congruence by contract. Co-ordination by contract is costly, however, where the two parties are bargaining in an unfamiliar situation and the hazards of contracting are great. The hazards to which we refer have been discussed elsewhere in the context of idiosyncratic exchange. Such problems arise when investments in specialised human or physical assets are required in order to complete the transaction in an economical way. With respect to the issues of concern to Chandler, the problems were especially severe when the mass production and sale of consumer or producer durables was contemplated. Distributors here would have to be induced to make specialised (product-and-brand-specific) investments and, once these investments were made, manu-facturers and distributors would thereafter often be dealing with each other in what essentially was a bilateral exchange arrangement. Given the hazards of opportunism that arise in such circumstances, both parties were reluctant to rely on autonomous contracting.

Note in this connection that Chandler did not observe vertical integration occurring in uniform degree in all industries. This is pre-cisely what one would anticipate when vertical integration is assessed in transaction cost terms. Thus vertical integration into distribution was negligible in some industries – standardised nuts and bolts being an example. In others, integration involved advertising and wholesaling but not retailing – branded consumer non-durables being in this category. In still others, integration included retailing and related support services – certain branded non-durables being among these. This progression is marked by the degree of transaction-specific investment, which is an implication of transaction cost theory. Other theories of vertical integration, by contrast, are silent on these matters.

This substitution of bureaucratic for market governance occurred in response to profit opportunities. But social cost savings also resulted. In the absence of other factors, net social as well as net private gains accrue when such organisational innovations appear.

Becoming multidivisional   The transformation of the modern corpor-ation from a functional to a multidivisional structure has been documented by Chandler.[5] This transformation is treated prominently in the *Markets and Hierarchies* volume (Williamson 1975, Chapters 8–9). Only a few comments are offered here.

Chandler characterised the reasons for the success of the multi-division structure thus:

> The basic reason for its success was simply that it clearly removed the executives responsible for the destiny of the entire enterprise from the more routine operational activities, and so gave them the time, information, and even psychological commitment for long-term planning and appraisal. . . .
> [The] new structure left the broad strategic decisions as to the allocation of existing resources and the acquisition of new ones in the hands of a top team of generalists. Relieved of operating duties and tactical decisions, a general executive was less likely to reflect the position of just one part of the whole. (Chandler 1966, pp. 382–3)

If Chandler is correct, this organisational change from a functional to a multidivisional structure served both to economise on bounded rationality, by relieving top executives of the more routine operational activities, and simultaneously to reduce sub-goal pursuit, which is a manifestation of opportunism. Inasmuch as most institutional choices involve trade-offs rather than Pareto-superior moves, this is surely quite remarkable. How was this accomplished?

The difficulties that the functionally organised firm encountered as it grew in size and diversity were attributable to diseconomies of agglomeration. The centralisation of what are effectively decomposable parts has adverse operating consequences of three kinds. First, attempts to achieve unneeded co-ordination generate overhead costs. Second, forced interdependencies give rise to congestion and other spillover costs. Third, opportunistic sub-goal pursuit is more difficult to detect and control as the degree of interconnectedness increases. Operating cost increases thus arise out of a failure to recognise essential decomposability. But the deficiencies of the functional structure went beyond these operating cost features. The functional form also served to confuse organisational purpose by failure to separate strategic from operating decision-making.

Although becoming multidivisional would not have been feasible without decomposability, the benefits of reorganisation required more than an assignment of semi-autonomous standing to natural sub-units within the firm. Becoming multidivisional further required the development of a strategic decision-making capability in the central office – indeed would have been hazardous to implement without this capability. The assignment of investment resources to high yield uses could be reliably accomplished only as the general office (i) had a sense of direction, (ii) was able to evaluate the merits of investment proposals originated by the operating divisions, and (iii) had the capacity to audit and assess operating division performance.

Removing top management from the operating affairs of the enterprise meant that, whereas bureaucratic control processes had governed previously, operating divisions were now governed in a quasi-market fashion. Thus divisions were assigned the status of quasi firms, and the central office assumed functions of review and resource allocation ordinarily associated with the capital market. As a consequence of these changes the goal confusion (or incongruence) that had previously reigned was supplanted by sub-goal clarity that was meaningfully related to enterprise objectives. The self-interest seeking that, when coupled with goal incongruence, had once drained the energies of the enterprise was now turned to productive purposes.

It is noteworthy that the transformation of the functional to the multidivisional form had little if any relation to technology. Organisational structure was altered, but the underlying technology remained the same in most instances. Thus although efficiency purposes were served, the economies driving the change and the economies that were realised were of a transaction cost rather than technological kind.

Bureaucracies and clans

The shift from functional to divisional structure has for the most part been completed in large US corporations (Teece 1979) and has been proceeding rapidly in Europe (Franko 1972). But a further question is what management 'style' ought to be practised in the large multidivisional enterprise. Issues relating to the 'economics of atmosphere' (Williamson 1975, pp. 37–9) arise in this connection. Ouchi has addressed the merits of bureaucratic versus clan-type management styles in a series of recent papers on this subject (Ouchi 1978, 1979, 1980).

To put the issue one way: What form of contracting ought to prevail within an organisation? As with market modes of contracting, there are two general options, which we designate as 'hard' and 'soft' contracting, respectively. Under hard contracting, the parties remain relatively autonomous, each is expected to press his or her interests vigorously, and contracting is relatively complete. Soft contracting, by contrast, presumes much closer identity of interests between the parties, and formal contracts are much less complete. This is the clan-type management style.

Although contract law specialists, sociologists, and others have long recognised soft contracting practices, the study of soft contracting has only recently come under scrutiny. Ian Macneil's (1974, 1978) work on 'relational contracting' is especially instructive. While it is beyond the scope of this paper to review the literature here, we nonetheless think it important to elaborate on the special problems that soft contracting encounters if it is introduced in an alien culture.

The basic argument is this: soft contracting, to be viable, needs to be supported by a more elaborate informal governance apparatus than is associated with hard contracting. Thus whereas the latter relies heavily on legal and economic sanctions, the former rests much more on social controls. As compared with hard contracting, soft contracting appeals more to the spirit than to the letter of the agreement.

Four points are relative in this regard. First, not all transactions need the additional supports afforded by soft contracting. Economising considerations would dictate that a distinction be made between those that do and that do not, and that each be organised appropriately. Second, the immediate parties to soft contracts are the ones who stand most to benefit from preserving the exchange. Accordingly, they have incentives to develop a bilateral (transaction-specific) trust relation. Third, the institutional infrastucture within which soft contracts are embedded also influences the viability of this type of exchange. And fourth, the design of transactions is a decision variable: depending on their confidence in the trading relations, parties will vary the degree to which trading hazards are introduced.

Trading hazards differ with the degree of transaction-specific investment and with uncertainty. The first of these hazards is obvious: Where investments are of a transaction-specific kind, parties will be unable to divert these assets to alternative uses of an equally productive kind. Accordingly, as the degree of asset specificity increases, additional governance supports are needed. The same applies as uncertainty is increased. The argument here is that the occasions to adapt the transaction to new circumstances increase as the degree of uncertainty increases. Since the incentive to defect from the spirit of the agreement increases as the frequency and magnitude of the indicated adaptations are increased, greater hazards are thereby posed.

Although the degree of uncertainty is commonly beyond the control of the parties, the degree of asset specificity is often theirs to determine. Thus, assume that a particular transaction is subject to an intermediate degree of uncertainty and the parties are attempting to optimise with respect to its transaction-specific features. Specifically, assume the following:

1. The transaction in question involves an employment relation.
2. Two different job designs are under consideration, one of a hard contracting and the other of a soft contracting kind.
3. Human capital skill acquisitions are involved for each job design: Under hard contracting the skills acquired are of a general purpose kind, while under soft contracting they are of a special kind.
4. Physical capital expenditures are identical whichever job design is adopted.

5. Assuming contractual continuity, the more productive job design is the one that involves special-purpose skill acquisition.

Whether this more productive job design is adopted, however, is problematical. In contrast to employees with general-purpose skills, employees who have acquired task-specific skills will be able to move to alternative employment only by experiencing a non-trivial productivity sacrifice in the process. In consideration of these added hazards, employers will be successful in inducing employees to acquire specialised skills only when the workers are either adequately compensated in advance for the hazards or when the job is adequately protected against opportunism during the course of task execution.

Holding governance structures constant, the wage premium needed to compensate workers against the added hazards may easily render the task-specific job design competitively non-viable, especially if workers are risk averse. The question then is whether this potentially more productive job design can be salvaged by surrounding it with transactional safeguards. This brings us back to the matter of bilateral trading relations and the institutional matrix within which trading takes place.

The 'special problems' of soft contracting to which we referred earlier are particularly great when soft contracting is introduced into an alien culture. The reason for this is that the entire burden of providing contractual safeguards falls entirely on the immediate parties to the transaction if background cultural supports are missing. Should one of the parties choose to defect, there is no further support for sustaining the transaction to which either can appeal. In contrast, where individual soft contracts are embedded in a soft contracting trading culture, defection is subject to added sanctions. The incentives to defect are accordingly reduced.

To some extent, the parties to the transaction may be able to devise procedural safeguards themselves. One example is the development of 'internal labour markets' whereby wages are assigned to jobs rather than to individuals, promotion ladders are defined, a sensitive grievance structure is devised, and so on (Doeringer and Piore 1971; Williamson, Wachter, and Harris 1975). But societal safeguards may provide additional security. This varies among economic systems. The 'clan' form of organisation that Ouchi (1978, 1979) has studied is much more viable in some cultures (e.g., Japanese) than in others (e.g., American).

The limitations of hard contracting are nevertheless great as the need progressively increases for successive adaptations to be made in response to uncertainty. Contracts simply fail to provide adequately for the appropriate responses in advance, and employees may engage in strategic bargaining. The more co-operative work relations associated with soft contracting have a clear advantage in these circumstances. The problem then is how to bring this off. This is a matter for which future research is plainly needed.

Other organisational design traditions
The literature on organisational design is vast, and we address only a small part of it here. Jeffrey Pfeffer's (1978) recent book on this subject distinguishes between longitudinal studies, managerial studies, and the power approach. He observes that most of the longitudinal studies have been preoccupied with measurement to the exclusion of theory (Pfeffer 1978, p. xiv). The work of Jay Galbraith (1973) and of Paul Lawrence and Jay Lorsch (1967) is in the managerial tradition. Pfeffer contends that this work is preoccupied with efficiency and effectiveness and neglects power and influence (Pfeffer 1978, p. xv), a tradition that he associates with Cyert and March (1963), Karl Weick (1969), and March and Olsen (1976). Organisational design issues are then addressed in terms of control, influence, and power.

Other organisational design approaches that go unmentioned by Pfeffer are the organisational ecology approach (Hannan and Freeman 1977; Aldrich 1979) and the theory of organisational structures advanced by Kenneth Mackenzie (1978). Inasmuch as efficiency figures prominently in both of these last two approaches, both are complementary to the Markets and Hierarchies approach. The power approach to organisational design, by contrast, is a very different tradition.

The neglect of power by the M & H approach is not to suggest that power is either uninteresting or unimportant. We submit, however, that power considerations will usually give way to efficiency – at least in profit-making enterprises, if observations are taken at sufficiently long intervals, say a decade. Thus the powers of heads of functional divisions and of their subordinates were vastly altered when functionally organised firms shifted to a multidivisional structure. Were power the only or the main organisational design factor, it is difficult to believe that large American and subsequently European businesses would have undergone such a vast organisational transformation over the past thirty years. From transaction cost and ecological points of view, however, the transformation, once started, was predictable.

Or consider Pfeffer's assertion that if 'the chief executive in a corporation always comes from marketing . . . there is a clue about power in the organisation' (Pfeffer 1978, p. 23). Viewed from a power perspective, the argument evidently is that the marketing people in this corporation have 'possession of control over critical resources', have preferential access to information, and are strategically located to cope with 'critical organisational uncertainty' (Pfeffer 1978, p. 17–28). We do not disagree with any of this but would make the more straight-forward argument that the marketing function in this organisation is especially critical to competitive viability.

Thus our position is that those parts of the enterprise that are most critical to organisational viability will be *assigned* possession of control over critical resources, will *have* preferential access to information, and will be *dealing* with critical organisational uncertainties. In some organisations this may be marketing, in others it may be R & D, and in still others it may be production. Failure to assign control to that part of the enterprise on which viability turns would contradict the efficiency hypothesis but would presumably be explained as a power outcome.[6]

Inasmuch as power is very vague and has resisted successive efforts to make it operational, whereas efficiency is much more clearly specified and the plausibility of an efficiency hypothesis is buttressed by ecological survival tests, we urge that efficiency analysis be made the centrepiece of the study of organisational design. This does not imply that power has no role to play, but we think it invites confusion to explain organisational results that are predicted by the efficiency hypothesis in terms of power. Rather power explains results when the organisation sacrifices efficiency to serve special interests. We concede that this occurs. But we do not believe that major organisational changes in the commercial sector are explained in these terms. The evidence is all to the contrary.

The Research Agenda
The Markets and Hierarchies approach to the study of organisational issues is relatively new as compared with other research traditions. Neither its power nor its limits have been fully established. Applications to date, however, have been numerous and mainly encouraging. Our discussion here merely suggests additional theoretical, empirical, and public policy applications.

General
As noted earlier, any problem that arises as a contracting problem or can be recast as one can usefully be examined in Markets and Hierarchies terms. This is not to suggest that the contracting paradigm should be applied to the exclusion of other research traditions. We nevertheless believe that insights not easily derived from alternative approaches can often be obtained by assessing transaction cost features. While sometimes these insights may be of a fragmentary kind, often they relate to core issues.

Inasmuch as transaction costs have reference to the costs of running the economic system, the useful comparisons are between alternative modes rather than between a proposed mode and a frictionless ideal.

Given that an explicit or implicit exchange is to be accomplished or a co-ordinated adaptation is to be affected, how should the transaction be organised? For many purposes, the analysis can be thought of as interface management. This applies within and between markets and firms.

Some specifics

Business history: markets to hierarchies   Transaction costs economics can be applied advantageously to the study of changing organisational structures through time. This is true both of organisational changes since the industrial revolution (Chandler 1966, 1977) and also pre-industrial changes (North 1978). A richer understanding of the economics of institutions is sure to emerge as business historians, industrial organisation specialists, economic theorists, and organisation theorists apply their collective talents to the systematic study of institutional issues. Transaction cost economising is, we submit, the driving force that is responsible for the main institutional changes (for an interpretation of Chandler's recent book in transaction cost terms, see Williamson 1980). Applications will include product market organisation and also changing labour and capital market forms of organisation through time.

Bureaucracies   Applications of Markets and Hierarchies to commercial bureaucracies will be concerned with interface governance. Specific organisational design applications (possibly with special reference to particular functions such as research and development) as well as general applications (again, the matrix form is in need of interpretation) should be possible. Additional empirical tests of the M-form and of other hypotheses can also be anticipated. Perhaps most important, the limits of internal organisation are poorly understood in relation to the limits of markets. The transaction cost approach appears to have much to offer for such an assessment. The ramifications are of interest both to worker-managed and to capitalist enterprises (Fitzroy and Mueller 1978). Whether recent developments involving employee participation in Europe constitute a contradiction to the efficiency hypothesis also warrants scrutiny.

Clans   The organisation of economic activity by greater reliance on clan-type structures requires study. Both the limitations of clans as well as the discriminating application of clan forms of organisation deserve attention. As between alternative forms of *internal* organisation, the clan appears to realise greater advantage in circumstances in which uncertainty is great. The argument needs to be elaborated and specific applications attempted, to service industries, high technology industries, and others characterised by extreme performance ambiguity.

The proposition that clan forms join high productivity with emotional well-being (low levels of alienation) deserves further scrutiny. As with other organisational panaceas, we believe that this is too simplistic. Rather the argument needs to be made in a more discriminating way that recognises transaction cost distinctions. The propositions that defection hazards are greater for clan forms, and that such forms are viable only when accompanied by additional governance supports, also warrants further study. Comparative international studies, in which hard versus soft contracting cultures are scrutinised, may be useful.

Public policy toward business   Public policy applications will also continue. This includes both antitrust and regulation. In the antitrust area, issues of strategic behaviour and fairness will come under special scrutiny. What has been referred to as the Decision Process Approach, which makes operational 'procedural rationality' (Simon 1978), would appear to hold promise for the microanalytic study of regulatory issues (Williamson 1979c).

Non-profit organisations   The organisation of non-profit enterprises, which are growing in economic importance (Weisbrod 1979), is intriguing and has hitherto evaded explanation of more than a partial or *ad hoc* kind. Whether the transaction cost approach will be illuminating remains to be seen. One of the problems with transactions in many non-profit organisations, as in service businesses, is that they are amorphous. Also the viability tests for non-profit organisations are often much weaker – partly because product market competition is weak, but also because an effective capital market displacement mechanism (takeover) is missing.

The study of government bureaux suffers from many of these same limitations. Once progress is made in studying non-profit organisations from a transaction cost (or any other) point of view, follow-up applications to government bureaus should be easy.

Conclusion

The Markets and Hierarchies programme of research is relatively young in comparison with other research traditions in organisation theory. Being young, it has its sceptics. We would not have it otherwise.

For one thing, we are inclined to be eclectic. No single approach applies equally well to all problems, and some issues are usefully addressed from several points of view. For another, we believe that most of the challenges can be met. Sometimes this may require extending the theory to apply to new circumstances. Sometimes it will require sharpening or qualifying parts of the argument. Formalising aspects of the argument may sometimes be needed and appears to be feasible. (See the recent paper by Hashimoto and Yu 1980 for developments of this last kind.)

The distinctive powers of the approach are attributable to its reliance on transaction cost reasoning and its unremitting emphasis on efficiency. While the particulars differ, the same approach to the study of transactions applies quite generally. The core methodological properties are these:

1. The transaction is the basic unit of analysis.
2. Human agents are subject to bounded rationality and self-interest.
3. The critical dimensions for describing transactions are frequency, uncertainty, and transaction-specific investments.
4. Economising on transaction costs is the principal factor that explains viable modes of contracting; it is the main issue with which organisational design ought to be concerned.
5. Assessing transaction cost differences is a comparative institutional exercise.

The approach is able to deal symmetrically with market and non-market modes of organisation and has successfully addressed a wide variety of organisational issues in a coherent way.

Those who prefer methodology and those who are averse to efficiency analysis will insist, with cause, that there is more to organisation theory than economising on transaction costs. We agree. We submit, however, that efficiency analysis is important to the study of all forms of organisation and is absolutely crucial to the study of commercial organisations. And we furthermore contend that the main test of a theory is its implications. So long as alternative theories are evaluated on this standard, we are confident that the Markets and Hierarchies approach will fare well in the comparison.

Notes

[1] J.R. Commons (1934) had urged such an approach much earlier, but both his efforts and those of other institutionalists were outside the mainstream of economic analysis and, except as they are dealt with in the study of economic thought, have been neglected.

[2] This was economics of a non-traditional kind. An efficiency orientation was maintained, but attention shifted from neoclassical production function issues to the study of transaction costs, in the spirit of J.R. Commons (1934), R.H. Coase (1952), and K.J. Arrow (1969).

[3] This assumes that it is costly for the incumbent supplier to transfer specialised physical assets to new suppliers. On this, see Williamson (1976a).

[4] The argument here follows Williamson (1979a, pp. 968–72).

[5] The path-breaking book here is Chandler's *Strategy and Structure* (1966).

Williamson's shift of emphasis from the factors that were responsible for managerial discretion to the factors, including especially internal organisation, that served to attenuate managerial discretion was much influenced by this book.

[6] Thus suppose that, from a competitive effectiveness viewpoint, marketing is the most important functional area. Suppose further that the founder and his progeny are engineers, and that each has worked his way up through manufacturing. Inasmuch as they have an ownership lock (power) on the system, the chief executive and his principal aides are appointed from these ranks. Although this has the efficiency benefit of coupling ownership and control, the firm may be vulnerable to market developments in relation to its rivals. Power explains the inefficiency (vulnerability) condition.

2 The Determinants of the Hierarchical Organisation of Industry
H. Daems

In several industries the co-ordination of activities, the allocation of resources and the monitoring of performance of establishments is administered by managerial hierarchies. These managerial hierarchies are operated by a central administrative office that, first, consolidates ownership over factories, laboratories, warehouses and sales offices and that, second, supervises the functioning of the establishments under its legal control. The large, diversified and integrated multi-unit establishment firms that dominate certain industries reflect the operation of these central administrative offices. The size, diversification and integration of, and the managerial control over, these multi-establishment firms has worried many economists and numerous studies were undertaken to assess the effect of these centrally administered organisations on the economy and society.[1] The question why managerial hierarchies came to administer certain industries has only recently received more attention. However, from the viewpoint of public policy, knowing why giant hierarchies developed is certainly as important as knowing their impact on society. This paper builds on recent work on institutional economics to explain why managerial hierarchies developed in certain industries.

The Facts
The extent of hierarchical organisation of modern industry is illustrated by the following statistics. In 1973, the non-communist world had 258 industrial companies each employing over 30,000 persons. The share of non-communist world employment of these companies in various manufacturing industries is estimated in Table 2.1. The data show that considerable differences exist among industries. Large-scale hierarchical organisations are most important in petroleum and electrical machinery. However, in textiles and apparel, wood, furniture, printing and leather large hierarchies are of no significance for organising industrial activities.

A similar but more detailed picture can be obtained for the United States. According to the 1972 *Enterprise Statistics* published by the

Table 2.1   Number of companies with over 30,000 people employed and their share in non-communist world employment for their industrial sector for various manufacturing industries for 1973

	Number	Share (%)
Food and beverages	31	20.5
Tobacco	5	38.1
Textiles and apparel	8	2.6
Wood	1	1.4
Furniture	—	—
Paper	8	15.9
Printing	—	—
Chemicals	33	39.5
Petroleum	14	72.1
Rubber	7	50.1
Leather	1	3.0
Glass, stone, clay	4	11.9
Primary metals	34	41.7
Metal products	10	8.8
Non-electric machinery	16	10.9
Electrical machinery	42	70.3
Transportation equipment	40	62.0
Measuring, optical, photographic	4	19.5
	258	

Non-communist countries
Developing countries are included

Sources: Calculated from *Fortune 500 US* and *Fortune 500 outside US* and various *United Nations Statistical Yearbook*

Bureau of the US Census, 447,170 establishments such as factories, laboratories, warehouses and sales offices were operated by firms in the manufacturing industry. Probably half of these establishments were independent firms. The others were administered by a central office which co-ordinated activities, allocated resources and monitored performance of several establishments. One-fourth of the total number of establishments were operated by 305 companies. On average each of these 305 companies employed 31,269 persons and none had fewer than 10,000 persons. The managerial hierarchies of these companies administered 352 establishments on average. All these companies were functioning in more than one industry. Table 2.2 shows that in the US also, large managerial hierarchies only became the dominant mode of organising co-ordination, allocation and monitoring in a limited number of industries. In petroleum, transportation equipment, tobacco and chemicals, co-ordination, allocation and monitoring were administered by managerial hierarchies. But in such other industries as

Table 2.2   Share of companies with more than 10,000 employees in total United States employment in various manufacturing industries, 1972 (%)

20	Food	25
21	Tobacco	71.1
22	Textiles	32.9
23	Apparel	9.6
24	Wood	4.8
25	Furniture	7.1
26	Pulp and paper	49.9
27	Printing and publishing	13.8
28	Chemicals	60.4
29	Petroleum	84.7
30	Rubber	41.6
31	Leather	42.1
32	Glass	33.9
33	Primary metals	59.9
34	Metal products	13.5
35	Machinery	37
36	Electrical machinery	64.4
37	Transportation equipment	80.3
38	Measuring and optical	33.5
39	Miscellaneous	12.4

Source: 1972 Enterprise Statistics, US Bureau of the Census

apparel, wood, furniture and metal products, managerial hierarchies were less prominent.

The picture obtained from the statistical data can be complemented by the historical findings of Professor Alfred D. Chandler Jr (1977). His recent work shows that large managerial hierarchies came to administer strategies of vertical integration from the 1880s onwards. These giant hierarchies operated successfully only in a few industries. Until the First World War, these industries were food and tobacco (milk, soup, cereals, meat, beer, distilled liquors and cigarettes), various standardised and assembled non-electrical machinery and equipment for private, industrial, administrative and agricultural uses (typewriters, sewing machines, harvesters, cash registers), chemicals (soap, paints, dynamite, soda), electrical machinery, equipment and supplies (cables, telephones, light and power generators), petroleum and also primary metals (steel). After the First World War managerial hierarchies came to operate in transportation equipment (cars first and airplanes later) and household appliances (refrigerators). From the 1920s onwards, managerial hierarchies not only administered co-ordination of vertically interrelated activities but they came also to manage strategies of product and geographical diversification. After the Second

World War the managerial hierarchies continued to grow in size in the aforementioned industries but as the statistical data showed the institution did not permanently spread to such other industries as clothing and furniture. In these industries the typical enterprises tend to remain single product, single function, single region, single establishment firms. These historical findings further document that managerial hierarchies only developed and survived in certain industries.[2]

A considerable amount of resources is being used to administer these multi-establishment organisations. A combination of various data in the *1972 Enterprise Statistics* leads to the suggestion that in the United States, 422,776 persons were employed to staff the central administration of these large companies at an annual cost of $6.2 billion which is approximately 6 per cent of the total payroll of these companies. Formulated differently, for every twenty-one employees in a large company there is at least one employee to administer co-ordination, allocation and monitoring. The amount of capital used for administrative purposes is impossible to estimate correctly from the census data but it is likely that it is not negligible.

These statistics and the historical findings suggest two conclusions. First, hierarchies are used to administer such fundamental economic functions as co-ordination, allocation and monitoring in certain industries but not in others. Second, the cost of administering certain industries is not negligible. In turn, these conclusions raise two closely related questions. Why are scarce resources utilised to administer the functioning of establishments? What determines the development of hierarchy in certain industries?

Previous Literature
The well developed literature on the economies of multi-plant operations, of diversification and of integration is relevant for answering the questions raised above. However, this literature should be extended in two ways. First, the technological and market conditions that make such economies realisable should be specified more precisely such that it becomes possible to explain inter-industry differences in the degree of multi-plant operation, diversification and integration. Second, and most importantly, the necessary conditions that explain why centralised administration by managerial hierarchies is required to capture the aforementioned economies must be spelled out. Until now most attention appears to have gone to the sufficient conditions. Managerial hierarchies are sufficient to capture economies of multi-establishment operations, of diversification and of integration. But are such hierarchies also necessary for reaping the benefits of diversification and integration? By focusing on the various institutional arrangements that establishments use to organise co-ordination allocation and monitoring

this paper develops the conditions that favour hierarchical organisation of industry. This focus was inspired by the pathbreaking work of first Ronald E. Coase (1952) and later, Oliver E. Williamson (1975) and Alfred D. Chandler Jr (1977).

A Choice of Institutional Arrangements

Co-ordination of activities, allocation of resources and monitoring of performance require communication of information about opportunities and actions. It is also necessary that compliance with contracts be enforceable to assure effective co-ordination. A rich variety of institutional arrangements exists to communicate information and to enforce compliance and thus to make possible co-ordination, allocation and monitoring. It is possible to dimensionalise institutions in such a way that three alternative institutional arrangements are distinguishable: markets, federations and hierarchies (Richardson 1972). As shown in Table 2.3, markets, federations and hierarchies differ in three ways: in the way they structure ownership, in the way they distribute returns and in the way they organise supervision to deal with the communication of information and the enforcement of compliance. Production and distribution establishments that are independently owned, that do not share returns and that do not mutually supervise one another rely on contingent prices to exchange information and to enforce compliance. In such industries with predominantly single product, single function, single establishment firms, activities are coordinated, resources allocated and performance monitored by prices and markets. In other cases establishments, while remaining independent, may try to pool returns to stimulate communication of information and compliance with contracts. Returns can be pooled in various ways; by sharing profits, by dividing markets or by centrally allocating orders. Such arrangements are called federations. Firms that are federated in this way rely on joint decision making for co-ordination, allocation and monitoring. Cartels are federations but not all federations are cartels. In some industries, particularly in Europe and Japan, firms are linked through extensive interlocking stockholdings. Such financial constructs are often called *financial groups* (Daems 1978). Such groups, however, do not rely on central administrative offices to supervise the group members. *Financial groups*, then, are not fundamentally different from profit pooling arrangements because the interlocking stockholdings ensure that the group members share in a complex manner in the total returns to the group. For this reason, *financial groups* are federations. There is another way for independent establishments to form a federation. Firms can indeed federate without pooling returns but by agreeing to mutual supervision. Franchising by hotels, fast food restaurants and soft-drink bottlers are examples of this

Table 2.3

TYPE OF INSTITUTION	DIMENSIONS Ownership	Returns	Supervision	EXAMPLES
Markets	Independent	No-pooling	No	Exchanges Contingent contracts
Federations {	Independent	Pooling	No	Cartels
	Consolidated→Pooling		No	Financial groups
	Independent	No-pooling	Yes	Franchising Interlocking directorship
Hierarchies	Consolidated→Pooling		Yes	Integrated and diversified companies

second type of federation. The last institutional arrangement to deal with information and compliance is the managerial hierarchy. Managerial hierarchies consolidate legal control over production and distribution establishments, consequently they also pool rewards and most importantly, they supervise the functioning of the estab-lishments. Vertically integrated and product and geographically diversified firms are hierarchical arrangements for co-ordination and allocation and monitoring.

The three alternative institutions are observable in modern in-dustrialised economies. In some industries hierarchies are used to co-ordinate interrelated activities, to allocate resources and to monitor performance. In some other industries federations dominate and finally there are many industries where markets are used for co-ordination, allocating and monitoring. The transition from one institutional arrangement to another is observable in mergers and divestitures. In this way studies of industrial organisation, concentration and mergers can be viewed as studies of why hierarchies or federations or markets are relied upon to organise co-ordination, allocation and monitoring. What is needed to explain the organisation of industry from this perspective is a theory why under certain conditions consolidated ownership and supervision (hierarchies) replace independent owner-ship without pooling and supervision (markets). Recent theoretical work in institutional economics provides extremely useful insights for developing such a theory (Davis and North 1971; Williamson 1975; Stiglitz 1975; Coase 1952; Alchian and Demsetz 1972).

In a profit-oriented economic system, it only makes sense for a group of production and distribution units to co-ordinate activities, to allocate resources and to monitor performance when co-ordination, allocation and monitoring lead to concerted actions among establishments that increase joint returns without lowering the return of one of the individual establishments. If no benefits can be obtained from concerted actions there is no point to use scarce resources to organise an institutional arrangement be it a market, a federation or a hierarchy for the exchange of information and the enforcement of contracts. It is well known from existing economic theory that in cases of production and/or demand externalities or interdependencies concerted actions lead to higher returns. Such is also the case when production establishments collude to monopolise supply. However, there is little in traditional theory to explain why institutional arrangements will be used to organise the concerted action. Production units could as well earn monopoly rents by means of tacit collusion among independent non-profit pooling sellers, as by means of cartels and holding companies or as by consolidating ownership and supervising the rate of production. Concerted action in the case of externalities and interdependencies could as well be organised by contingent contracting between independent units, as by pooling returns, or as by supervising actions or by consolidating ownership. Why, then, is it that under certain conditions concerted action is organised by means of hierarchies and under other conditions federations and markets are used? Formulated differently, what are the conditions that lead administrative offices to provide managerial services in exchange for legal consolidation and supervision instead of market contracting between independent establishments? If no answer exists to these questions, then the aforementioned institutional arrangements are irrelevant for economic activity. Such would also imply that all the commonly used statistical measures of sellers concentration based on the degree of legal independence of the suppliers are irrelevant for measuring monopolising power and that the statistical measures of integration and diversification cannot teach anything about the benefits of integration and diversification. Indeed, both measures implicitly assume that consolidated ownership makes a difference. Since most economists are not ready to accept the conclusion that institutional arrangements are irrelevant (why else would institutions exist?), a need exists to find the determinants that affect institutional choices.

The Determinants of Hierarchy

The determinants of hierarchy are easier to discuss if the argument is developed in three successive steps. In the first step it is assumed that the three institutional arrangements have the same installing and operating costs and that the difference between the various institutions results in differing effects on the joint return to concerted actions.

Formulated more accurately, we start out by assuming that the pay-off to the joint activity is a function only of the contractual relations existing between the co-operating units. In a second step the assumption of step 1 is dropped and attention is focused on the differences in installing and operating costs of the three alternative institutional arrangements. In the final step the two previous steps are combined to discuss the net advantage of a particular institution.

The first step implies that the institutional arrangement that leads to the highest joint pay-off be adopted by the participating units. The following example illustrates this reasoning. If the total joint return to monopolising supply is higher through consolidated ownership and supervision (hierarchy) than through independent units and profit-pooling (federation), we expect multi-unit hierarchies to be used for monopolising supply provided – as was assumed above – the costs of installing and operating a hierarchy and federation are equal and not higher than the costs of tacit collusion. Similarly, if the joint return to concerted action in the case of an externality is higher under hierarchy than under any other institutional arrangement we expect hierarchy to be the only institution to deal with externalities and interdependencies.

However, the argument as yet fails to explain why it is that joint returns are influenced by the particular institutional arrangement governing the co-operation between units. Upon reflection it is clear that the explanation must come from the superiority of a particular institution in handling the exchange of information and the enforcement of compliance needed for the co-ordination allocation and monitoring processes in the joint activity. A particular institutional arrangement can only achieve for an extended period of time, higher joint returns on concerted actions than other institutional arrangements with equal installing and operating costs if it communicates information better and/or enforces compliance more effectively.

The superiority of a particular institutional arrangement is not absolute but is dependent on the *specific* needs for information and compliance. In some cases a concerted action of interdependent units requires a considerable exchange of complex information and a tight enforcement of compliance. In other cases the full pay-off to the joint action can be achieved with a limited amount of simple information and without policing compliance. Then, it remains to be clarified why different concerted actions lead to different needs for information and compliance. Concerted actions are the results of explicit or implicit transactions between co-operating units. These transactions are responsible for differences in the need for information and compliance. Recently, Professor Oliver Williamson has identified the three critical dimensions of every transaction as being: the degree of uncertainty involved in fully completing the transaction, the size of transaction-specific investments, and the frequency of recurrence of the transaction (Williamson 1979b). The third dimension is less relevant at this point but will be of critical importance in the second step of the argument when operating costs of institutions are discussed. The first two dimensions of a transaction have important implications. The larger the uncertainty about successfully completing transactions and concerted actions in a particular industry the greater the specific needs for information and compliance in that industry. Transaction-specific investments are easier to describe with reference to some examples. The marketing of some perishable products requires highly specialised equipment. In such cases, transactions between processing and distributing units require investments for unique and highly specific uses. Often the selling of complex products requires special knowledge about specifications and special servicing. In this example again, transactions between manufacturing and distributing units are only possible when transaction-specific investments are made. The greater the amount of resources that is irreversibly committed for specific or transacting-specific purposes the more the need exists for tight compliance. Since hierarchies, for a variety of reasons, have superior enforcement mechanisms and information networks, it seems plausible to postulate that consolidated ownership and supervision will be more used in industries where the co-ordination, allocation and monitoring processes of concerted actions are subject to considerable uncertainty or require resources for highly specialised and unique uses.[3]

It is unreasonable, to assume, as was done in the first step of the argument, that the costs of organised concerted action are independent of the particular institutional arrangement used. This brings us to the second step of the argument. In reality, the costs of installing and operating an institutional arrangement are a function of the type of institution chosen. Co-ordinating activities, allocating resources and monitoring performance through market contracting is costly because resources are needed to collect information and to enforce contract provisions. The costs of hierarchy come from two sources: first, the consolidation of ownership stimulates shirking and second, the supervision consumes resources.[4] Because of profit-pooling, federations are also subject to shirking costs and the recurrent negotiating process is likely to consume a considerable amount of resources.

The frequency with which transactions must recur to sustain a concerted action between co-operating units over a longer period of time is important for comparing the cost advantages of the various institutional arrangements. The total costs of installing and operating a hierarchy are probably constant or slightly increasing with the frequency of recurrence. Federations face lower fixed costs than hierarchies but have some variable costs for every transaction that is being negotiated. This implies that federations face increasing total cost with respect to frequency of recurrence. Market contracting has the lowest fixed cost but the highest variable cost. In this case total information and compliance cost for organising concerted actions is nearly proportional to the frequency with which such actions need to be negotiated. These cost conditions suggest that economies exist in organising the concerted actions of establishments with hierarchies when the frequency of transactions between these units is high.

In many cases the costs of installing and operating an institutional arrangement are also affected by government regulations and taxes. The costs of forming a new hierarchical arrangement by merger are influenced by corporation taxes and by anti-trust legislation. So are the costs of organising a federation in the form of a cartel prohibitively high in the US and in some cases in Europe because governments have outlawed cartel arrangements. The costs of using market mechanisms for co-ordinating vertical interdependencies is sometimes affected by sales taxes.

Both previous steps can be combined to discuss the net gain to organising co-ordination, allocation and monitoring by a particular institution. Institutional arrangements, very much like technologies, compete with one another. In a competitive world with free institutional choices those institutions will survive that promise the highest net return to the co-operating units in the long run. This leads to an important conclusion. Hierarchies rival with federations and markets to provide co-ordination, allocation and monitoring. This rivalry is termed as *institutional competition*. It is only when hierarchies promise a higher net return in the long run than other institutional arrangements that they can hope to survive over the long haul. It was shown that the superiority of a hierarchical arrangement is not absolute but depends on specific conditions. These conditions vary among industries and they are influenced by the needs for information and compliance. Hence hierarchies will be more successful in certain industries than in others. Hierarchies will tend to operate in industries where exchange of information and enforcement of compliance is important because of large uncertainty about successful completion of transactions, because of transaction-specific investments and because of high frequency of recurrence of the transactions. The argument implies also that when multi-unit hierarchies are used as a dominant institutional mode in a particular industry it must be because hierarchical arrangements lead to higher returns than non-hierarchical arrangements.

Hypotheses

The concept of institutional competition enables us to formulate two hypotheses. *First*, multi-establishment enterprises that consolidate ownership and organise supervision will only be successful in a limited number of industries. Also, multi-establishment enterprises will be operating in the same industries in different nations, provided governments do not impose legal and fiscal obstacles to the choice of institutional arrangements. The characteristics of these industries are discussed below. *Second*, in these industries large-scale enterprises will be more profitable than non-consolidated and single establishment firms. It is very important to stress that the hypothesis does not imply multi-establishment enterprises to earn high returns if compared with all enterprises in the economy. It is only *within* certain industries that integrated and diversified enterprises out-perform single product, single establishment, single function firms in the long run. In those industries, also, the stability over time of integrated and/or diversified enterprises should be larger than the stability of non-integrated and/or non-diversified firms. Such firms will be attracted to these industries during the upturn of the industry's business cycle when the cost of expanding the hierarchy of the existing firms further is larger than the benefits of such expansion. During a downturn the non-integrated, non-diversified firms will be forced out of the industry. Thus, over the course of an industry's business cycle differences in stability of integrated and diversified firms and non-integrated and non-diversified firms will be observable.

To permit a test of these hypotheses the precise characteristics of the hierarchically organised industries must be derived from the arguments developed in previous sections of this paper. Three characteristics will be important: (i) the research intensity of the industry, (ii) the extent to which demand in the industry is dependent on supplier provided information and (iii) the size of the industry's material input requirements.

Research intensity stimulates consolidation of ownership and supervision by hierarchies for several reasons. One reason is that research and development activities must build on production and marketing experiences for improving processes and products. This exchange of experience and knowledge makes production and marketing activities interdependent with research and development activities.[5] Such interdependence makes concerted actions advantageous. But the transactions needed to organise the concerted actions are subject to large uncertainties and require some transaction-specific investments. One source of uncertainty is the presence of information impactedness which occurs when the parties involved have unequal access to knowledge and information. Another source is the public goods nature of knowledge. Under such circumstances and without proper institutional arrangements the co-operating units will most likely exploit the information impactedness to their own advantage. Such opportunistic behaviour in turn makes joint action difficult to sustain over the long haul. Another reason is that when research laboratories, in response to a variety of factors invent new processes and products or suggest new applications, transfer of this knowledge involves highly uncertain transactions. Again the sources for this uncertainty are information impactedness and the public goods nature of knowledge. In most cases transaction-specific investments are needed also. Consolidation of ownership and supervision will often be the most efficient arrangement to make sure that the return on the invention is fully appropriated and to learn about genuinely new opportunities for further improvements. As a consequence it is to be expected that research intensive industries will tend to be organised by hierarchies and multi-establishment firms will dominate under such circumstances.

In some industries, market demand is a function of supplier provided information and services. Indeed in markets for consumer durables, processed foods and standardised equipment for business uses the potential customer is confronted with a choice problem under uncertainty. The customer has imperfect information about possible uses of the product, reliability, quality and after sales servicing. The manufacturer attempts to widen the market by reducing the customer's uncertainty. One way for the manufacturer to reduce this uncertainty is to rely on branding. Brand names allow the supplier to communicate information about the product to the customer. However, once a brand name has gained customer acceptance it must be protected from free riders and distortions. Free riders, in this case, are competitors who try to profit from the specific investments in the brand by copying the product as closely as possible. For the protection of their brands most manufacturers need to rely on close co-operation with the distributors of their products (Porter 1976). Distortions in the brand image with respect to quality are likely to arise when the product has to move through successive stages of processing and distribution before it reaches the customer. Often different units in different locations are responsible for successive stages. Close co-operation between these units is needed to sustain product quality and brand image. Another likely source of brand image distortions, this time not only with respect to quality but also with respect to servicing, arises when several independent manufacturing establishments try jointly to exploit the economies of scale in branding. Again a very tight co-operation will be necessary to prevent brand image distortions. Both protection against free riders and brand distortions, therefore, require joint actions. Transactions are needed to organise such joint actions. Not only is uncertainty about successful completion of the transactions large but also are often transaction-specific investments involved. In most cases, consolidated ownership and supervision will be most efficient in handling the specific information and compliance needs. But in some other cases federations will be used. Market contracting is unlikely to survive for long in these circumstances because of the costs involved in writing and enforcing complex contingent contracts. In general, then, we expect multi-unit hierarchies to be used in industries where demand is dependent on branding. It is not possible to obtain a perfect measure of branding but advertising expenditures measured as percentages of sales are close enough proxies for the extent of branding industry by industry.

Industries that require a large volume of specific intermediate products for their activities tend to be transacting with specialised suppliers on a recurrent basis to acquire such goods. Very often quality and timely delivery are critically important for a least cost operation. Close co-operation between users and suppliers will be needed. It was already suggested before that the specific information and compliance needs of recurrent transactions make it profitable to economise on transactions by consolidated ownership and supervision. Thus, industries that consume a high volume of special intermediate products will rely on hierarchies for organising the vertical interdependence. It is proposed that the dependence of an industry on intermediate inputs be measured by the ratio of value of intermediate products and services to total sales. The larger this ratio the more the industry will be hierarchically organised.

Empirical Evidence

Several empirical studies, although some written with a different perspective in mind, lend support to the basic hypotheses of this paper. Papers by Mahityahu Marcus (1969), Richard C. Osborn (1970), Harold Demsetz (1973), Michael E. Porter (1979) and Robert J. Stonebraker (1976) found that returns are positively influenced by firm size in certain industries but not in others. Since the size of firms is in most cases an accurate estimate of the extent of multi-establishment operations and of the use of managerial hierarchies, their research findings come as no surprise. Marcus observed that the dependence of the rate of return on firm size varied from industry to industry but he failed to indicate whether the industries, where size had a positive effect, shared common characteristics. Osborn first, and Demsetz later, showed that performance differences between the largest firms and the smallest firms in an industry depend on the concentration ratio. In most cases, industries with large managerial hierarchies will also be the most concentrated industries. The Demsetz findings, then, lend support to the hypothesis. The empirical findings of Michael Porter are of particular relevance. He found that the rate of return for the largest firms in an industry were positively and significantly influenced by advertising intensity measured as the share of advertising expenditures in sales, suggesting in this way that where advertising was low, large firms had it more difficult to out-perform small firms. Finally, Stonebraker undertook to explain the profit risk of small firms. He found that profit risk and failure rate of small firms was directly related to advertising intensity and most importantly to R and D expenditures. These findings suggest that research and advertising intensive industries will be less successfully organised by small firms, presumably single establishment firms.

Further tests of the hypotheses were obtained from new statistical tests. Data for these tests were obtained from the *US Census of Manufacturers* in 1972 and *IRS Source Book of Corporation Income 1972*. The dependent variable is the extent to which managerial hierarchies are used to administer co-ordination, allocation and monitoring of establishments in particular industries. The spread of such hierarchies is reflected in the appearance of multi-establishment firms. Therefore it was decided to measure the extent of the hierarchical organisation of an industry by the share of multi-establishment firms in total employment of that industry. This variable was labelled HIER. Multi-establishment firms tend to operate in several industries at the same time. In order to minimise the risk of measurement biases resulting from multi-industry operations industries were defined at the two-digit level. This broad definition of industry makes overlapping between industries less likely. Two other dependent variables were constructed. One variable measures the share of employment in companies with over 10,000 people and is called TEN. The other measures the share of industry employment in multi-industry companies and is indicated by MULTI. The correlation between these three dependent variables is extremely high, as can be seen from the correlation matrix, Table 2.4.

According to the hypotheses inter-industry differences in HIER, TEN and MULTI, should be explainable by reseach intensity, advertising intensity and by the size of the input requirements. Research intensity (RND) was measured by the ratio of expenditures on applied

Table 2.4   Correlation matrix of dependent variables

	TEN	MULTI	HIER	Average	Standard deviation
TEN	1			0.39	0.25
MULTI	0.93	1		0.69	0.20
HIER	0.92	0.99	1	0.76	0.16

research by product (*not* by industries) to sales for that product. The data was obtained from publications by the *National Science Foundation*. The advertising-to-sales ratio (ADV) was computed from *IRS Source Book on Corporation Income*. Sales minus value added over sales based on Census establishment data was labelled INP and was taken as an estimate of the need for material inputs.

The regression results are reported in Table 2.5. They support the hypotheses advanced in this paper. It is only in industries where the need for communication of information and enforcement of compliance are large because of research and development activities, advertising and large input requirements that hierarchies will be used to administer co-ordination, allocation and monitoring of establishments.

This brings up the second hypothesis. It was argued that in those particular industries where multi-establishment firms have a competitive advantage because of their particular way of organising, such firms must out-perform single establishment firms. A direct test of this hypothesis is not possible. But since multi-unit firms tend to be much larger than single unit firms an indirect test can be devised that exploits this size difference. The technique employed was inspired by Demsetz's work. The IRS industries for 1972 were regrouped in four size classes: Class 1 for firms with assets under $500,000, Class 2 for firms between $500,000 and $5,000,000. Class 3 for firms in between $5,000,000 and $50,000,000 and finally Class 4 for firms beyond $50,000,000. For every size class accounting rates of return (profits before taxes plus interest over total assets) were calculated. These rates of return are called R_1, R_2, R_3 and R_4. Several writers have argued that the profit data in the bottom IRS size class are unreliable because of the under-reporting of profits by small corporations. Hence we construct Class 1–2 that includes all firms in Class 1 and Class 2. The rate of return for that class is labelled R_{12}. Next the following differences are defined $R4MR1 = R_4 - R_1$, $R4MR2 = R_4 - R_1$, $R4MR3 = R_4 - R_3$, $R4MR12 = R_4 - R_{12}$. If research activities and advertising necessitate consolidated ownership and supervision for efficient handling of information and compliance we expect the performance difference between large firms and small firms to be positively associated with research intensity and advertising-to-sales ratios.

Because of the under-reporting in Class 1 it was decided not to limit tests of the positive association to R4MR1 but also to consider R4MR2 and R4MR12. The IRS data allowed for a study of forty-one industries. Since research and development data were not available for all these industries a dummy variable was constructed to capture research intensity. RND01 equals 1 when on the basis of NFS data we had reason to believe that the research expenditures in that industry were more than 10 per cent of total business receipts. RND01 was put equal

Table 2.5

Dependent variable	Constant	ADV	RND	NP	R^{2a}	F/statistic
TEN	-0.441 (1.824)*	5.337 (1.312)	6.887 (3.148)**	1.294 (3.129)**	0.403	5.279*
MULTI	0.082 (0.435)	6.020 (1.887)*	5.668 (3.304)**	0.877 (2.705)**	0.419	5.570**
HIER	0.242 (1.518)	5.232 (1.952)*	4.497 (3.121)**	0.745 (2.736)**	0.406	5.337**

* 5% significant level
** 1% significant level
[a] Adjusted for degrees of freedom

to zero in the remaining industries. An alternative and more strict measure was used by raising the cut-off point to 20 per cent. This variable was named RND02. Table 2.6 reports the results of the regression analysis. The hypothesis is supported quite well by the data. Industries characterised by large research and development activities and by large outlays for advertising are most profitably organised by large firms; presumably such firms are also multi-establishment firms. As could be expected equations 1 and 2 perform less well in the regression analysis. Indeed, in Class 1 the under-reporting makes stochastic noise on profits so large that it lowers the coefficient of determination. In equations 3 and 4 the stochastic noise is reduced and the positive effect of advertising and research intensity are clearly observable. The similarities of these results with equations 7 and 8 are worth noting. Equations 5 and 6 show that the positive effect of research intensity tapers off when the size class is increased. This suggests that once a certain size is reached, organisation of research and development does not require further expansion of firm sizes. However, such is not the case for advertising.

The tests reported here, then, support the view that large hierarchies develop in some modern industries in response to specific needs for communication of information and enforcement of compliance. The result also suggests that such hierarchies because of consolidated ownership and supervision are a more efficient arrangement for organising certain industries than other non-hierarchical arrangements.

Conclusion

This paper has suggested a new perspective for studying the organisation of industry by focusing on the various institutional arrangements that production and distribution units use to organise concerted action. The search for an efficient organisation of information and compliance was central to our analysis. Institutional competition assures that the most efficient arrangement will be used for the co-ordination of activities, the allocation of resources and the monitoring of performance. In some industries the organisational advantages of consolidated ownership and supervision provide diversified and integrated multi-establishment firms with a competitive superiority for administering concerted action. The results are concentration. But such concentration is a product of a search for efficient organisation in a competitive economy.

Notes
[1] The literature on this subject is so extensive and also so well known that I have decided not to attempt to give a bibliographic reference.

Table 2.6

Dependent variable	Constant	ADV	RDNO1	RDNO2	R^{2a}	F statistic
1. R4MR1	-0.0067 (-0.4249)	0.9417 (1.6362)	0.0332 (1.7744)*		0.08	2.82
2.	-0.0015 (-0.1127)	0.8012 (1.3970)		0.0377 (1.9511)*	0.09	3.17
3. R4MR2	-0.0282 (-2.1347)*	1.3425 (2.7730)**	0.0334 (2.7730)**		0.19	5.92*
4.	-0.0247 (-2.2049)*	1.1857 (2.5213)**		0.0432 (2.7237)**	0.24	7.64*
5. R4MR3	-0.0309 (-2.9314)*	0.9917 (2.5673)**	0.0049 (0.3950)		0.10	3.34*
6.	-0.0284 (-3.0631)**	0.9858 (2.5350)**		0.0004 (0.0325)	0.10	3.25*
7. R4MR12	-0.0177 (-1.3678)	1.2159 (2.5506)**	0.0277 (1.7918)*		0.15	4.723
8.	-0.0153 (-1.3793)	1.0821 (2.3248)*		0.0371 (2.3673)*	0.20	6.10*

* Significant at 5%
** Significant at 1%
ᵃ Adjusted for degrees of freedom

[2] Ongoing historical research suggests that such was also the case in the UK, Germany and France. See also Alfred D. Chandler Jr and Herman Daems (1980).

[3] For a discussion of enforcement mechanisms of hierarchies in economic terms see Daems (1980).

[4] See the statistics in the beginning of the paper for an estimate of this second source of costs.

[4] For an interesting analysis of this interdependence see Christopher Freeman (1974), especially Chapter 5.

3 Between Market and Hierarchy*
O.H. Poensgen

I. Introduction
Among the principal forms of organising and co-ordinating human
work we find the economically self-contained family or group of
families ('hunting band' in Jay's (1973) term) – more generally, the
group held together principally by non-economic goals. Second, there
is the peer group formed for the pursuit of economic goals with every
participant also belonging to at least one different group with a non-
economic basis of association; third, the hierarchical organisation;
fourth, associations or federations of peer groups or of hierarchically
organised entities, and fifth, the market. This order reflects a
decreasing strength of bonds of the persons involved, a decreasing
length of the time of association per day or measured in years, a
decreasing number of needs satisfied by the association and an
increasing substitutability of one partner for another.

The above forms are points in a continuous spectrum singled out for
their distinct properties. To see this we only have to idealise hierarchy
as an arrangement where, once the employment contract is fixed for a
determinate length, further communication concerns the actions of the
hierarchically organised party only and potentially covers every detail
of what, how, by what means, when, and where the other party has to
perform. In contrast, in the market (in its extreme forms) buyers and
sellers meet who know nothing of each other, who do not expect to meet
and contract again, and who exchange for monetary considerations only
a completely fungible good, here and now, with the result that the price
and quantity are the only objects of communication.

We can give names to some of the points in the continuum between
hierarchy or peer groups on the one side and markets on the other.

* This paper was prepared for the Conference on Markets and Hierarchies, held at
Imperial College, London, 2–4 January 1980. A few changes were made as a result of the
very stimulating discussion. I am particularly indebted to Messrs Herman Daems and
Oliver E. Williamson.

The computations reported in this paper were performed by M. Marx and E. Schiffels
on a TR 440 at the University Computation Centre financed by the Deutsche
Forschungsgemeinschaft. Part of the research reported here was financed by a grant from
the Deutsche Forschungsgemeinschaft whose support is gratefully acknowledged.

There is the multi-divisional enterprise, a hierarchical organisation which, however, uses the market mechanism for two purposes: (i) to regulate the flow of goods and services between divisions of equal rank and (ii) to regulate cash flows between the top of the firm and the divisions. The top, however, reserves the right to supersede the market mechanism at any time by fiat. If the division is a separate legal entity we have reached the next point, that of the parent–subsidiary relationship. Here, instances where the hierarchical mode is invoked are far less frequent and, more important, the areas of activity where it is operative decrease in number. This is done either by providing the sub-unit with its own capability in accounting, electronic data processing, finance, the legal domain, etc., obviating the need to accept or render services from other parts of the organisation or, alternatively, by also subjecting such services to the price mechanism. The lower the parent's share in the subsidiary, the further we expect to find an organisation along this road. The same holds if the parent company is no longer operative but a holding company.

Even if companies are not tied by ownership, there may exist hierarchical elements in the relationship. Price leadership in an industry provides an example. More commonly, non-market elements typical of the relationships within a peer group can be discerned, such as agreements to share knowledge or even profits, undertaking joint ventures and, most importantly, regulating how to deal with third parties with respect to prices, quantities, time of delivery, abode of customers served, type of product delivered, product specifications, services rendered, terms of payment. Depending on the subject of the agreement, the number of potential areas covered, its legality and enforcement we may speak of cartels, meeting of the minds, conscious parallelism, tacit or overt collusion. We are addressing ourselves in particular to three of these intermediate forms of economic forms of organisation, i.e. interlocking directorates, cartels and parent–subsidiary relationships. We ask below which tasks each form will serve and what conditions will favour a more complete adoption of hierarchy, i.e. merger. We see those tasks as strategy formulation, providing inputs, disposing of the outputs and organising the process.

Strategy   Some of the indicators of a successful strategy are growth of the firm, demonstrated innovativeness, high and stable rewards both intrinsic and extrinsic for the factors of production, in particular, labour and capital, and low risk of loss of capital or jobs. To be able to implement a successful strategy it is desirable to put together a balanced mix of growing and non-growing sectors; to transfer funds (and other resources) from those parts of the organisation generating it to those needing it most in view of the objective.

Input   The task is to procure those resources (personnel, material, parts and services, means of production, finance) that are needed from the outside with reasonable certainty in the required amount and kind.

Output   The goods and services produced must be disposed on profitable terms without large and unforeseeable fluctuations in the prices obtained, quantities delivered, and without interference from third party (such as governmental action, boycott, picketing or adverse publicity).

Organisation   The above must be organised. We list as the main tasks of organisation, division of labour, allocation of resources, scheduling, monitoring and co-ordination in the sense of effecting changes during the process to adjust to the unforeseen or unforeseeable, all applied to both the production and distribution of the fruits of the joint efforts. In doing so, those directing these efforts implicitly acknowledge bounded rationality of themselves, other personnel and third parties; uncertainty for all parties; often non-coinciding, if not opposing objectives of others pursued with opportunism ('self-interest seeking with guile', in Williamson's words, 1975, p. 26). To continue in Williamson's vein, all of these have as a consequence that not all relevant information existing somewhere is available to the firm (the condition of 'information impactedness' obtaining).

The organisational literature for a number of years has discussed the relationship of an organisation with its environment including the direction of the relationship, its tightness, and kind (Child 1972). Various models have been advanced such as the information processing model (Dill 1958; Lawrence and Lorsch 1967; Duncan 1972), the resource dependence model (Aldrich and Pfeffer 1976), the natural selection model (Aldrich 1979). We can test and compare those models. To do so we could link systematically the variables mentioned in those models to the organisational mode (market vs. hierarchy) taking the various industries as points of observation. Alternatively, we could examine changes over time in both sets of variables. We may do this in a later paper. Here we will restrict ourselves to drawing a connection from one particular variable, i.e. competitive pressure to changes in the hierarchical mode in a rather impressionistic way.

Competitive pressure in its relationship to organisation understandably enough is a variable of particular interest to economists (see Rumelt 1974 and other students of Bruce Scott, e.g. Franko 1976). Organisational sociologists have either paid more attention to its subjective correlate, i.e. a feeling of stress (Child 1972) or turned to other variables such as variability and complexity of the environment. The latter point has been made by Staw and Szwakowski (1975) who along with March and Simon (1958), Cyert and March (1963),

Khandwalla (1972, 1976) and Kieser (1974) are notable exceptions to this generalisation.

To test our hypotheses we use empirical data on German manufacturing firms and industries. These data were gathered within the scope of a larger project with the title 'Context, Organisation and Performance' (see also Thonet and Poensgen 1979). We start with firms tied by interlocking directorates but not by ownership, this relationship being the loosest and least hierarchical one among those discussed.

II. Interlocking Directorates

The law and the functions of the board
German Corporation Law (*Aktiengesetz*) requires every corporation (*Aktiengesellschaft*) to have two boards, a managing board (*Vorstand*) constituted exclusively of full-time corporate officers and a supervisory board (*Aufsichtsrat*) made up solely of outsiders, no joint membership of the boards being admissible. The supervisory board's duties go well beyond the rights of supervision. It is also charged with appointing and discharging the members of the managing board; it can stipulate, and usually does, that certain major decisions are not taken and transactions are not performed without its prior consent. It has equal voice with management in determining dividend policy. The law sets a minimum of three for the number of members and a maximum that varies with size up to an absolute maximum of twenty-one persons. We have collected detailed data (Schiffels 1979) on all members of all corporations in fifteen (out of thirty-one) branches of manufacturing for the years 1961–5 covering 629 *Aktiengesellschaften* or about 45 per cent of all German manufacturing corporations in existence during that time span. Information was available on 8849 seats of supervisory boards (or 6969 individuals). The average size is 6.4 seats per board. This figure was rather stable over time. German law during that time (changed in 1976) provides for two-thirds of the members to be appointed by the shareholders, one-third by employees among themselves and among representatives of trade unions.[1]

The language of the law leaves considerable leeway regarding the actual motives, both in appointing someone to the board and with respect to the kind of influence exerted by the board member. Such motives may include the exercise of ownership rights with respect to business and dividend policy, the safeguard of debt capital and the satisfaction on the Law on Co-Determination (*Mitbestimmungsgesetz von 1976*). But it is of particular interest to us that board composition may reflect the co-optation representatives of the environment to defuse threats (such as potential competitors) or to recognise or deal with chances that present themselves to the corporation or even to create those chances, e.g. by getting preferential access to customers or suppliers.

Co-optation

When we ask ourselves what purposes board members can serve we find:

- Expertise; for example, bankers will presumably be most qualified in advising how to obtain and manage funds.
- Establishing relationships that help in getting the required *inputs* (money; materials; parts; services) on desirable terms and without interruption.
- Establishing relationships that help in selling the *output* in the required quantities on desirable terms.

In the case of almost all companies all members of the managing board participate in the meetings of supervisory board. Thus, the meetings of the supervisory board provide a convenient opportunity to get to know each other's character and possibilities and establish a relationship of trust. The regularity of board meetings ensures that the relationships do not lapse if there are no current problems; it even ensures that a relationship exists once it is needed.

We have no statements by the persons elected or electing others about the motives in choosing a board member. Data are available, however, about the organisation that is a board member's principal employer, and we can make some inferences from those. About 4.6 per cent of board members are former members of managing boards including those that were managers of other companies. They may sit on the boards to ease the passing of the reins of management into younger and less experienced hands. In other cases, a board seat may be the terminal reward for faithful service or for backing the successor. We cannot separate the two explanations, which in any case do not exclude each other.

About 2.7 per cent are university personnel or members of research institutes. Members or employees of the federal or local governments including parliaments (about 1 per cent of which may sit on the board as the governmental 'representatives') represent 4.1 per cent. For about half of the board members we also have their area of training. For 6.6 per cent of cases the training is in natural sciences. Most of those members, it seems reasonable to assume, have been elected for their expertise rather than to be of assistance in getting inputs or disposing of outputs. This conclusion is less convincing for the 20.7 per cent who have a training in engineering. For the 24.7 per cent with a training in economics or business administration or the 40.7 per cent with a legal

Table 3.1 Board representation of customer industries

IC	Industry	Number of major customer industries	Percentage of output sold to them	Percentage of companies in industry with at least one manager of customer industry on the board [a]
07	Chemical	4	30.43	26.47
10	Plastic products	10	40.04	37.50
16	Iron and steel	6	57.69	16.40
17	Non-ferrous metals	7	64.79	29.50
18	Metal structures	3	14.33	16.70
21	Shipbuilding	1	2.33	25.00
22	Electrical machinery and engineering	3	24.85	27.80
24	Metal fabricating	6	26.16	21.00
25	Toys and jewellery	0	0	0
27	Pulp and paper	5	58.77	31.70
29	Leather	0	0	0
30	Leather products	1	12.33	0
31	Textile	4	36.79	30.60
33	Flour and other mill products	1	19.83	7.70
37	Food, tobacco, beverages	1	12.92	3.70
	Averages	3.5	26.75	18.27

[a] Includes some double counting since the figures are obtained by adding the percentages for the individual customer industries and a given company may have representatives of several companies in different customer industries on its board

training it is not possible to disentangle expertise and relationships helpful in the market place or even collusion as motives.

We now turn to co-optation of persons from customer industries. This type is the one that is most common according to a report by the US Federal Trade Commission (1951, p. 36). We list for the fifteen industries given in Table 3.1 those manufacturing and mining industries which bought a non-trivial amount of the industries' output. 'Non-trivial' was arbitrarily defined as 2 per cent or more of the total output. We leave out agriculture, construction, trade and services as potential sources of board members. Firms in those branches are generally small, dispersed and not represented on the board except for banks, which were treated separately. We then calculate percentage of firms that have co-opted one or more managers of a firm in the customer industry to the supervisory board. Our principal hypothesis is:

The larger the percentage of output sold to another manufacturing industry the larger the percentage of companies that co-opt managers of that industry as members of the supervisory board.

The results are presented in Table 3.1.

Roughly speaking, the higher the share of output sold to other manufacturing firms, the more frequent are customer firms represented on the board. If we take the individual data from the synthetic manufacturers as a customer of the chemical industry etc. to food, tobacco, beverages as a customer of 'Food, Tobacco, Beverages' and run a correlation this impression gets confirmed. The correlation coefficient of $R = 0.25$ is significant, but not high.

We can also hypothesise that the more concentrated the customer industry is, the higher the probability that a single person from that industry can provide the useful information required about the industry and the larger the output he possibly can commit his own firm to buy; that the bigger the company whose manager is asked to sit on the board, the more prestige he will bring to the supervisory board; and that the lower the profitability the higher the pressure to select board members on the basis of their usefulness (rather than to please past members of the managing board or to have a board management is 'comfortable' with). To test these hypotheses we run a regression of the percentage of companies in a given industry (BOARD) that has at least one manager of a firm in a customer industry as a member of its supervisory board. Our independent variables are

Output: percentage of output sold to that industry
KZ6:   share of the six largest firms of the customer industry in the output of the customer industry
Size: median size of firm (thousand employees) within the customer industry
Profits: profits before interest and taxes divided by total capital
Imports: imports in per cent of industry within the customer industry

Results:
Board = $2.95 + 0.29Output$ $n = 48$ $R=0.26$ $F=3.28$
                                                      $p=0.09$
Board = $-0.23 + 0.30Output + 0.14KZ6 - 0.28Size$ $R=0.34$ $F=1.98$
           (0.16)   (0.09)   (0.21)   n.s.

Profits and *Imports* have no significant effects.

If we repeat the analysis leaving out intra-industry board representation (and intra-industry input-output relationships) all correlation vanishes. Since intra-industry interlocking directorates can be explained by a desire for concerted monopolising behaviour, co-optation of customers thus does not seem a significant consideration in constituting the board.

We next do the same analysis for industries delivering inputs to the industry whose board we are considering. By and large we get the same results. On the average, the representation on the board per per cent input is slightly lower than per per cent output (0.56 vs. 0.70).[2] But this may be a statistical artifact.[3]

Running the same regression as above with the input data we get:

$Board = 1.60 + 0.33 Input$ $n = 69$ $R = 0.40$ $F = 12.98$
           (0.09) $p < 0.001$

$Board = 1.99 + 0.32 Input - 0.12 KZ6 + 2.65 Size$ $R = 0.50$ $F = 7.27$
           (0.09)   (0.07)   (1.0) $p < 0.001$

Aside from the fact that the concentration ratio that has the 'wrong' sign

Table 3.2   *Board representation of supplier industries*

IC	Industry	Number of manu. suppl. in industries	Percentage of inputs required	Percentage of companies within row ind. with at least one manager of supplier industry on the board [a]*
07	Chemical	5	45.52	34.7
10	Plastic products	6	57.40	25.0
16	Iron and steel	5	55.11	18.0
17	Non-ferrous metals	4	47.24	11.8
18	Metal structures	5	55.74	16.7
21	Shipbuilding	7	59.87	37.5
22	Electrical machinery and engineering	6	47.07	50.1
24	Metal fabricating	7	53.18	18.1
25	Toys and jewellery	9	39.00	0
27	Pulp and paper	7	37.59	52.8
29	Leather	0	0	0
30	Leather products	6	44.05	11.1
31	Textile	3	46.85	40.1
33	Flour and other mill products	3	7.04	23.1
37	Food, tobacco, beverages	2	22.17	7.4
	Averages	5	41.19	23.14

and size now appears as a significant contributor, the relationship between share of inputs purchased from a particular industry and representation of that industry on the board, is stronger than the corresponding relationship for inputs. Furthermore, it does not vanish once intra-industry data are removed.

Extending the analysis to persons who sit on the supervisory boards, both of a given industry and its supplier or customer (rather than have a manager of a supplier or customer firm sit on the supervisory board of the focus firm) does not change the results materially.

We are, thus, driven to the conclusion that interlocking directorates mostly are the accidental results of two unrelated companies wanting to have the same qualified person on board. We thus wonder whether indeed interlocking directorates are all that important or dangerous in Germany as supposed in the American literature ('the practice of interlocking directorates offends laws, human and divine')[4] or by American legislatures in passing restrictive measures.[5] We question whether the loose ties co-opting directors or managers of other firms are really of much help as intimated earlier in orchestrating behaviour or coping otherwise with a highly competitive environment.[6] We tend to concur with Stigler's (1968, p. 261) dictum:[7]

Interlocking directorates are a clumsy technique even when one desires to co-ordinate the activities of two firms.

We got even further than this, putting forth the hypothesis that just because it is such a poor instrument in concerting behaviour of firms within the same industry and in structuring relationships with suppliers and customers, increased competition will cause firms to make less use of the board for these purposes and rather use it for one or more of the remaining ones.

To test this we look at the development of interlocking directorates over time. Over the last twenty years several developments have occurred to lower protective walls around the economy (for example, tariffs and transportation and communication costs have gone down, anti-trust laws and competition from previously underdeveloped countries have greatly strengthened).

As a result the average West German manufacturing company's profit before taxes and interest as a percentage of total assets has fallen fairly steadily from 20 per cent per annum in 1965 to 14 per cent per annum in 1976. The stronger the competition by foreigners, the less the given corporation can hope to cope with the environment by means of a board constituted of the representatives of German firms.

In Table 3.3 we notice a substantial decrease in interlocking directorates. In part this may be explained by a drop in the number of companies (1961: 562; 1966: 576; 1970: 495; 1975: 392). But the drop

Table 3.5 Interlocking directorates

IC	Industry	1961 same	all 15	%	1966 same	all 15	%	1970 same	all 15	%	1975 same	all 15	%
07	Chemical	37	142	26.0	37	126	29.4	37	109	33.9	29	88	33.0
10	Plastic products	0	13	0	0	28	0	0	17	0	0	7	0
16	Iron and steel	53	179	29.6	45	145	31.0	33	99	33.3	31	78	39.7
17	Non-ferrous metals	4	63	6.3	4	57	7.0	3	39	7.7	2	24	8.3
18	Metal structures	7	65	10.8	9	49	18.4	8	36	22.2	8	36	22.2
21	Shipbuilding	2	13	15.3	2	13	15.4	2	28	7.1	0	15	0
22	Electrical and mechanical engineering	29	133	21.8	23	117	19.7	18	90	20.0	17	76	22.4
24	Metal fabricating	8	61	13.1	6	40	15.0	7	41	17.1	3	27	11.1
25	Toys and jewellery	0	10	0	0	14	0	0	12	0	0	7	0
27	Pulp and paper	0	66	0	0	60	0	2	33	6.1	0	23	0
29	Leather	2	12	16.7	4	10	40.0	2	7	28.6	0	2	0
30	Leather products	2	21	9.5	2	16	12.5	2	8	25.0	0	5	0
31	Textile	84	195	43.1	79	169	46.7	55	111	49.5	41	73	56.2
33	Flour and other mill products	9	22	40.9	3	22	13.6	4	22	18.2	0	15	0
37	Food, tobacco, beverages	4	72	5.6	4	68	5.9	0	35	0	5	25	20.0
	Sum/Average	241	1067	22.9	218	934	24.06	173	687	25.18	136	501	27.2

The numbers in the column lettered 'same' state the number of companies in the same industry that companies in the row industry are related to via interlocking directorates; the numbers in the column lettered 'all 15' give the number of corporations in all fifteen manufacturing industries considered here which have interlocking directorates with one or more of the corporations of the row industry.

We count as interlocking directorate every case where at least one member of the supervisory board of a company sits on the managing or supervisory board of one or more corporations of the row industry.

Companies related by ownership have been excluded.

Only interlocking directorates between corporations (Aktiengesellschaften) are considered.

Interlocking directorates for only fifteen of thirty-one branches of manufacturing cover about half of all such interlocks. Thus, the percentage of all interlocking directorates is understated by about 50 per cent, the percentage of interlocking directorates within the same industry is overstated by the same amount because every interlocking directorate is counted twice.

in directorates from 1067 to 501, i.e. by 50 per cent, is more pronounced than that of companies which amounts only to 30 per cent. Furthermore, the smaller the circle of remaining companies, the more useful interlocking directorates are. If their number drops nonetheless we must consider this as confirmation of our hypothesis that a more competitive environment with more foreigners competing renders contacts between domestic companies less helpful.[8]

It would be desirable to next investigate how well co-optation to the board works as a strategy to cope with the non-economic environment, in particular in response to concerns of environmentalists, to the movement against nuclear energy and finally consumerism – if it can be termed a non-economic issue. Owing to lack of information this cannot be done here.

III. Cartels

Interlocking directorates may provide opportunities for concerting behaviour of two or three firms, but those opportunities are much too haphazard with respect to the firms whose representatives meet, the number of participants is too small for many purposes, the times of meetings are not geared to the appropriate timetable to handle a problem and so on. At best, it seems, interlocking directorates may serve as the nucleus of crystallisation for an agreement. Now Williamson (1979, p. 240) has argued rather persuasively that

the absence of legal prohibitions to collusive contracting is not what prevents comprehensive collusive contracts from being reached. Rather, elementary bounded rationality considerations explain this condition.

Those agreements that are most suited to foster the objectives of profit and stability of the potential participants are outlawed as practices conducive to restraint of trade. As a result they often can only be inferred from the effects. In addition they are difficult to distinguish from other forms of behaviour such as meeting of the mind, conscious parallelism, tacit collusion or just oligopolistic behaviour in general. There is an exception to this statement. In Germany there are certain types of agreement which are legal, enforceable, and, most important for our purposes, for which official and public notification of the authorities is a condition of legality and enforceability. We are referring to the types of cartels set forth in the Law Against the Restraint of Competition (*Gesetz gegen Wettbewerbsbeschränkungen*) as exceptions to the general prohibition of contracts, associations and decisions designed by firms to change production or market conditions in such a way as to restrict competition.

These cartels – in the following the term will refer only to legal ones – are contractual agreements between legally separate entities competing with each other in the market for inputs or outputs. The agreements reduce one or more decision parameters of the partners.

Traditionally the various forms of cartels have been assigned to one of two groups of cartels. 'Higher order cartels' fix prices, set quotas (market shares) or quantities, divide the market by area or kind of customer or type of product. In their advanced form of sales syndicates they take a large step towards merger. (Pooling of profits would be the final step short of merger.) The law frowns particularly on higher order cartels. Only some types are admissible at all, and even for those, specific permission must be obtained in advance. 'Lower types of cartels' may refer to anything else, in particular, terms of sales including rebates, etc. Here, in general, no prior permission but just notification is required, the Federal Cartel Office (*Bundeskartellamt*) retaining the right to veto the agreement during the three months following notification.

On 1 January 1979 a total of 227 cartels were in force, of which 76 were 'lower cartels' and 151 'higher cartels' (Bundeskartellamt 1979). The vast majority of products is not covered by any cartel of any type, let alone by cartels restricting several parameters of competition. Only very few firms in Germany belong to any cartel at all. Those who do belong to one usually manufacture and sell rather homogeneous and humdrum 'old' products.[9] This picture does not change materially if we study all applications for cartels instead of cartels in force (i.e. successful applications).

The results are just what we expect if we consider Oliver Williamson's statement (1975, p. 239):

A contract between two or more parties will be attractive in the degree to which: (i) the good service or behaviour in question is amenable to unambiguous written specification; (ii) joint gains from collective action (agreement) are potentially available; (iii) implementation in the face of uncertainty does not occasion costly haggling; (iv) monitoring the agreement is not costly and (v) detected non-compliance carries commensurate penalties at low enforcement expense.

Such is likely to be the case if the product is homogeneous; if expected losses, in the case that no co-operation is reached, continue to be large; the number of persons or entities that have to act in concert is small; the persons involved have a common cultural background; in particular the same objectives and the same attitude towards chiselling; opportunities to meet are frequent, or meetings are easily arranged; buyers are not changing and report fully prices offered (as under competitive bidding; Stigler 1968, p. 48). Thus, collusion is most promising for homogeneous products if the share of imports in domestic sales is small, the industry is highly concentrated and the product late in its life cycle. The latter has been reasoned by Heuss

Table 3.4 Cartels in Germany, 1961–76

Year	Applications for cartels[b] 'higher' cartels Cumulative	Change	'lower' cartels Cumulative	Change	Sum	Cartels legally in force[a] 'higher' cartels Cumulative	Change	'lower'[c] cartels Cumulative	Change	Sum	Cartels in force at end of year
1961	123		82		205	44		56		100	100
1966	188	65	132	50	320	92	48	85	29	177	168
1970	244	56	152	20	396	152	60	97	12	249	213
1975	295	49	169	17	464	192	40	108	19	300	211
1976	315	20	171	2	486	204	12	109	1	313	211
End 1976						131		80			211

[a] Total number in force at any time between 1961 and 1976.

[b] Cartels as defined in 'Gesetz gegen Wettbewerbsbeschränkungen', para. 4; para. 5, 2, and 3; para. 5 a and b; para. 6–7, i.e. cartels exempted from the legal inhibition of agreements resulting in the lowering of competition as set forth in para. 1, GWB (cartels providing for rationalisation, but also affecting prices, cartels providing for product specialisation, for co-operation of small and medium-sized firms, cartels concerning exports and imports). These cartels can be expected to affect price, quantity, area of distribution, line of product sold or several of these.

[c] All other cartels, in particular those establishing common terms of sale or product norms.

(1965, pp. 230–61) and Oberender (1973, as quoted in Tuchfeldt 1978, p. 451). They argue that late in the life cycle the transparency of the market increases and competition is mainly carried out via price and quality.

Now most products and services on the market do not fit remotely the conditions just outlined. Thus, we should not expect many products to be covered by cartels.

Earlier in the paper we stated that competition in Germany had become substantially strengthened by a number of developments. Our hypothesis is that this favours stronger forms of associations over weak ones. Applied to cartels we expect a shift of the relative emphasis away from 'lower cartels' to higher cartels. To test this we examine the applications for cartels and cartels in force for the years 1961–76 distinguishing higher cartels and lower cartels. As the figures in Table 3.4 show both the applications and the permissions for higher cartels have increased substantially faster than those for lower cartels. The ratio of higher cartels in force to lower ones has shifted from 44:56 (=0.78) to 130:80 (1=1.63), i.e. reversed itself. This, by the way, confirms that price, quantity, market share, area of distribution, type of customer served and indeed the main competitive parameters rather than other ones such as terms of sale and service.

We summarise stating that under a rather narrow set of conditions cartels are a form of organisation between market and hierarchy that can be of help in obtaining inputs and selling outputs at favourable and stable terms. In the domain of firms' strategy and organisation cartels do not seem to be helpful as their participants are separate legal entities with different owners. Only part of their activities and the attaining of objectives is covered by cartels. It seems to us, however, that very little empirical research has been done on cartels, in particular the situation on the participants before forming a cartel, number and size of participants and the effect of the cartel.

IV. Capital Ownership

Berle and Means (1932) maintained that the modern capitalistic economy is characterised by a separation of ownership and management, and more importantly by dispersion of ownership that is so pronounced that owners in effect cannot control management, management then being free to pursue goals different from those of the owners. They also maintain that such separation and dispersion of ownership increases over time. These theses turn out not to be true for Germany, as shown elsewhere for companies listed on the stock exchange (Thonet and Poensgen 1979, p. 26). In addition, the usual categorisation of manager-controlled vs. owner-controlled companies overlooks a most important third category, i.e. companies controlled by another company.

We confirm this by extending the analysis to unlisted companies as well as examining all manufacturing companies in all branches of manufacturing except brewing as listed by the Federal Office of Statistics (*Statistisches Bundesamt*) for 1975. There was a total of 748 companies. Information and ownership was available for 666 companies. The findings are shown in Table 3.5. Thus, it emerges that the normal company in as far as it has another company as the largest owner is owned by another operating company.

Having established the importance of the phenomenon we will ask what purposes in our list on p. 55 are served by capital ownership.

Strategy

Equity participation, i.e. ownership, may be close to indispensable for the transfer of funds between parts of an industrial combine. The subsidiary may also be kept out of profitable areas where the parent company is active. Of course, the effect would be particularly large if the subsidiary were to be totally or partially closed down. Thus minority interests create difficulties with respect to the use of the assets (*usus*), the definition and distribution of the income (*usufructus*) and the change including disposal (*abusus*). The German Corporation Law (*Aktiengesetz*) has tried explicitly to provide for both the needs of

Table 3.5   *Manufacturing companies by type of ownership, 1975*

Largest owner	Number of firms
(1) A person, family group (214) or holding company (70)	284
(2) Dispersed (no owner holds more than 20%)	26
(3) Operating company in manufacturing (280), banking (41), insurance company (2), co-operative society (7)	330
(4) Others (investment funds, 0; foundations, 6; trade unions, 0; Federal Government, 0; State, 2; Municipal, 1; others, 8)a	17
(5) Non-assigned but belonging to categories (1), (3) or (4)	9
	666
NO INFORMATION AVAILABLE	82
Total	748

The figures cover all manufacturing corporations (*Aktiengesellchaften*) except breweries.

a   These figures understate dramatically the influence of goverment because the government administers its large industrial interests via a holding company, in particular the VEBA company.

the parent company in directing the subsidiary and the protection of minority owners. It provides for a formal contract of dominance (*Beherrschungsvertrag*) which provides that the management of the dominant firm can give direct orders to the dependent one without working through the shareholders, the supervisory board, appointment of pliant members to the management board, etc. (It also provides rather elaborately for the protection of minority stockholders.)

Nonetheless, such machinery is rather cumbersome and we would expect that in order to serve the function of transferring funds and integrating operations completely into that of a parent company full ownership is the normal state of affairs. This in principal is a testable proposition. Transfer of funds should be a particularly important objective in Germany since there is so little financing via new equity.

The second strategic purpose mentioned on p. 55 was to put together a balanced mix of growing and non-growing sectors. To do so a company may try to acquire a much smaller company pioneering in a related field, possibly even developing substitutes to the acquirer's product. The acquiring company is likely to be large, inflexible and bureaucratic and will probably rely much on rules and decisions from the top in its co-ordination efforts and ways to adapt to changes. Fields characterised by fast and novel technologies, however, usually require decentralisation, intensive monitoring of the environment and technological development as well as fast decisions instead of decisions delayed by the passage through several layers of a large hierarchy. Pay for experts may be higher than for experts in other technological fields. Co-ordination may occur via agreement by peers or by settling issues within a team rather than via regulations or the established hierarchy.

Large companies will recognise this. They will also be aware of the fact that it would be very difficult to modify and keep differentiated (in the sense of Lawrence and Lorsch 1967) a part of the original company without creating demands for more decentralisation, higher pay scales etc. in other parts of the company. It thus may be easier to buy an existing company and not integrate it too closely into the existing industrial group.[10] Majority ownership may suffice.

Reduction of uncertainty via diversification is a third strategic purpose for acquiring a stake in other companies. Companies in non-related fields would serve best for this purpose. Here, even minority ownership might do. If financial means are limited, smaller stakes in more companies might even be superior to full ownership in a few firms.

Inputs, outputs and competition

There are, however, other areas of uncertainty, such as uncertainty relating to the supply of inputs, i.e. of raw material, intermediate products, services, know-how, rights, licences, mineral rights, rights of way, etc. The uncertainty may be with a respect to price, quantity, quality, timeliness. As pointed out by Williamson (1975) bounded rationality, opportunism plus the small numbers problem make it difficult if not impossible to eliminate this uncertainty by writing contracts covering future contingencies. Instead it seems to be more feasible to integrate backward by buying the source of materials etc. This strategy was very common one or two generations ago as pointed out by Chandler (1977). Since then, very often developments have occurred to diminish the uncertainty, increase the number of suppliers, increase familiarity with the products, the know-how and improve information processing capabilities. All of these are developments favouring a shift towards the market rather than the hierarchy (Williamson 1975, p. 10). As reported above the responses to our interview questions bear out our assertion that getting supplies generally is not a major problem. It is a normal state of affairs for a capitalist economy that the market is a buyer's market not a seller's market.

This suggests that forward integration is a more important strategic purpose than backward integration, one of the methods being the creation of captive customers by their acquisition. In Germany forward integration was fairly frequent until the 1960s, i.e. as long as the German market had walls around it. As pointed out on p. 62 these walls, however, have been breached or tunnelled since. Once the market was opened to all commerce, integrating forward just meant carrying the problem of selling output to a later production stage, usually a stage subject even more to competition from abroad since the value per pound on the average was higher and the freight cost per dollar value correspondingly lower. It also meant that management had to be expert in two or more markets and technologies, those for the intermediate products and those for the final product. As the competitive pressure also affected the intermediate stage, the manager of the final products, where competition was fiercest, rebelled against a top management that restricted their sources of supplies to internal ones. Franko (1976) has described in detail the pressures forcing the European and especially German companies to abandon the more centralised functional structure and adopt the divisional structure with its semi-autonomous managers and internal markets. In other words, the pressure is away from hierarchy and towards the market. Thus forward integration is not expected to play a major role within industrial groups.

Since we have ruled out successively conglomerate diversification, forward and backward integration on the one hand, and since we have demonstrated on the other that the normal state of affairs for a company is to have an operating parent company, we must expect most parent–subsidiary relationships to link companies in the same industry. Companies linked by ownership can do everything members in a cartel can do, only better, because monitoring can be substantially extended beyond behaviour visible in the market. In addition disputes can be settled by fiat and gains cannot be kept but must be delivered to a parent company. This diminishes incentives to opportunism. While this may be true, its significance probably is small as far as fixing of prices and quantities goes. Cases are rare where adding subsidiaries to a parent company will give the combination cartel-like dominance of a market. Other activities of the cartels, especially those of the lower order ones plus product specialisation may be more helpful especially in saving costs even if the combined market is small.

We turn now to the evidence for the hypothesis that horizontal combinations are most common. To test the hypothesis we investigate all known ownership ties (largest to fifth largest owners) for the 666 companies mentioned in Table 3.5). There are 975 owner-owned ties with the owned always being a non-brewing manufacturing corporation (*Aktiengesellschaft*). While in 382 cases the owner is an operating company only in 226 cases it has the legal form of an *Aktiengesellschaft*. Table 3.6 examines 151 ties between manufacturing more closely. [1] We interpret this as substantial support of our hypothesis. With respect to the within-industry category, however, we must admit that they may hide a number of supplier-buyer relationships. The percentage of ties, however, is far larger than the corresponding share of industry output

Table 3.6   Linkages of manufacturing corporations to other manufacturing corporations, 1975 (excluding breweries)

105 or 70%	of ties are with companies within the same branch of manufacturing[a]
27 or 17%	of ties are with companies outside the same branch of manufacturing but within the same sector[b] of manufacturing
13 or 9%	of ties are with companies to an industry in an adjoining sector
6 or 4%	of ties are with companies in unrelated industries, i.e. where no strong supplier–customer relationship can be expected

[a]   226 − 151 = 75 firms were active in fields other than manufacturing, i.e. banking, insurance, agriculture, mining, construction, transportation, communication, electric power generation, trade, and other services.

[b]   7 sectors of manufacturing were defined by us: 1. food and kindred products; 2. (other) consumer goods; 3. intermediate products; 4. capital goods; 5. industry producing both goods for consumption and intermediate products; 6. industries producing both consumption and capital goods; 7. industries producing both intermediate products and capital goods.

sold to other manufacturing firms. This can be seen by inspecting input-output tables (DIW 1975).

We recall that in the case of interlocking directorates (see Table 3.3) intra-industry ties accounted for only 25 per cent of all ties vs. 70 per cent here. We interpret this to mean that collusion or, put more neutrally, co-ordination of firms within the same industries very easily gets bogged down by conflicts over markets, areas, products, prices and decisions to reduce or expand capacity. In such cases ownership ties are required to resolve the conflict. They give a much more powerful lever to force management of two or more firms to act in concert. On the other hand, to get the co-operation of a supplier or customer no such stick is needed; interlocking directorates as well as other forms of co-operation which are in the mutual interest of firms will suffice.

Organisation

Among the tasks mentioned on p. 55 we have not yet discussed organisation. A number of pertinent questions were addressed to managers of eighty-eight firms in four industries (chemical, electrical, metal fabricating, textile) chosen from all manufacturing firms for detailed interviewing.

We asked two questions regarding the division of labour:

- In which areas does your firm render services to related companies which are equivalent to more than 10 per cent of the total budget of the corresponding department of your firm?
- Are services rendered to your company by related companies the value of which exceeds 10 per cent of the budget of the appropriate department of your firm?

There were fifty-five companies describing themselves as members of an industrial group, either dominant or dependent or dominant with respect to one company, dependent with respect to another company. The percentage of companies where services were either received or rendered to the extent described above are listed in Table 3.7. The questions were restricted to the staff functions listed here, i.e. excluded production and marketing as well as activities abroad. Some of the figures are quite low, because the particular function is not performed at all (OR) or not separable from other work (market-research, special studies).

Co-ordination may extend both to organisation structure and organisational procedure such as planning, techniques, the accounting systems and personnel practices. Organisational innovation may be transferred particularly easily between companies with ownership ties. If the parent company exercises its influence we expect it to transplant

Table 3.7   Percentage of fifty-five companies receiving from or rendering staff services to related companies by area

EDP	40
Finance	34
Law	33
Taxes	31
R & D	29
Special studies	25[a]
Organisation	18
Marketing research	13
Operations research	7
Other	18

[a]   Cost reduction, choice of location, routing of traffic, etc.

her own structure or her own procedures. This may be so either because it has been tried and found to be superior to alternatives or because this makes it easier to work with subsidiaries or to influence them in substantive areas.

By and large, for such procedures to be transplantable the parent company must be an operating company active in the same sector of industry, say manufacturing. If the subsidiary is much smaller than the parent company such transplanation may still be dysfunctional for the subsidiary.

Control may be effected by means of either procedures or persons. We asked the firms of our sample to what extent the format of the reports to the parent company or even the system of accounts of the subsidiary were prescribed by the parent or dominant company. Out of fifty-three related companies answering the question thirty-three termed such influence as comprehensive; twenty responded that only a few basic data were prescribed and required.[11]

We also asked whether and in what area personnel below the managing board of the dependent company may be told to obey orders coming directly from persons within the dominant company bypassing the managing board of the dependent company. Out of forty-seven dependent companies investigated nine report this for at least one of their functional departments. Other organisational arrangements by the dominant firms to institutionalise its influence are of more practical relevance. If the dependent company is made to report to the managing board of the dominant company in its entirety we find this to be an indicator of much relative freedom for the dependent company. If the management, however, reports to a single member of the managing board, as is the case for about one-third of the companies reporting to a parent company in our sample, it depends on the function of the member within the dominant company how much freedom the dependent company has. If he is the company counsel or in charge of finance or a similar function, the influence probably still is weak. If, however, he is head of marketing or production or a product group, influence is likely to be much stronger, in particular if the subsidiary is a marketing company (e.g. abroad), a company producing inputs for the dominant company or one manufacturing products within the product scope of the industrial group. If the dominant company is very large, occasionally the management of the dependent company is made to report to a head of group that is not even a member of the managing board.[12] This usually points to the fact that the dependent company in effect is just a well integrated part of the larger business combined. In such cases, a part of the product spectrum or a particular market is assigned to the dependent company and the company itself may even be incomplete, i.e. not have all the functions necessary to exist as an independent entity. The converse may also be true.

While we have not investigated the forms of control in detail as they are linked to other variables it seems to us that managements of parent's companies have much relative freedom in shaping their relationship to the management of subsidiaries. The results of this subsection on organisation suggest to us that among its sub-tasks as listed on p. 56 only the division of tasks (including products) among the members of an industrial group and the allocation of monetary resources plus monitoring are of major import. In principle, this is testable; we do not have sufficient data, however, to do this thoroughly.

V. Mergers

As far as we can see, virtually all of the tasks described on p.55 could also be accomplished by a combination of a parent company and its wholly owned subsidiary. The formal act of merger may just remove some of the costs and delays associated with maintaining the legal institutions of management board and supervisory board, keeping separate sets of accounts, balance sheets and like. It may also make clear to all concerned that a former company is now fully integrated and stripped of the vestiges of independence.

If the situation before the merger was one of less than 100 per cent ownership, the merger removes the difficulties (discussed on p. 69ff) in implementing the strategy of an industrial group when there is minority ownership in some of its members. Of course the mergers we observed may start from any ownership, none, partial or full. It therefore would be incorrect to seek the merger motives exclusively in those advantages that distinguish full ownership in a separate legal entity from a complete integration; instead the points discussed in the section on capital ownership also apply.

Table 3.8   Mergers in Germany, 1966–78

Year	Number of mergers
1966	43
1967	65
1968	65
1969	168
1970	305
1971	220
1972	269
1973	242
1974	318
1975	448
1976	453
1977	554
1978	558

23 GWB requires notification of mergers involving market shares of 20 per cent or more or sales of at least DM 500 million or 10,000 employees of all partners combined.
Source: *Bundeskartellamt* (1977, p. 138 and 1979, p. 115)

Mergers by size, type and over time

The results presented in earlier section of this paper lead us to expect that the increase in competitive pressure in Germany has fostered merger activities. Table 3.8 shows the figures for mergers that the Federal Cartel Office (*Bundeskartellamt*) was notified of, as required by the Law Against the Constraint of Competition (*Gesetz gegen Wettbewerbeschränkung*, GW). As predicted the number of mergers is increasing almost year by year. Large firms or more precisely firms operating in industries where on the average firms are large play the largest role in those mergers although, of course, the number of firms available from mergers drops drastically with size.

Table 3.9   Mergers by size, 1970–76

Sales of participating firms combined in DM millions	Number of mergers	Numbers of participating firms	Classification by sales of participating firms individually
Below 250	128	273	2594
250–500	75	159	246
500–1000	265	598	451
1000–5000	804	1880	1113
Above 5000	967	2465	971
Total	2239	5375	5375

Firms involved in several mergers are accounted repeatedly.
Source: *Bundeskartellamt* (1977, pp. 144–5)

From our discussion of capital ownership we would expect most mergers to be horizontal ones. This turns out to be the case.

Table 3.10   Mergers by type, 1970–76

Type	Number of mergers		Per cent of total
Horizontal		1652	74
without diversification	1214		54
with diversification	438		20
Vertical		302	13
Conglomerate		285	13
Total		2239	100

The classification of conglomerate mergers by the Federal Cartel Office is more inclusive than ours. Thus, the reported percentage is above the figure reported by us for conglomerate linkages by means of capital ownership.

Source: Bundeskartellamt (1977, p. 148)

Mergers and cartels as substitutes
Combining the industry-by-industry data on the frequency of mergers with the corresponding data on cartels permits us to throw some light on the motivations of both mergers and cartels as well as on the appropriateness of dividing cartels in higher order and lower order ones. In Table 3.11 we calculate zero-order Pearson correlations for higher order and lower order cartels in force (at the end of 1976) with mergers (1970–76) within the same industry, on the one hand, and mergers outside the industry, on the other. There are twenty-five observations, one for each of twenty-five industries for which the Federal Cartel Office makes the data available. The correlation between higher cartels in force and mergers within the same industry is substantial and significant: all other correlations are low and insignificant. We interpret this as follows:

1. Mergers within the same industry and higher cartels to a certain extent are substitutes for each other – in industries where we find the ones we also find the others.
2. Motives for higher and lower order cartels apparently are different or, put differently, the classification of cartels into higher-order ones and lower-order ones make sense – so would economic policy making that same distinction.
3. The motive for mergers with a firm outside one's own industry differ from those for mergers within one's own industry.

These observations cannot be explained by technological economies of scale because we would then expect lower order cartels to be correlated to within-industry mergers. The motive therefore presumably is to increase market power. We must take care, however, against passing a judgement to the effect that such mergers reduce competition. The merging firms may be second-tier firms who hope to establish a countervailing power to those in the first tier.

Table 3.11   Cartels and mergers correlated

	Mergers	
	within the industry	outside the industry
Higher order cartels	0.51**	0.06
Lower order cartels	0.16	–0.09

Number of industries: 25
** Significance at the $p = 0.01$ level
Source: *Bundeskartellamt* (1977) and own calculations

Mergers within vs. without the acquirer's industry

If we look at the average size of acquired firms it turns out that firms acquired within the own industry have average sales of DM 150 million. This is about three times the figure for sales of firms acquired outside the own industry (DM 55 million). This confirms our hypothesis that the acquisition within the own industry serves to buy out a competitor and to build up monopoly power whereas the acquisition of a firm in another industry more often has a goal to acquire know-how (technological motivation) (cf. p. 69). For the acquisition of market power is the more effective the larger the acquired firm is. In acquiring know-how, however, it is more economical to buy a small firm with the appropriate specialisation. The first point is borne out by Table 3.9. Three out of four mergers within the own industry are classified by the Federal Cartel Office as 'without diversification'. Kaufer (1979, pp. 8–20) suspects that many acquisitions of other firms occur to remove that much capacity from the market and he presents some evidence. We conjecture that many purchases within the industry are made by firms that try to lower the distance to the very largest one.[13]

We have attempted to explain merger activity 'within' and 'without' the industry by means of multiple merger models. It turns out that we are able to explain 90 per cent of all 'within industry' mergers simply by introducing the number of possible combinations (which is a function of the square of the number of companies in the industry (above a certain, large size)) without any attention to circumstances which vary from industry to industry, such as economies of scale, competitive pressure, pace of change, effect of the business cycle and alike.

If we introduce into our regression the profitability of the industry (profits before interest and taxes divided by long-term capital averaged for the years 1971–5) variance explained rises from 90.35 to 94.4 per cent. This means that profitability explains more than 40 per cent of variance left after introducing the number of potential merger partners.[14] The figures tell us that mergers are not something resorted to if the firm is in dire straits, on the contrary, on the average 'within industry' mergers are more frequent in industries that are doing well. Our findings at least raise doubts as to whether horizontal mergers raise efficiency.

These results lead us to expect that the number of mergers outside the own industry is a product of the number of firms within the industry of the acquirer and the number of firms in the industry of the acquired. The number of mergers involving firms in two given industries, however, is so small that we cannot deal with it appropriately. Since the number of firms in other industries is large in relation to the number of firms within the own industry the number of potential partners outside the industry is practically independent of the industry, i.e. is a constant. Thus, we expect the number of mergers outside the own industry and the number of acquirers to be linearly related. Indeed it turns out that the variance explained is 31 per cent ($R = 0.56$; $p < 0.01$).[15]

If we further include measures of absolute and relative firm size, concentration, average sales of acquired companies (all of which prove significant in a multiple regression model), total variance explained, while not quite as large as in the 'within industry' one, is still very large (90 per cent). It means that only 10 per cent of inter-industry variance remains for the effects of interaction between the industry of the acquirer and the industry of the acquired, e.g. the proximity of industries in which existing know-how in technology or marketing can be used or that are important as suppliers or customers.

VI Conclusion

It is only under competitive pressure that organisational arrangements begin to approach their optimum state. This is the obverse of the famous dictum coined by Hicks (1935, p. 8): 'The best of all monopoly profits is a quiet life.'

While there are numerous devices of co-ordination within the spectrum between market, association and hierarchy, increasing competitive pressures will lead firms in their relationship to other firms either to revert to market relationships or to advance to hierarchy – the centre cannot hold. Thus, we have seen interlocking directorates tend to be of little use in the best of circumstances and are of declining importance when the economy is highly competitive. Cartels as both non-market and non-hierarchical devices have some uses, but only in a rather stagnant environment which limits the extent to which they are adopted greatly. This would be less true for cartels which fix prices, assign quotas etc., but those not only encounter legal obstacles but are also severely threatened by competitive firms without. Looking at the bonds provided by capital ownership we must distinguish between conglomerate industrial groups, vertically integrated ones and those operating within the same industry. The passage to a later stage in the life cycle as well as increasing competitive pressure will reduce the usefulness of the bond and drive them towards the market, the same forces will drive horizontal combines towards a strengthening of hierarchy albeit through merger. In all cases these forces work against the more loose associations.

Notes

[1] The mining and the iron and steel industry are an exception. They are covered by a different law which provides for 50:50 proportions plus a neutral member.

[2] 18.27/26.75 (botton row of Table 3.1) and 23.14/41.19 (botton row of Table 3.2). respectively.

[3] Strictly speaking we do not count board members that are managers in firms of the inputs industries but count the number of companies that have one *or more* managers of firms of a given input industry on the board.

[4] Statement attributed to Judge L. Brandeis by Helferding, US Federal Trade Commission 1951, p. 3.

[5] Interstate Commerce Act of 1887 (as amended), Clayton Act of 1914, Communications Act of 1934, Civil Aeronautics Act of 1938, to name but the pre-war statutes (US Federal Trade Commission 1951).

[6] At best it may be of some use if there are few firms in the industry, a hypothesis confirmed by Schiffels (1980). He finds a positive correlationship of $R = 0.24$ ($p < 0.001$) between the rate of concentration of the focus industry and the number of interlocking directorates.

[7] I am indebted to Schiffels for this quote and the one by Brandeis.

[8] One can argue that the above argument rests on the assumption that the expected number of interlocks is proportional to the number of companies and that this is not a good or tested assumption. However, taking the various industries as different observations, we can regress the ratio of interlocks 1975/61 on the corresponding ratio for the number of companies and companies squared. This should indicate (i) what percentage of the decline is indeed explained by the reduction in the number of companies and (ii) what the shape of the relationship is. We get:

Interlocks 1975/61 $= 0.16 + 0.50$ number of companies 1975/61

$n = 16$; $R = 0.47$; $R^2adj = 0.16$; $F = 3.67$; $p = 0.075$

It turns out that the square term does not make any contribution at all (instead it reduces R^2adj). The relationship is weak, not quite significant, and, if anything, linear. Thus the drop in directorates cannot be attributed (to more than 16 per cent) to the change in the number of companies.

[9] R&D-intensive firms producing new equipment with recently invented or modified

processes possibly have a device of their own of concerting behaviour if they want to reduce competitive pressure. We are referring to pattern pooling and cross-licensing. This device, however, encounters strong resistance by the Law and the practice of the Federal Cartel Office.

[10] There are other advantages, such as limitation of liability, maintenance of goodwill associated with the firm's name, both in the eyes of customers and employees, establishing or keeping separate product images useful in different segments of the market, etc.

[11] We have not investigated the hypothesis that companies operating in the same industry prescribe more closely the reports and the system of accounts to their subsidiaries.

[12] In our sample this was true for five out of forty-five reporting relationships.

[13] A remark by Scherer (1970, p. 111) points into the same direction: 'Another effect of the postwar merger wave was to increase the quality of firm sizes within the population of the largest firms.'

[14] The partial correlation between profitability and the number of merger holding the number of merger partners constant is 0.64; the relationship is positive and highly significant ($p < 0.001$, F = 13.4).

[15] As to be expected a quadratic term for the number of firms within the own industry by itself explains far less variance (18 per cent).

PART III

4 The Invisibility of Power in
Economics: beyond markets and
hierarchies
M. Bauer and E. Cohen

The success of a theory – especially one which is mainly based on tried
and tested concepts – gives rise to problems: what explanation can be
given for the sway exerted by supporters of the institutional school[1] not
only over economists and sociologists but also over students of large
organisations? Many critiques have been made of the model of pure,
perfect competition and market equilibrium. Prior to the institutional
school, many economists had substantially altered the classical theory
of the firm: the hypothesis of atomicity was replaced by that of oligopoly;[2] the hypothesis of the homogeneity of products by that of product
differentiation and monopolistic competition (Chamberlain 1953); the
hypothesis of market transparency by that of market opacity and the
uncertainty and unequal distribution of information (Von Neuman and
Morgenstern 1944); the hypothesis of universal rationality by that of a
plurality of possible rationalities;[3] the hypothesis of a single decision-
making centre by that of a multiplicity of actors influencing the choices
made (March and Simon 1958; Cyert and March 1963); and the hypothesis of the market as the only means of allocating goods by that of
market failure and hence by the study of public or indivisible goods
(Arrow 1951; Buchanan 1968). All in all, this theory, which was static,
ahistorical, equilibristic, individualistic, and which discounted the
phenomenon of power, was unable to account for the functioning of
large industrial firms, i.e. of the dominant actors in contemporary
economic life.

What do the theorists of institutional economics add to these critical
analyses? Is what they offer merely a reorganisation of this body of
criticism? Is their theory a new bridge between economics and the
sociology of organisations – two disciplines that have generally ignored
each other's achievements? Is the theory a restructuring of economic
knowledge based on the propositions of information theory and the
cybernetic model? Or is it the old liberal ideology dressed up in new
clothes to suit large organisations? A detailed study of the conceptual
framework, the analytical propositions and implicit hypotheses in the
theoretical work of one of the most prominent theorists of institutional

economics will enable us to specify some of the reasons for the theory's attractivenss and to define the essential features of an alternative approach which, starting from the main problems raised by Williamson, does not gloss over the reality of domination or assume the existence of a social consensus.

I. Markets and Hierarchies: the foundations of organised liberalism

To analyse the hypotheses implicit in an approach that claims to be free of ideological or partisan preliminary entails a detailed study of its theoretical framework, its logic, and its corollaries.

Conceptual framework

Williamson has embarked upon a twofold project: it is both theoretical and political. The task he undertakes is to break away from the analysis of an abstract market and to replace it with one entailing the study of relationships between economic actors with bounded rationality, motivated by individual projects, and possessing only partial information. In so doing, he puts forward a unitary approach that, by rejecting the traditional gap between the study of the internal functioning of the organisation and of its environment, concentrates on the study of either inter- or intra-organisational social relations. Here, a sociological approach contributes to a revival of economic theory. The author thus seeks to improve our understanding of the origins, forms and effects of economic concentration so as to generate more enlightened and therefore more effective action by public authorities.

To aid understanding of economic phenomena, Williamson proposes a grid based on negotiation and transaction costs. In the uncertain and complex world of modern economic activity, we are faced with the crucial problem of reduction of uncertainty, which is particularly costly to control. However, the organisation cannot reduce totally this uncertainty without endangering the very idea of a viable, human society. The problem, therefore, is to establish a dynamic balance which in the long run avoids the twin pitfalls of disorder and paralysis. Neither all-out competition between micro-units nor totalitarian bureaucratic organisation can meet this theoretical challenge. Williamson uses informational economics to assess the effectiveness of the different forms of company organisation and of the economic system.

More precisely, the unitary approach offered by Williamson distinguishes between human and environmental factors with all these factors left floating freely in the atmosphere, and looks at their interrelation. But although this approach in general responds to the body of criticism directed at classical microeconomic theory, it does so in a particularly reductive manner. For example, uncertainty is never qualified but merely quantitatively assessed (as opposed to the theory of games, which allows for different forms of uncertainty); the strategy of each of the members of a possible oligopoly is never specified unless it be to contrast 'true' oligopoly to one that conceals domination by one of its members. The bounded rationality of the actors, which is intended to contrast with the universal model of profit maximisation, actually results in a minimisation of transaction costs (a new universal form of rationality?), which is far from a detailed study of the different preference functions guiding the action of the various agents. The actor's opportunism, which does indeed enable a distinction to be drawn between seeking monetary gain and other forms of remuneration, is never itself related back to particular choices. The development of the concept of 'information impactedness' marks an advance over the view of information as free and equally distributed, but it does not permit the analysis of the different qualities of information or of its utility value. Finally, there is the question of the atmosphere that should characterise this general climate, which cannot be precisely estimated in accounting terms, but which is generally admitted to be essential by all actors in the system studied.

In short, this is a particularly formal approach which enables the author both to replace the unrealistic model of control via the market with negotiated control, and to substitute for the unreal model of the programmed hedonistic robot (the theory of individual behaviour in liberal economics) the model of conflicting groups representing different orientations and settling for a partial optimum. Only an explication of this formal model – through an analysis of its logical corollaries – can permit the evaluation of its validity and usefulness.

Theoretical propositions and empirical testing

Williamson tests his analytical framework by studying six of the main forms of economic organisation, while at the same time trying to explain the main transformations to the socioeconomic system and proposing the political means to ensure the improved functioning of the system.

(a) From peer group to the simple hierarchy   Although co-operation and peer groups emerge as the first organisational forms capable of absorbing uncertainty, of controlling the indivisible and socialising risk, their proper functioning presupposes great informational expenditure. Williamson is thus able to account for the general emergence of the hierarchy as the favoured means for reducing these transaction costs and eliminating 'free rider abuses'. The economics of information thus enables one both to rediscover the iron law of oligarchy and to dispel scientifically the cream of self-management. Moreover, as the author notes, it is the cost of negotiation rather than the direction of the action

that should determine the forms of social action.

While not wishing here to drag in the debate on the irreducible value of the direction of a social action, we would nevertheless mention that there are instances in which, even purely from the point of view of economic effectiveness, the peer group emerges as being more effective than the simple hierarchy: experiments in job-enrichment, particularly in self-managing groups, provide an illustration of this since they allow for less expensive and higher quality total production than hierarchical organisation of the Taylorian type.

(b) The creation of the complex organisations as a structuring of simple hierarchies: the example of vertical integration   An organisation becomes vertically integrated because it needs to reduce uncertainty over its supplies and/or sales. The same objective can undoubtedly be achieved by the negotiation of long-term contracts, but Williamson claims that this is a more expensive operation than merging: mergers are therefore to be preferred. His approach appears to disregard the stakes in such a process of vertical concentration. Two examples, taken from the history of a French industrial group, suggest that the operations of vertical integration cannot simply be explained as an attempt to minimise transaction costs.

At the end of the last century, Megatube,[4] a smelting firm, was trying to expand. As it did so, it confronted not only the cartels of raw material suppliers (coal and iron), but also the large integrated steel companies. The firm's initial policy – and this indeed illustrates Williamson's claims – was to negotiate long-term contracts. But soon Megatube developed production activities in raw materials sectors itself. Can this policy be explained as an effort to reduce transaction costs? In fact, the policy was an expression both of the firm's inability to take over a firm producing raw materials and of a deliberate plan to shape by its presence the development of the raw materials sector. This example emphasises that a given firm cannot always choose between long-term contracts and mergers. The example also indicates that Williamson's theory does not enable one to account for the initiator of integration: an integration of smelting firms towards raw materials is not equivalent to an integration of coal firms towards the smelting industry, unless one assumes that the firm is not an actor with a policy plan.

Fifty years later, this same firm, which had in the meantime grown considerably, opted for marked integration and began offering complete water-supply systems. One reason was, of course, to reduce uncertainty on the side of its customers. But there was also a deeper motive: to determine by its presence the consumption of a particular productive good. In pursuing this policy, the firm was asserting its ability to define the world of market goods, and it thus emerged as not only an economic but also a sociopolitical actor. If the process in question is reduced to an effort to lessen uncertainty, this perspective becomes lost; the transactions between actors rightly remain in the centre of the analysis, but their specificity and their content disappear.

(c) Creation of the 'M-form' The process by which organisations develop, and which according to Williamson enables firms to absorb a maximum of uncertainty, must nevertheless reach a limit for two reasons. First, there is a real risk of a new market being reconstructed within the organisation (the development of intra-organisational uncertainty); second, because the system thus formed becomes increasingly difficult to govern on account of growing conflict between different internal sub-groups. The solution that was historically developed to solve this problem was the invention of a new organisation, the multi-departmental, product-market (M-form) organisation. Sloan's organisational innovation, which became rapidly widespread, allowed for double economy in transaction costs, for it separated the non-interdependent sub-systems, which could thus be individually controlled, and enabled a general control system to ensure coherence between the different directions taken by each of these sub-systems in relation to a global aim.

The sociohistorical analysis of Megatube has enabled us to establish the non-inevitability of this kind of reform: Megatube, which had considerably diversified its production throughout the first half of the twentieth century, preserved a functional (U-form) organisation until the early 1960s, all the while maintaining a high level of economic efficiency. How, then, can we explain that 'the structure did not follow the strategy' (Chandler 1966) and that the firm did not collapse under transaction costs that became increasingly prohibitive? To understand this phenomenon – which not only challenges Chandler's theories but also casts doubt upon the viewpoint advanced by Williamson – requires a shift in our interpretative framework.

If the firm was able to maintain its high level of performance, it did so because it could win and keep the loyalty of its members and maintain the coherence of its sub-units. The collective memory which it built up for itself, its control procedures, and the support it finally obtained – all enabled the firm to co-ordinate a complex organisational system without having to undertake organisational reform. Indeed, we believe that the success of the M-form derives not as Williamson states from the differentiation it carries out upon the cybernetic sub-system, but from the fact that it enables a homogeneous culture to be created within the firm. No matter how important the formal properties of an organisational structure and the actual content of a particular ideology (the ideology of decentralisation and of the entrepreneurial model), these are effective only in so far as they ensure consensus between the members of the organisation and compatability between the sub-objectives of each of its sub-units; all other ways of creating an internal culture in the firm would lead in the end to the same result. As Hirschman (1978) notes, every organisation must develop mechanisms that can win the loyalty of its members.

Our observations of many French firms have shown that the M-form was almost never used to generate harmony among the different sub-groups and thus to produce a consensus about the firm's avowed aims. Are we dealing here with a case peculiar to France, a Latin country which rejects any kind of consensus and which, in industrial organis-ation, has experienced only 'corrupted M-forms'? Or should we not rather interpret this 'corrupted M-form' – with which Anglo-Saxon countries are also acquainted – as the preferred strategy by which a small number of people achieve domination over large groups? We shall only recall here that in the most 'decentralised' American firms, control procedures are standardised and highly detailed, 'methodologies' proliferate (plans, sales manuals, personnel management handbooks . . .), the centralisation of financial resources is not challenged, and major corporate decisions are discussed only by a small group. These are all strategies which undoubtedly reduce uncertainty and transaction costs, but which, as they affect social organisation and power relations, are utterly disregarded by Williamson.

(d) Relations with shareholders and internal control   Williamson's unitary theory also allows him to throw new light on the old discussion of the conflict between the supporters of internal control and those who back the capital-owner's power. The theory of the absorption of uncertainty and the minimisation of transaction costs can actually account for the progressive rift between the shareholders and the managers of the firm. According to Williamson managers are freed from the dominance of the financial market so as not to be exposed to the characteristic uncertainty of this environment. And if the reaction of the shareholders to this transfer of power was so weak, it was because of the transfer simultaneously allowed for structuring the financial market, for more efficient control of large firms, and hence for more profitable investment opportunities.

Williamson goes on to provide a theoretical basis for the managerial ideology of competence; but at the same time, he dismisses what is socially important in this transfer of power. What is the effect of such a transfer on the firm's policy? This is a question which Williamson never considered and one to which, moreover, his theory provides no answer. The formation of large firms and the resulting centralisation of power makes it vitally important to define the orientations adopted by those who run them: do they aim only at economic efficiency or do they attempt to realise other sociopolitical aims? Galbraith (1967), to cite only one example, has developed the theory of the compatibility between seeking satisfactory (non-maximal) profits and extending the domination of a particular group over society. Clearly, this involves reduction of uncertainty. But what is the nature of the social order that has thus been created?

(e) The necessary market failure of the dominant firm   This last problem is not avoided by Williamson, who explicitly foresees the dangers of the systematic effort to reduce uncertainty by the large organisation: the dominant firm is one which has reached the limits of this process as it monopolises a fixed market. Although he is but little concerned with the social effects of this phenomenon, he nevertheless rediscovers the concerns of many writers who have discussed the dangers of monopoly. For him, the absorption of uncertainty can never be complete, for if uncertainty disappears in the environment, it reappears in the organisation which is then unable to deal with it. Inertia, bureaucracy, the exacerbation of internal conflicts and the rift between the top and the bottom – these factors undermine monopoly from within. How then does it happen that these monoliths take shape and endure? This is the question that Williamson addresses.

In seeking to explain the emergence of such monsters Williamson believes we should not look to the logic of the development of a firm that has become dominant (it is justifiable for a firm to attempt to minimise transaction costs) but rather to the non-functioning of the firm's existing or potential rivals. A dominant rival may, of course, have profited innocently from innovation, from the foresightedness of its management, or simply from historical chance. But these advantages of the 'first-mover', even if reinforced by the development of a specific know-how, would have had to be challenged by existing rivals or even by the entry of new competitors. If the market fails in its regulatory function – and Williamson's conceptualisation cannot account for such failure except in terms of illegal and predatory practices or historical accident – then it is to the state as an actor that the author turns for remedy.

But it is not because he has eliminated from his scheme of analysis the social dimension of the firm's activity that the author is unable to account for the domination which many large firms today exercise over some economic actors?

In our view, far from being reprehensible exceptions to the theoretical principle of competition, the practices of competition–collusion are the very essence of firms' policies. For example, throughout its history, Megatube was simultaneously engaged in competition and collusion, the latter bearing on a specific aspect of its policy: depending on the period, the policy to be 'frozen' would be that of prices, technical innovation or prospecting for new customers.

An economic situation, therefore, cannot be characterised either by a state of competition or by a state of *entente*; it can be defined only by the 'object of the collusion' *and* the 'place of confrontation'. It thus becomes vitally important to know which actor is responsible for defining both the strategic and frozen resources and to discover where he derives the authority to do so. The resources available to this actor do not consist exclusively of information, nor can his specific action be understood merely as an effort to reduce uncertainty. On the contrary, what is really at issue here is the discretionary power of the actor for defining the functioning of the economic system in which he operates. Thus the advantage of the 'first-mover' is best assessed in terms of domination. One is then better able to understand how the advantage of this 'first-mover' is perpetuated: dominated competitors no longer have a choice of strategic resource and must act in an economic world where the rules of the game have been defined by their chief adversary.

By thus separating the concepts of competition and monopoly, one can also account for some of the paradoxical propositions put forward by Hirschman: monopoly, far from being antithetical to competition, is one of the preconditions for its proper functioning; this fact, moreover, is well understood by some large firms that organise their monopoly artificially by creating a variety of competing brands. This resulting competition, which is always limited to specific products, prevents the emergence of organised protest, and unsatisfied consumers have to settle for switching to another brand produced by the same firm.

Finally, the state, as an actor, cannot be considered *a priori* as an impartial judge who will guarantee the proper functioning of a competitive system. Where is the boundary between the actors of the political system and those of the economic system? Who can prevent large firms from influencing, if not dictating, decisions of the public authorities in industrial matters? Our studies have in fact shown the great ability of industrial leaders to bring about a convergence, under extremely varied conditions, between state policy and the firm's interest. Should there be any resistance, industrial leaders can play upon the internal contradictions in the state apparatus, profiting in particular from the stability of their own positions in contrast to the rapid turnover of political figures.

(f) Oligopoly: ideal type or ideal solution?   Once monopoly has been banished by Williamson – either with the aid of his theory or with the aid of the state – the economic system can achieve a certain dynamic

balance *vis-à-vis* the problem of dealing with uncertainty. Oligopoly, assisted by small innovators, simultaneously ensures minimisation of transaction costs, retains an amount of uncertainty which it is able to handle, and thus guarantees the renewal of the world of goods. Williamson returns to large firms organised according to the divisional (M-form) model to reduce uncertainty to the maximum. The competition maintained by these firms within the oligopoly ensures partial control of the residual uncertainty. Finally, small innovators, thanks to their flexibility, can easily exploit new opportunities and therefore represent a useful disruptive factor which helps the large firms to renew their production.

Far from becoming reified, the economic system now emerges as a dynamic system in which both large and small firms coexist in mutual and collective interest: small firms enable large ones to develop, and large firms offer small ones the opportunity of seeing some of their innovations implemented on a large scale. This description of the relations linking large firms and small innovators would seem to account for the pattern of development of many of the traditional product sectors; it thus runs counter to the generally accepted propositions about the generative function of the large firms in research and development. It is moreover compatible with the creative role of the science industries which, on account of their complex organisation, are able to control this particular type of uncertainty. Williamson's conceptual apparatus, therefore, makes possible the theoretical establishment of a dynamic balance which reconciles individual interests and the general interest. The social order is legitimised along with the economic interventions of the state, which, in the name of the general interest, roots out practices that do not conform to this balance.

Before proceeding further, we should register our surprise at this exclusively legal conception of the state's role in economic life. How can one pass over the state's determining role as an economic actor, as a customer but also a producer, as a research organiser but also a financier? How can one neglect the importance of the various coalitions between sub-systems of the state and industrial groups, in which what is at stake is not only the transformation of a particular economic system but also the control of a world-wide geopolitical 'equilibrium'?

Implicit hypotheses
Going beyond the detailed analysis of the internal logic of Williamson's theory, we will now transfer this theory to the actual field of economic and sociological knowledge and attempt to explicate the implicit hypotheses upon which it is based.

(a) Information: a bridge between exchange and production? What is

Williamson's position in relation to the great debates which, since the nineteenth century, have set classical economists against Marxist economists, with the former viewing the economic world as an endless chainwork of markets governed by exchange, and the latter by contrast giving priority to the social relation established in production? In relation to the liberal school – particularly the marginalist theory – Williamson makes a double break, thus anticipating many of the criticisms customarily made of this school. He replaces impersonal exchange by relations between actors and institutions. But in giving central importance to the concept of information, he integrates the processes of exchange and production into his theory: the exchange of information is an act of production which has its own cost. Is this, then, the analysis of a new 'Capital', namely information?

This is in fact a new political economy in which the strategic variable around which all social relations are structured is the possession of information. The author is able to account simultaneously for the development of the organisational forms and of the economic system as a function of the cost of information and information transactions. He also explains the importance assumed today by processing of information in the production of goods.

Nevertheless, his theory does not deal with the analysis of transformation and of the production of information. How is this new strategic resource distribution among the actors? In whose hands does it lie and against whom is it used? Although Williamson does not explicitly foresee this question, he gives the impression that it is a resource that almost uniformly infiltrates the whole social body. Everyone possesses information, and therefore power, and marks out for himself a free space which, under certain conditions of shrewdness and insight, he is able to develop. But this harmony can be explained only by abandoning the analysis of production: Williamson remains a supporter of exchange, even though for the exchange of goods he may substitute the exchange of signs.

(b) An institutionalist who ignores the actors   The special contribution of institutional economics is to focus analysis on specific actors motivated by a particular project, characterised by bounded rationality, who set up relations of alliance and conflict. With regard to actors, Williamson is interested only in the firm; he takes no notice of the economic action of many other agents, e.g., the consumers, the scientific and technical community, the state.

When the state does appear in his scheme, it is only in its legal function. The central position it has held in economic life since the 1930s is disregarded: the contemporary state assists research, promotes the development of the leading industries, comes to the assistance of industries in difficulty, and through its macroeconomic policies defines some of the rules of the game and controls the system.

A more exact study of the state's economic action would no doubt stress that the state's different partial policies do not express a unique and coherent economic–industrial plan. State institutions are in fact a multitude of different administrations, each with its own more or less explicit, more or less accepted plan, each enjoying a certain autonomy and therefore able to intervene in a specific manner in the economic field. An institutional theory which disregarded these splits, tensions and peculiarities would fail to achieve its object.

To take one other collective actor, we note the absence of consumers in Williamson's conceptual scheme. From this point of view, Hirschman's position is more coherent, following an institutional approach. His approach in fact derives from the paradox of classical economics which, although based on the concept of the all-powerfulness of the consumer, aspires to account for the functioning of an economic system in which the consumer has no say. Everything, including even competition, is designed to ensure the consumer's docility and loyal attachment.

Williamson reports the same paradox; in institutionalist theory, two hypotheses can explain the place of the consumer. Either he is a passive actor, and to understand how the economic system functions and is transformed, does not require accounting for his actions, although it would nevertheless be necessary in this case to account for his passivity. Or else – and this would appear to be Williamson's position – the consumer is the central actor who governs the system in his role as arbitrator over competitors; and here, we again encounter the hypothesis, dear to the classical writers, of the consumer king.

As an institutionalist, Williamson disregards many of the real economic actors, being interested only in the firm and in the statist police and relegating the production of the other actors to the uncertain background of the environment. Thus, he essentially defines the economic system in the same way as did the classical economists, even though his description of this system is less unrealistic.

(c) An economics of consensus   The actors studied by Williamson enter into negotiation; indeed, the cost of these negotiations is the focus of his analysis. These actors are opportunists and have a bounded rationality: the *a priori* existence of conflicting interests and divergent plans is resolved in negotiation. This analysis supposes that agreement is always possible, that conflict is always negotiable, and that in the long run profits are shared and that there exists a common reference point: the economics of transaction costs.

This analysis leaves many questions unanswered. What becomes of actors who challenge the reference point: those who prefer self-management to the hierarchy because the existence of the hierarchy cannot be reduced to any particular informational cost; those who prefer the monopoly that generates protest to the oligopoly that produces fraudulent competition; those who do not resign themselves to seeing their future designed, planned and produced by a small group, even if this is the solution which minimises transaction costs; those who would like to see widespread social discussion developing around major changes in society, even though the transaction costs may be great?

Williamson's theory presupposes general consensus on the values, the choices of organisation and the forms of life: all is negotiable, all divergences can be reduced.

(d) The new version of liberal theory   Williamson's initial project consisted in re-thinking microeconomics, theories which could not easily be reconciled with the existence of very large firms. But in the last analysis, his theory repeats the basic assumptions of liberal economics, changing only the terms.

- This is an economics of exchange, even though goods are replaced by information.
- The reconstructed system of exchange spontaneously tends towards equilibrium; true, it is no longer an invisible hand which commands, but rather the combined action of large organisations and the statist police.
- There exists a universal rationality, the minimisation of transaction costs being substituted for the maximisation of utility.
- The pursuit of each individual of his own interest leads finally to the collective welfare.
- The small number does not destroy competition; thus the condition of atomicity is redefined.

Overall, the author remains a prisoner of the traditional principles of economics, even though he replaces abstract categories by artificial actors. The institutionalist outlook does not alter the way in which economic phenomena are apprehended: it is classical liberal economics dressed up in the colours of the large firm. This new clothing is by no means innocent, for it legitimises the dominant forms of economic and social organisation in the developed countries.

II   Towards an Economics of Domination

Analytical framework

Like Williamson, we also wish to account for the functioning and evolution of economic organisations in their 'environment' by giving priority to the study of the relationships between actors. But because sociology has long since shown that these relationships cannot be reduced solely to negotiated exchange and influence, we propose here an approach which distinguishes between social relations in accordance with what is at stake. Four types of social relations are considered:

(a) The relation of domination   which refers to the ability of a group of actors to impose on others the manner of functioning of a social system or of the major transformations within this system. The reproduction and also the transformation of this system represent the stakes over which the class struggle is waged. Domination, whatever form it may take, always involves recourse to pure violence and the belief of those dominated in the legitimate character of this relationship. This social relation thus makes it possible for a group to impose on others the content and organisation of work activities, the forms of individual and collective consumption, the rules of the game in a given economic sub-system, and even a certain relationship with nature. It is, then, a highly asymmetrical relation, one that is irreversible during any given period: those dominated cannot help but react to this relation, which they must endure.

(b) The relation of influence   which may be defined as the ability of a group of actors to ensure that, in negotiation with another group of actors, the terms of compromise they obtain should be favourable to them. It is assumed that the framework of the negotiation is itself the outcome of a relation of domination, and that the relation of influence is therefore occasionally unbalanced. In the relation of influence, the conflict can be resolved by negotiation, which is not the case in the relation of domination. The relations of influence develop at the core of what is called the policy system, and may in the end lead to predetermined role structure.

(c) The relation of authority   which belongs to a role structure, that is, a system in which there is expectation of orders and expectation of obedience. This relation is asymmetrical. The holder of authority, however, in exercising his function is doing no more than demonstrate a power inherent in the definition of his own role, a power which for this very reason sets limits on his ability to predetermine the behaviour of his subordinates.

(d) *The relation of production*   which develops through an act of transformation applied to a symbolic or material product; this process occurs according to principles partially derived from role structure. A relation of production will therefore be analysed chiefly in terms of an individual or collective actor's degree of autonomy and in terms of the nature of the knowledge and know-how.

The relations of domination, influence and production develop just as much within the firm as within the relations between the firm and its 'environment'. Thus one can speak of a relation of domination towards a market, a competititor or sub-contractor, and likewise towards a professional group within the firm. Similarly, relations of influence arise in negotiations designed to establish an *entente* with rivals or an agreement with the state, as well as within the policy-making system of the firm itself. Finally, relations of production may equally well develop in the activity of buying or selling a product, service or patent (we will later speak of relations of exchange) as in the production of technical goods by a firm, for instance in a workshop or an accountancy service.

This heterogeneity of social relations prevents us from viewing the market or a hierarchy in a uni-dimensional perspective: the market is no longer seen as a given imposed upon economic organisations but rather as the social production of a system of actors which we refer to as a SAUM (*Système d'Acteurs d'un Univers Marchand* – the system of actors of a market universe). The internal organisation of firms is not interpreted in terms of simple or complex hierarchies, but must be seen in terms of differentiated power systems which then need to be reconstructed.

Instead of regarding the market as an entity outside the firm, a whole that is more or less stable, more or less complex, more or less homogeneous, more or less uncertain, but always constraining, we intend to analyse the system of actors, which incorporates the firm and the social relations that develop within it. These actors, i.e. the firm studied and its competitors, the different forms of state apparatus, one sub-group or another in the scientific and technical community, and the consumers, all in fact set up relations of domination, influence and exchange in order to introduce a new partition in the market world. Thus they constitute a SAUM whose functioning they simultaneously define. The conceptualisation advanced here challenges the notions of branches, sectors and industries as givens, and aims instead at accounting for their actual existence.

To account for the production and functioning of a SAUM and for each of the actors involved in it, one must perform differential analysis on its different power systems. We shall be using the term SD (*système dirigeant* – directive system) to refer to the system of actors who develop relations of domination; SP (*système politique* – policy system) for the system of actors who establish relations of influence; and SO (*système organisationnel* – organisational system) for the system of actors who maintain relations of exchange and/or production within the framework of a system of authority. The study of the specific social production of each of these systems and of their interconnectedness thus becomes the object of our analysis. Here, we shall restrict ourselves to applying these concepts to the study of the large firm.

The directive system of the large firm shapes the system of actors which develops the relations of domination both in the SAUMs in which the firm is engaged and within the firm itself. This exercise of domination is reflected both in the development of the rules of functioning for one (or several) SAUMs in which the firm participates and in the definition of the strategic resources of the firm and its pattern of development.

The action of an SD can be analysed with regard to both the transformation of the *univers marchand* and the formation of a specific firm. In fact, an SD defines the firm's activity, its products and markets (i.e. the SAUM(s) of which it forms part), and it can even go so far as creating new SAUMs or changing radically the functioning or the boundaries of existing SAUMs. In any case, in so doing, it produces an original combination of modes of accumulation and patterns of development.

The *structure of the mode of accumulation* is defined by the structure of the resources around which the firm's activity is organised. One cannot provide an *a priori* typology of the modes of accumulation: they can only be reconstructed by the observer who (at least at this first level of analysis) cannot avoid noticing the breaks. Provisionally – and with respect to the last century – we can define eight modes of accumulation, each characterised by a central resource: in the market model – transport; in the artisan model – knowledge of a trade or craft; in the industrial model – the takeover by technology of workers' know-how; in the market-control model – the control of consumption; in the technological model – the establishment of new market connections and the reorganisation of scientific knowledge; in the military– industrial model – the relation with the state; in the informational model – the control of information; in the financial model – the level of profitability alone.

These modes of accumulation have been reconstructed from an analysis of the major choices made by the SDs of the firms studied. In spite of the connotation of the different terms used to define the various modes of accumulation and their strategic resources, one should not automatically conclude that a particular professional group occupies a privileged position in either the political system or the directive system. On the contrary, this relation between a potentially hegemonic professional group and the dominant mode of accumulation should be the object of study. While in the society at large these different modes of accumulation coexist, they are combined in a more or less specific way in a large firm.

The *structure of the pattern of development* is understood to mean the system of relations that the observer can construct between the different SAUMs in which the firm is actively engaged. Historically a large firm often results from initial development in a single SAUM, and the firm's development might be described in terms of this dimension. We can also discern internal growth, concentration, vertical integration, product differentiation, product range, technological transfer and diversification. The two last-mentioned possibilities, which cast doubt upon the initial choice in the utilisation of accumulated resources, constitute an 'eccentric' development; in the other instances, we are concerned with 'autocentric' development.

Eccentric developments, which have been frequent in recent years, can no doubt be interpreted as a way for the SD to consolidate its discretionary power by not relying even on the radical development of a single SAUM. The combination of the concepts of mode of accumulation and pattern of development may enable one to account for an original strategy of restructuring an industrial system adopted successfully by certain groups, i.e., diversification within a sector through the takeover of firms, the result of which is a change in the dominant modes of accumulation in the newly absorbed firms.

It should be emphasised that the definition of the specific SAUM (or SAUMs) of which the firm is part, and the production of an original structure of modes of accumulation and patterns of development, derives from one and the same action.

Through the nature of the relations it establishes between these different SAUMs, the SD of a large firm can not only redefine the sectoring of the market world, but also predetermine the work content of the firm's organisational units. By its choice of diversification, it can separate the firm's different activities and can decide whether or not to develop any one of these activities: e.g., to invest heavily in a new market, to create one, or even suddenly to withdraw.

What enables us to distinguish the SD of an industrial group from the other systems is not the position of the actors who make up the SD in terms of their affiliation to the firm – for the actors in the SD of an industrial group may be either inside or outside the firm – but rather the ability of this system to introduce its choices into the firm's organisational system. In order to do so, the SD makes use of a policy system (SP) over which it wields power.

It should be added that the SD may or may not be sub-divided into different specialised sub-systems and that it may serve as a point of consensus for the 'major orientations' of the firm or as a forum for airing more or less openly declared conflicts between antagonistic groups. Finally, the study of the manner in which the SD exercises its sway over the SP enables us to assess its real ability to exert domination.

The large firm's *policy system* ('*système politique*' – SP) shapes the system of actors of the industrial group that is involved in relations of influence (both within the firm and with external actors) that have been created to control its position in the different SAUMs in which it participates, and hence to activate all the resources granted to it by the SD. Thus, the SP defines the *firm's policies* as well as its norms, role structures and information circuits, which lead to the formation of the organisational system over which it exercises control.

By definition, the SP's work consists in introducing – both within the organisation of the firm and in the different SAUMs to which it belongs – the choices made by the SD, and consequently in impressing upon these groups the fact of the SD's domination. Nevertheless, these choices cannot be automatically converted into a set of decisions and the SP's autonomy is therefore relative. To explain the specific nature of the SP's activity, we describe the results of its production in terms of partial policies and general policies. By contrasting these policies with the choices of the SD, one is able to specify the SP's margin of manoeuvre.

A firm encompasses distinct activities – manufacturing, sales, finance, research – each of which corresponds to action objectives that can be described as partial: each of these activities is in fact undertaken by a specific group which implements its particular knowledge (and know-how) to promote a special material or symbolic production. Thus the chain of objectives and of means of action defined by each SP for each of these activities reflects certain rationalities or 'logics of action' (LA).[5] A partial policy will be defined by assocating an activity with the structure of LA, either of which one may be dominant.

To describe the content of a firm's policy, it is necessary to combine two approaches. First, the observer must clarify the implicit rationality of the action developed by a particular policy system. Thus, for instance, the dominant LA of a commercial policy may be either sales progression or short-term profitability or the firm's reputation or market occupation, etc. To discriminate between these different possibilities, we must not only analyse commercial practices in terms of indicators that are always specific to the activity studied, but also relate them back to the firm's past practices and to those of its rivals; this process enables us to uncover discontinuities, conflicts and changes of orientation. The variety of partial policies that can be profitably studied to account for a firm's action, and the diversity of the ways of functioning of the SAUMs within which the action of the firm's groups is developed, prevents any *a priori* evaluation of these indicators and of their meaning. All the same, one cannot remain satisfied with merely this analysis of content, for a policy actually acquires meaning only when it is related to the choices and exigencies of the SD. Thus two policies which might be described as identical when judged using the same grid of indicators may in fact turn out to have very different significations, and vice versa.

The characteristic feature of an industrial group's SP is that it splits into different specialised (and hierarchised) sub-systems – so great is the variety of problems, constraints and decisions. This fragmentation should also be considered as a preferred way of exercising domination. Consequently, the analysis of an SP concentrates secondly on its manner of differentiating and establishing hierarchies, each of the sub-systems being characterised simultaneously by the stakes at play and by the relations of control it maintains with the other policy sub-systems.

Each of the policy sub-systems revealed by the analysis must be characterised in several ways: by the structure of objectives it produces, defined in terms of *logics of action*, by the conditions that enable an actor to gain access to the sub-system, by the object of consensus and the possible conflicts by which it may be shot through, and also by its ability to transform the organisational system and thus impress upon it the fact of its domination.

The large firm's *organisational system* ('*système organisationnel*' – SO) is the system of actors which controls the tension between the requirements of the policy system which imposes norms and regulations on the SO and the technical exigencies resulting from the relations of production. Its functioning is particularly dependent on the constraints imposed by the firm's various policy sub-systems, the tangible expression of which is to be found in the different forms of the division of labour: the extent to which the behaviour of the actors is predetermined and the manner in which knowledge and know-how are combined and put into practice.

A system of authority then intervenes to impose the requirements of the SP at the level of the SO: nevertheless, the fact still remains that this system, even when combined with a considerable number of rules, is unable to determine completely the behaviour of a social group, no matter how small and specialised it may be. As Michel Crozier (Crozier 1978) has shown, 'games' develop within this organisational system, but with actors whose effectiveness remains limited as to their ability to introduce striking transformations in the running of the firm. In order to acquire an accurate understanding of this limitation one must actually study the problem of the conditions governing the transformation of an organisational system into a policy system.

It should be stressed here that these three systems (SD, SP, SO) do not entail sub-division of the firm's real actors according to their hierarchical levels: firstly because an actor's official position is not a reliable indicator of the relations he establishes, and secondly – and more importantly – because in the conceptual scheme the levels are analytical and the actors abstract. It is by empirical research that we are able to establish whether the 'director' of a company is acting simultaneously in the SD, the SP and even the SO, whether his activity is restricted almost exclusively to the SD level, or, conversely, whether it is excluded from this system. Once we had started work in an industrial group, the first phase consisted in setting out from an analysis of the social relations established by the actors, and hence in constructing these different systems, distinguishing their junctures and interrelations, and defining the manner of operation.

Some of the results of analysis
The usefulness of the analytical scheme presented above can ultimately be proved only by the interpretations it makes possible. Given the limitations of space for this paper, we have not been able to demonstrate through detailed empirical examples how this conceptualisation has enabled us to understand the history of economic sectors as different as those of aluminium, fresh dairy products, or hydraulic pipes, and to describe the development of the large French firms investing in these sectors, and to account for their strategies.

Here we shall restrict ourselves to formulating certain general propositions developed from the comparative study of the case histories of three large French firms. The dogmatic nature of this presentation should be understood as the result of an attempt at synthesis, and should not lead us to forget the specificity, the singularity and the richness of each of the sociohistorical analyses which we have presented elsewhere.[6]

As a centre of private power, the large firm wields wide discretionary power in its relations not only with the state and the scientific community, but also with consumers and with its competitors. Our analysis did not confirm the theories favouring the domination of firms by state apparatus, and it demonstrated that even in a state with a large degree of central economic planning, the directors of firms are able to attract the full range of state aid for their own projects: in the histories of all three firms studied, state action resulted only in the consolidation of the firm's power.

While the firms occasionally monopolise the production of certain sub-groups in the national scientific community, they also keep a fairly consistent watch over all scientific and technical innovations, and are capable of acting very swiftly – and with powerful financial backing – to implement these innovations in order to modify the world of goods.

The control exercised by these large firms over consumption is based not only on the activation of various forms of know-how (in marketing, publicity, training, etc.) but also on agreements between producers and on the opportunities open to diversified firms of controlling 'competition' between substitute products.

The nature of the relationship between competing firms is seen in the process by which an *'entente'* is established, structured, and later challenged, as in the formation of a new *'entente'*. Through this new agreement the content of certain partial policies is frozen and the relative value of the strategic advantages of each member to the agreement is assessed: the manner of functioning of the SAUM to which the firms belong becomes the focus of conflict between the firms. Through its ability to make and break agreements with its competitors, a firm imposes on the different actors in the SAUM the nature of new strategic resources, thus producing qualitative changes to the market. A firm's initial technological or commercial advantage predicts very poorly the extent to which that firm can maintain long-term domination over a particular SAUM.

There are no relations of simple determination between the formal composition of an SD (whether in terms of capital ownership or of statutory position) and the choices it exerts over the firm's modes of accumulation and the pattern of development. Thus, two firms operating in the same SAUM, with formally identical SDs, successfully carried out extremely different industrial policies. Conversely, important changes in the capital structure of another group did not lead to a change in its industrial strategy. Consequently, to account for the firm's main choices, an analysis of its internal power system, and particularly the structuring of its SD, of the methods of recruitment and training of its members, of its memory and its hold over the firm's SP, is necessary.

An industrial group is controlled by the firm's government which is always limited in number to a few people. These people cannot be characterised by their subordination to the owners of capital, for under some conditions, the SD can actually render itself autonomous of the owners, thus forming an internal SD. The conditions for entering the SD are difficult to stipulate. To be sure, ownership of capital is not a necessary resource, and professional competence – all the more so when it is 'certified' by a diploma – is not a sufficient resource; but a certain interrelation between competence (largely acquired within the firm) and relational capital (which may represent a particular form of the relationship towards ownership) can help us explain how access is gained to the SD of a large firm.

Through centralisation of the financial policy, the government acquires the means of mobilising major resources so as to ensure large-scale involvement in a new sector, or even to encourage the development of one sector over another by causing the 'cash-flow to circulate'. In some firms, this circulation may nevertheless remain limited, reflecting the influence exerted by some departmental heads. All the same, the SD largely determines the development of the group's different sectors through the divisions it makes in the group's various activities, i.e. through the spheres of activity it assigns to each department.

Management training is carried out within the firm itself, and may be interpreted as a training both in the politics and in the policy of the firm. This means, first, the progressive acquisition of the ways of thinking needed to make choices about the firm's modes of accumulation and pattern of development, bearing in mind especially the history of the organisation and of its past projects. Second, it means methodical training in the forms of control over the industrial group's policy and organisational systems, as well as in the ability to exert influence over other public or private power centres.

The partial and/or general policies produced by the firm's different policy sub-systems express rationales or 'logics of action' which, to be understood, must be related to the choices and demands of the SD and the strategies of competitors. Consequently, a professional group in which the members have all received the same training – or, one might say, have been cast in the same mould – can, over a relatively short period, evolve radically different policies (in terms of LA), and may do so without making any appreciable alteration to the content of its work. Conversely, several different professional groups, can, over a long period and within a single SAUM which is changing its manner of functioning, act collectively following the same LA. The analysis of firms' policies cannot therefore be based on an *a priori* scheme of LAs and of indicators; it must examine the relationships between the products of the different systems (directive system, policy system, policy sub-systems) centring on reconstructed problems, always bearing in mind the characteristic features of the SAUMs in which the industrial group participates.

Most conflicts may be interpreted as confrontations between policy systems, different LAs and organisational units. Only by analysing all these different levels can we account for the way they emerge and are resolved. The rare open conflicts that arise over the selection of patterns of development and modes of accumulation are resolved in a radical manner, the SD thereby indicating which conflicts can be tolerated and which cannot.

The establishment of the empirical limits of a policy system (and of the various policy sub-systems) is both a subject of analysis and a result of research. The reconstructed policy system is, however, characterised by splits into more or less specialised sub-systems, the manipulation of which provides the SD with one of its favoured means for exercising domination.

Purely functional organisation has everywhere disappeared, nor does divisional organisation into Products and Markets (the model of the DPO and of decentralisation) exist at all. But it should, however, be pointed out that these units never possess all the functions necessary to define general policy for a given SAUM. We have proposed a new model of organisation to account for this phenomenon: *'functional organisation, partly dismembered and recombined'*. Here one will recognise the broad features of Williamson's M-form, with the difference that here we are not dealing with an exceptional case but with a dominant and widespread form. This model implies that one is concerned at root with a functional organisation, and it stresses the fact that only a limited number of functional divisions have been dismembered and regrouped.

Although one may establish a connection between the changes in a firm's modes of accumulation and patterns of development and changes in the functioning of its SD, these changes are not necessarily manifested through changes in the structuring of the SP or in the organisational structure. 'Structure does not always follow strategy', even in a situation of economic efficiency.

The very concept of an organisation has been redefined as an original social product of the firm's policy system. It thus becomes impossible to account for a firm's characteristics – and particularly for the modalities of the division of labour and the mechanisms that define the tasks it accomplishes – without examining the interconnection between the three systems, SD–SP–SO.

In describing how authority and control are exercised, it is not enough merely to contrast personal authority, impersonal rules or cybernetic control; rather, it is the specific combinations of these three possibilities which enable us to compare organisations and to account for their development. An administrative policy cannot be analysed exclusively in the formal terms of authority and/or control mechanism. The effects of this policy likewise determine the content of the work of the firm's different professional groups through crystallisation of the knowledge the firm produces. Two models for the capitalisation of knowledge can be specified: the 'skimming-off' model described above and the 'washing-out' model (the mechanisation of social knowledge), developed very early in the marketing units.

While the SD and the SP may be the centres where new 'power knowledge' is created (cf. the invention of the pattern of development and the modes of accumulation of policy-making knowledge . . .), the same is also happening in the organisational system, which operates chiefly by the transference and combination of crafts: the firm as a whole must be considered as a centre for the production of knowledge. In the organisational system, the creation of new knowledge through the displacement and combination of old knowledge is all the more effective when there is an active policy system which, through its control over the organisation, seeks to introduce the choices made by the SD.

III Conclusion

By replacing the unrealistic and impersonal mechanisms of the market with the study of the strategies of specific, organised actors, the institutional school appeared to make a breakthrough rich in theoretical and political implications. The doors, however, which for a moment stood ajar, were immediately slammed shut again. The theory proposed was in fact no more than a new form of the old liberal theory based on social consensus, the effectiveness of competition and general negotiation. Even the role of the state – although it becomes increasingly visible – has been reduced to a quasi-legal function.

We have argued that by introducing the firm into a system of actors – bearing in mind the heterogeneity of the social relations and systems – it becomes possible to account for the functioning and evolution of the firm. An institutional economics, therefore, should assume control over *all the actors* involved in the definition of a particular market universe, list and define the different *types of relations* established, study the *actual content of the projects* developed and thus reconstruct the conflicts, *both negotiable and non-negotiable*, which set the actors against each other.

In abandoning the reductive formalism which aims more at disregarding problems that have nonetheless been perceived than at solving them (the existence of an alternative form of organisation, with or without hierarchy, the existence of power within the market and the organisation, the bounded rationality of the actors, etc.), institutional economics should be concerned with the social productions of all the actors engaged in a particular market. If this concept is taken into account, it clearly changes the definition of economic problems; but this is in fact the condition for establishing a relation between economics and the sociopolitical conditions on which it is based.

Carried to its ultimate conclusions, this theoretical break makes it possible to locate the quasi-monopoly of large organisations in societal production, a production which these organisations achieve through the organised silence of those dominated. Everything, including competition, is so arranged that the voice of the dominated should never be heard and that the choices of the leaders should appear to be inspired by rationality. Williamson, far from being open to the new demands of consumers, the public and the users, limits himself to defining the conditions of their domination. An institutional economics on the other hand should favour new forms of collective expression and contribute to the formulation of a theory that would link the societal projects of the entire group of actors, regardless of whether these projects relate to work units, to the running of large organisations, or to the determination of major industrial choices. Only when this conflict, in all its dimensions, is incorporated at the very centre of analysis does an institutional theory of economics begin to acquire meaning.

Notes

[1] Proof is given by the numerous articles that have followed the publication of the works of Williamson (1975), and Hirschmann (1970), and even by the very organisation of this symposium.

[2] Of numerous works on oligopoly, we might mention, among the models for price determination, those of Cournot, Edgeworth or Chamberlain; among the studies on concentration those of Blair and Houssiaux; and among the analyses on barriers to entry, that of Bain.

[3] Ever since Baumol replaced the search for maximum profit with the search for a maximisation of turnover compatible with profit constraint, many writers have devised functions of preference or utility which the firm might endeavour to maximise.

[4] A small local smelting firm, founded in the mid-nineteenth century, this firm specialised very early on in the manufacture of cast-iron water pipes. After attaining an almost monopolistic position on the French market, it now holds an extremely important position on the world market for the manufacture of water pipes, and, as a result of various mergers, has become one of the largest French industrial groups.

[5] Here we have adopted the term proposed by L. Karpik in 'Le Capitalisme technologique', *Sociologie du travail*, no. 1, 1972.

[6] For a fuller presentation of our analytical scheme and our research results, see: M. Bauer and E. Cohen, 1981.

5 Markets and Hierarchies: efficiency or domination?
A. Francis

Introduction

Apparently working entirely independently both Alfred Chandler (1977) and Oliver Williamson (1975) have virtually simultaneously developed rather similar explanations for the emergence of the giant corporation. Their fundamental argument is that under certain conditions co-ordination of collective action can be conducted more efficiently and cheaply by means of an administrative hierarchy than by transactions conducted in the market place. Thus under pressure of competition many firms have engaged in vertical integration. More-over, at least according to Chandler, the larger the throughput of business down the vertically integrated chain the greater does the advantage of hierarchy over market show up. Thus with increasing returns to scale of throughput the larger firm has the comparative advantage and hence there is a tendency to concentration.

What I wish to show in this paper is that neither Chandler's nor Williamson's arguments lead, on the basis of economic considerations alone, necessarily in the direction which they suggest. By the example of the rise of factory production and the emergence of the large corpo-ration I try to argue that where hierarchy is chosen in preference to market as a means of conducting transactions, this is not always because it is in some sense technically a more efficient means of transacting, but because it allows one party to dominate the other and act against their interests.

Chandler and Williamson on the Merits of Hierarchical Co-ordination

Chandler's *Visible Hand* is first and foremost a 'history of a business institution and a business class' (Chandler 1977, p. 1) and not a treatise on economic theory. His presentation of the 'markets and hierarchies' argument is thus less well-developed than that of Williamson. Chandler merely explains that central to the explanation of the managerial revo-lution in American business is that 'business enterprise took the place of market mechanisms in co-ordinating the activities of the economy and directing its resources' and that such internalisation of activities has many advantages. The main one is that 'the internalisation of many units permitted the flow of goods from one unit to another to be administratively co-ordinated', and that the consequently more 'effective scheduling of flows achieved a more intensive use of facilities and personnel employed in the processes of production and distribution and so increased productivity and reduced costs' (Chandler 1977, p. 7). Chandler states that when the volume of economic activities reaches a certain level then 'administrative co-ordination [is] more efficient and more profitable than market co-ordination' (Chandler 1977, p. 8).

Williamson's argument is much more subtle and complex. For Williamson the following set of factors are necessary before hierarchy shows a comparative advantage over market as a means of conducting transactions. (It should also be noted that Williamson prefers to speak of transactions rather than of co-ordination. The latter is something that may or may not follow from a set of transactions and so transactional analysis is prior.) Firstly the transactions, for hierarchy to have a comparative advantage, are conducted under conditions of uncertainty/complexity and so the constraint of bounded rationality operates. Secondly transactions take place under conditions of small numbers exchange, either *ex ante* or *ex post* or both and so opportunism becomes a viable strategy. These two sets of factors together lead to a condition of information impactedness. Finally those parties to the transaction must all be pecuniary gain maximisers who place a low cost or indeed a positive benefit on the atmosphere of hierarchical organisation. Under all these conditions hierarchical organisation would have superior productivity consequences and thus would be adopted.

Williamson then explores the extent to which these conditions usually obtain in the employment relation, in the set of transactions between intermediate product markets, and in the capital market as it relates to the supply of capital to business units. These three areas are those represented in Scott's (1970) three stages of company growth, i.e. the emergence of the business enterprise in the form of factory production, its growth into the larger single product multi-functionally organised firm, and finally the maturation into the divisionalised, diversified giant corporation. Williamson suggests that his conditions occur for the replacement of market transactions by hierarchically controlled transactions at each of these three stages and thus offers a cogent explanation for Scott's empirically based model. However, there appear to be some substantial flaws in the argument which Williamson makes which renders more problematic the question of why such giant firms emerged.

A Critique of Williamson

Chandler does not deal, in *The Visible Hand*, with the rise of factory production itself. Nevertheless Williamson's explanation for this is identical in shape to his argument for the rise of the vertical integrated firm and partly because factory production is temporally prior to vertical integration, and partly because I am more familiar with some evidence about just how such factory production came about in the US and Europe. I want to examine closely this stage of Williamson's argument before considering the question of vertical integration.

In explaining the emergence of the simple hierarchy and the employment relationship in production Williamson suggests that the conventional explanations based on technological indivisibilities and non-separabilities are inadequate and should be replaced by a consideration of the transaction costs incurred in using such technologies and by a consideration of transaction costs more generally.

In so far as I understand his argument it is that it is not the steam engine which gave rise to the capitalist but original sin. Williamson argues that indivisible technologies, in the form for example of the steam engine and the mill building, could be monopoly owned and sold for hire, and this of course was the situation that obtained in many US and UK machinery factories with their systems of inside contracting (see, for example, Nelson 1975 and Gospel 1977). However, such inside contracting cannot in most cases be of the complex contingent claims form on account of bounded rationality (so Williamson claims but does not satisfactorily substantiate), while sequential spot contracting is hazardous where suppliers acquire non trivial learning-by-doing advantages and an absence of opportunism cannot safely be presumed. The learning-by-doing condition is, of course, what gives rise to the small-numbers condition. Thus collective organisation arises instead. Similarly what prevents technological non-separabilities, e.g. the specialised operations in the famous pin-making factory, from being uncoupled via a normal sales relationship plus buffer stocks is usually the difficulty of transacting in circumstances which give rise to opportunism and information impactedness, rather than a straight technological imperative or the cost of maintaining the higher stocks.

However, if we try to apply these hypotheses to what we know about the emergence of factory production there appear to be some difficulties. Firstly we should note that one of the prime requirements which Williamson sets up for the transition from market to hierarchy to occur, namely that both parties should be pecuniary gain maximisers, does not appear to hold in this context. Landes, for example, in *The Unbound Prometheus* draws attention to the practice of the supposedly typical worker under a putting-out system to 'carouse the Saturday of pay, the Sabbath Sunday, the "Holy Monday" as well; dragged himself reluctantly back to work Tuesday, warmed to the task Wednesday, and laboured furiously Thursday and Friday to finish in time for another long weekend' (Landes 1969, p. 59). Each week they should, in Williamson's terms, drive a sequential spot contract with the travelling merchant over how much output and for what remuneration they would produce over the next period. The merchants, however, were nearer to being pecuniary gain maximisers and in a time of rapid rising demand for their products were having to spend an increasing proportion of their time travelling round the countryside finding additional putting-out workers. With the peasants' propensity for leisure, and hence backward-sloping supply curve for labour, sequential spot contracting was not up to the task of persuading the workers to produce as much as the merchants wanted. This in itself, without the additional impetus created by the availability of steam power and other new technologies, was enough, according to Marglin (1975), for the merchants to change the nature of the contract they were offering. In fact the merchants then contracted with other parties, notably women and children from the workhouses of the Midlands who could not be said to be in a strong sellers' market for labour, and the form of contract was what Simon (1957) would term an authority relation. Williamson identifies this as in essence similar to spot market contracting, but the subject of the contract was now their labour power rather than a certain quantity of cloth. Once contracted to work so many hours per day output was kept up by the kind of 'driving' techniques described by Nelson (1975). All this seems to have very little to do with the hazards of information impactedness under *ex post* small numbers sequential spot contracting, and much more to do with the imperfections of the labour market and the rather weak bargaining position certain groups seemed to have under those circumstances. It is certainly not an argument for the relative technical efficiency of hierarchy over market as a mode of engaging in transactions.

If we turn now to a conisderation of those industries using skilled labour, or what Williamson terms a high level of task idiosyncrasies, it appears we can again rework the causality. Nelson, in his study of the origins of the new factory system in the United States, observes that the system of 'inside contracting' persisted in the machinery factories of the North East until the early twentieth century. According to Williamson such a system should have suffered substantial difficulties for the reasons outlined above. Certainly the contracting system did not appear to be that of the contingent claims type, and thus is in line with Williamson's hypothesis about bounded rationality. But why did the system of sequential spot contracting persist for so long when it gave rise to opportunistic behaviour? At least two features of the inside contractor system would appear to be troublesome. The one is that of bilateral monopoly which Williamson identifies. In this case both parties are likely to spend a great deal of time bargaining over each spot contract and each party will be dissatisfied at this unproductive use of their time. A change to a less time-consuming mode of reaching agreement over price etc. would, in the absence of some value being placed on the activity of bargaining itself, be in both parties' interest assuming the alternative mode did not involve some higher costs being incurred. The other problem with inside contracting is the opportunism that can arise as a result of information impactedness. Assuming that the essence of the inside contract is over the price for a job, and the price cost is very dependent on the time the job takes to do, then the two major areas of negotiation are over the price per unit of time that is to be paid and the length of time the job should take. The two factors are collapsed into the one variable of price for the job in the negotiation but there are the two areas of uncertainty around which information becomes impacted. In the first area, that of price per unit of time, then the employer/client has impacted knowledge because he knows how much profit there is in the job and how much he can afford to pay and still come out on top. There is every opportunity for opportunistic behaviour here on the part of the employer/client. In the second area, that of the time a job will take, the craftsman/operative has the advantage and the information because of his skill and experience in knowing how long it will take him to perform the necessary tasks. Guarding this knowledge is something that craft unions/guilds have realised to be important since time immemorial, of course. (These two areas are other than another major one noted by Williamson, which is the problem of non-trivial learning and how this can be exploited by first-movers. This problem according to Williamson can be solved notionally by charging for the first-mover advantage in the establishment of the first contract but fails for the obvious difficulties of building that into the contract.)

The problem of information impactedness on the employers' side could only be resolved by the inside contractors setting up on their own account, so avoiding the middleman position of the entrepreneur. This is impossible when the entrepreneur owns and leases to them the technologically indivisible factory. The problem of information impactedness arising on the other side can be resolved either by the employer setting up a system of obtaining the same knowledge about normal lengths of times for jobs as is held by the craftsmen, or more generally those performing the idiosyncratic tasks, or by persuading such people to do the work on a different form of contract, e.g. under a direct employment relationship. It is difficult to see what advantage there is to the craftsman to fall in with this arrangement. He loses his own opportunity to be opportunistic without the employer giving up his similar opportunity. All he gains is the time to engage in productive work that he otherwise spent in lengthy bargaining in his relation of bilateral monopoly with his employer. We have already shown that there is evidence that many workers actually have a preference for leisure over work, even when the latter is paid for and the former not, and it can by no means be certain that a positive value is not placed by the employee in the activity of bargaining with his employer. In these circumstances it is not surprising to find that craft workers did not wish to change from an inside contracting mode to an employment relationship. Because the work is skilled and craft groups maintained control over entry to their occupations, then employers could not, unlike the case of the early unskilled textile workers, find an alternative source of recruits in a weak labour market position and give them an all-or-nothing choice of no work or work only under an employment contract. The alternative strategy by the employers of reducing the impactedness of the information of the operatives would thus seem to be the likely outcome and this is what a number of recent critics have suggested is what Taylorism was fundamentally about.

Rose (1978) and Braverman (1974), for example, have suggested that Taylor's skill was not so much in generating *new* knowledge about the speed and techniques with which work could be done but, in Williamson's terms, reducing the impactedness of the information. That is, it is argued that knowledge about the most efficient way to perform their jobs may well have been possessed by individual workers but kept from management so that they could not know if 'soldiering' was taking place. By studying and timing work patterns in detail Taylor was able to reproduce this information in a form available for management to plan production on the basis of known possible levels of production, monitor performance closely to ensure that targets were reached, and impose sanctions in the event of failure. It is noteworthy that Taylor's schemes required very substantial numbers of people in staff positions checking on performance after the work study research had been done. This interpretation of Taylorism suggests, in other words, that once again it is not that the new organisational form is technically more efficient, but that it increases managerial control.

The argument I am trying to develop is threefold. Firstly I am arguing that it is not at all clear that replacement of market by hierarchy in the development of factory production was in the interests of both principal parties to the contract, the employers and the workers. Secondly the evidence does not unequivocally suggest that the organisational innovation resulted in greater technical efficiency in handling the transactions and therefore in co-ordinating the activities taking place within the factory. It appears quite possible to view the evidence as supporting just as strongly the hypothesis that hierarchical co-ordination offered tighter control over the workforce by the employers and thus an ability to achieve their objectives at the expense of the workers' objectives. Thirdly, that if these first two arguments are correct then it is not possible to predict from an examination only of the economics of the situation when a switch from markets to hierarchies obtains. To explain such a shift requires consideration of the surrounding social and political context which enabled the employers to exercise power. This is a rather different argument to that of Williamson and Chandler which maintained that the new arrangements offered a better economic solution at the system level.

The Case of Vertical Integration

A similar argument to the one above can be made about vertical integration. As mentioned above Williamson suggests that the reasons for vertical integration are the same as those for the emergence of the employment relationship. He argues that the problems between suppliers and users of intermediate products of using either complex contingent claims contracting or sequential spot contracting are the same as those experienced by employers and workers and lead to the same institutional solution, namely the adoption of hierarchy.

Chandler, firstly in his *Strategy and Structure* (1962) and then in the more detailed and complex *Visible Hand* (1977) shows that the usual pattern of company growth is the following. Given, for whatever reason, the appearance of a new entrepreneurial opportunity the clutch of firms which get into the product market area first grow with the market, and if the market area is a high growth one, grow fast. For those firms which ultimately become very large there is at some stage a process of vertical integration, either forwards or backwards or both. This vertical integration stage may, but not necessarily, be preceded by horizontal integration through merging with other companies in the industry. The crucial vertical integration stage comes about because, according to Chandler, the manufacturer cuts those transaction costs which are incurred by having to buy raw/unfinished materials and to sell the finished product to, for example, wholesalers, by merging with the suppliers/customers. Those hierarchically co-ordinated transactions are cheaper, Chandler argues, than those co-ordinated through the market if the volume of the flow of goods is high. Thus only in some industries, notably those producing a high volume of standardised, nationally distributed, mass or process-produced goods, were these economies in co-ordination costs to be made.

There are a number of possible objections to this argument. The first is that, as in the case of the inside contractor, there may be many cases in which it would not be in the interests of the small supplier, or the small buyer, to merge with the large company which it was marketing.

The small-scale owner may prefer to maintain control over his own enterprise and continue to engage in the, perhaps costly, haggling involved in marketing supplies or purchase with the large enterprise rather than reduce transaction costs by accepting hierarchical control at the expense of being taken over. Whether or not a takeover occurs would then depend on the power of the larger company over the smaller to force him to cede control. This in turn would depend among other things on the ownership structure of the firms and the interests the ownership groups had.

A second more major objection follows from Williamson who would argue that the transition from market to hierarchy does not occur because of the general superiority of the latter form of transacting over the former given a high volume of transactions, but only when certain specified conditions are met. In the particular case of vertical integration, the information impactedness condition is crucial. It is noteworthy that in the retailing industry, for example, there is a surprising absence of vertical integration. In the UK, and I understand that this is not untypical, it is very rare to find a retailer who has integrated backwards into manufacturing, though it is not at all uncommon to find manufacturers who have integrated forward into retailing. This striking asymmetry would not exist under the simple Chandler hypothesis of the superiority of hierarchy. However it can be explained in some measure by reference to the high level of information retailers have about prices and quality of manufactured products and the fact that the relation between manufacturer and retailer rarely reduces to small-numbers exchange. Thus there is in the market relationship very little opportunity for opportunistic behaviour on the part of the manufacturer, and thus no disadvantage to the retailer in continuing with a market relationship. On the other hand the primary reason for the manufacturer integrating forward into retailing often seems to be to create a situation of information impactedness on their side *vis-à-vis* the customer. To take the case of the Singer company documented by Chandler, the consumer who happens to go into a Singer shop in the High Street is likely both to obtain less information about comparative performance and prices of sewing machines in general, and more likely to be 'driven', to use Nelson's not inappropriate word for the activity of foremen in factory workshops, than the consumer who chooses to purchase a machine in a multiple store.

This introduces a third major objection, and that is the element of power that can be involved in the hierarchical as compared with the market relationship. When an entrepreneur integrates either backwards or forwards by taking over a supplier or customer he is not just buying the possibility of setting up an hierarchical relationship over the transaction between the two parties but is also entering into the equivalent of an employment relationship/authority relationship with him. That is, the entrepreneur now has the power to direct the supplier to supply only to him, and the customer to take only his goods. This latter case may well be of crucial significance for a manufacturer integrating forward and setting up a distribution network to get his goods to the final consumer. With an authority relationship over the 'wholesaler' and even 'retailer', as for example in the case of Singer, the manufacturer can order that it is his goods which are distributed and promoted to the retail customer, even though the wholesaler, if he had been free to transact through market mechanisms, might have chosen on cost or quality grounds to stock and distribute the product of an alternative manufacturer. This seems to me to be clearly different from the Chandler and Williamson arguments in both the reason for the adoption of hierarchy and in its social and economic effects. If either or both of the first and the third of the objections above can be sustained then it follows that, in a number of instances, the pressure to merge may come from only one of the parties in the contracting relationship, and whether or not vertical integration will occur may depend on the relative power position of the two parties.

The Problem of Domination

So far I have suggested that in many cases markets are replaced by hierarchies as a result of domination by one party over the other rather than by mutual agreement on the basis of an expectation of mutual benefit. I have also suggested that in a number of cases the major benefits accruing from the switch arise from the resulting domination within the hierarchical relationship rather than because of a reduction in transaction costs.

This poses two important questions about the nature of domination. The first concerns the relationship between domination and hierarchy. The second is of concern in any ongoing debate in this area between economists and sociologists, and that is the relationship between domination and monopoly.

Weber, the father of theories about the rationalisation of society and hence of the emergence of the bureaucratic form of organisation, has of course something to say about both these questions. He suggests (Weber 1978, p. 943) that 'there are two diametrically contrasting types of domination, viz., domination by virtue of a constellation of interests (in particular: by virtue of a position of monopoly), and domination by virtue of authority, i.e., power to command and duty to obey'. The argument I am suggesting here about the role of domination in considerations of transaction costs appear at first sight to relate precisely to these two types of domination. Hierarchies emerge because of domination by virtue of a constellation of interests (often only those of one party in the transaction), and hierarchy shows an advantage by virtue of domination by authority. While I think the reason for emergence fits the Weberian formulation (which itself is not considered, or at least made explicit, by Chandler or Williamson) the role of domination within hierarchy needs further exploration.

The way in which Chandler and Williamson both appear to claim that hierarchy offers advantages over market is as follows. If A has to transact with B then either they do this in the market place or else move into the hierarchical transaction mode in which case a third party, C, enters the scene. This third party is the bureaucratic mechanism set up, presumably under joint agreement. It is C who stands in hierarchical relationship to both A and B. A and B remain on the same level and both stand to gain the same transaction cost reduction and also lose the same atmospheric benefits of autonomy. However, certainly in the case of the employment relationship and I would argue often in the case of vertical integration, a different hierarchy is instituted. This is one in which A now stands over B or vice versa. In this case A and B are not equal in the costs and benefits they incur and the advantage in the transaction is not simply that third party arbitrage offers a solution to market failures induced by Williamsonian factors. Now either A or B, whoever stands below the other in the new hierarchy, is forced to accept ('has a duty to obey') whatever transaction is proposed by the other, so long as this is within the terms of the authority relation in which they now stand. It is very likely that the outcome of transactions under this type of hierarchy will be markedly different, and be much more within the interest of the dominant party, from the outcome under the arbitrage hierarchical relation that one would imagine would be set up if the two parties had mutually agreed to merge for their common benefit. It is possible, and maybe probable, that in the former case, where one party to the transaction comes to dominate the other, that the advantage accruing to the instituting of hierarchy comes from the domination itself, whereby the dominated party now does what the dominant party prefers, as least as much as from a reduction in transaction costs.

With regard to the question of the relationship between the concepts of domination and monopoly, this is of some importance to the extent that if the two concepts are not synonymous then economists cannot handle the problem entirely by themselves. If the argument is accepted that domination plays a role in the formation of hierarchies then economists should pay much more attention to the extent to which firms have a monopoly position within the labour, product and capital markets. However, though Weber observes that a position of monopoly is the particular case of the exercise of domination by virtue of a constellation of interests, and though this has served as the basis for sociological theories of the basis of power, it should be stressed that sociological treatments of power have extended beyond considerations merely of labour, capital and product market structures. One feature sociologists would draw attention to would be that monopolies of resources other than money may be a source of power, e.g. access to status positions in the community and access to knowledge. A second feature would be the identification of the constellations of interests themselves and the role of class in this. For example, particularly bearing in mind the case of vertical integration, identifying the interests of financiers/bankers and attempting to identify whether or not they stand as a class with regard to their possible common interests, and whether industrialists occupy a different set of class interests would be a worthwhile sociological activity. A preliminary attempt to do this is contained within Francis (1980). Thirdly there is the process of legitimation whereby domination becomes to be exercised by virtue of authority and not just by virtue of a position of monopoly. Which groups/classes in society, if any, are in a particularly advantaged position to hasten this process?

And also mention must be made here (and the list of contributions which sociology might make to a discussion of the role of domination in this context is by no means exhausted) of the *way* in which power may be exercised. Of particular note here is the exposition by Lukes (1974) in which he argues that an individual or group's own perceived interests may be the subject of manipulation of other powerful parties. For example, one way of exercising power is when one company has enough resources at its disposal that it can directly confront another company and attempt to take it over even when that company feels that it is not in its interests to be taken over. But a second way of exercising power would be manifest under circumstances where it may be possible for the more powerful company to engage in behaviour which leads to the other company coming to a false view about what its own interests are. This other dimension of power is additional to the exercise of a monopoly position in the market place and not amenable to economic analysis.

Conclusion

I have argued that while Williamson's organisational failures framework offers much insight into the process whereby hierarchies replace markets, and in particular into why the employment relation and vertical integration occur, it understates the exercise of domination in the process. A necessary refinement of the organisational failures framework is to drop the notion of system interests and substitute a thorough-going analysis of the interests of the various parties to the transaction. In addition further analysis should be done of the various power resources each party has at its disposal so that an attempt can be made to identify the exercise of power both in the influencing of perceived interests and in the way in which hierarchies are introduced. It may then appear that many of the vaunted efficiency advantages of hierarchy over market are either less, or at least more one-sided, than have so far been suggested.

6 The Organisational Failures Framework and Industrial Sociology
P. Willman

Introduction

Williamson's 'Markets and Hierarchies' (henceforward MH) attempts to come to terms with the influence of sets of factors which more conventional economic analysis would define simply as extra-economic. Williamson clearly believes that his organisational failures framework has a wide applicability in social sciences, and applies it both to relations between firms and to those between employers and employed (Williamson 1976b). In this paper, I want to assess the relevance of the MH perspective for sociologists and industrial relations analysts concerned with the latter.

In 'Markets and Hierarchies' (1975) Williamson seeks to apply the assumptions of seller opportunism developed in the organisational failures framework to transactions for labour. The central concern is to indicate inviability of contingent claims and sequential spot contracting in the face of seller opportunism, and to argue the transactional rationale for the development of internal labour market structures as solutions to opportunism which economise on bounded rationality. In assessing this work I wish to argue that, although an 'institutional' focus and a concern to see how organisational dynamics can substitute for more traditional economic categories may appeal to some sociologists, Williamson incorporates certain assumptions which are sociologically questionable. His concern with the *remediable* difficulties of industrial enterprises induces a rather one-sided application of the organisational failures framework which focuses almost entirely on worker opportunism. Partially because of this, he develops a rather unsatisfactory notion of 'atmosphere' which leads too readily to the acceptance of internal labour market structures as solutions to opportunism. More systematic sociological work on the employment relationship gives a rather better explanation of the underlying problems.

Section 1 focuses on the problem of remediability, and indicates the consequences of accepting opportunism as a feature of both buyer and seller behaviour. Section 2 illustrates the implications of this for internal labour markets and discusses the idea of 'atmosphere'. Section 3 discusses sociological work in the area, from which certain conclusions follow.

The Problem of Remediability

It has become reasonably commonplace to incorporate into glib sociological rejections of the validity of modern economic microtheory some strictures about the value-laden character of economic concepts, and to note the relatively close relationship between description and normative judgement in much economic work. Indeed, such strictures are often presented in such a way as to imply that such value probelms are no longer relevant to the 'correct' sociological approach (Hyman and Brough 1975). Such rejections are hardly constructive: vigorous rehearsal of the 'value problem' in social theory generally is usually an imperfect prelude to empirical work searching for some useful 'mix' of concepts drawn from different social–scientific disciplines.

Having said this, it may seem rather perverse of me to suggest that the prescriptive elements in MH pose severe normative difficulties. Nevertheless, I believe this to be the case. But these difficulties emerge at a rather more concrete level than those conventionally criticised. They emerge because Williamson discusses his extra-economic mechanisms in terms of remedies to institutional 'failure' which are distinct and in some cases superior to those of the market. A number of hoary old sociological problems emerge. The search for 'remedies' presupposes prior identification of 'problems': the approach must deal with purposive action in a non-economic way. The emergence of 'problems' implies interest-divergence which may or may not have some social–structural basis. In turn, interest-divergence problematises the search for a solution. These issues deserve more detailed discussion.

Williamson is concerned with the relative efficiency of markets and internal organisation as modes of executing similar sets of transactions. His concern with 'comparative institutional choice' leads him to discuss the efficacy of different contractual 'modes' in minimising transaction costs. Hence 'Remedial frictions . . . constitute the conditions of interest' (Williamson 1975). The end-point – the reduction of transaction costs – is uncontroversial both for the theorist and, presumably, for the social actors involved. Although extra-economic mechanisms are discussed, they are evaluated in terms of their ability to encourage developments which are themselves unproblematic for conventional economic theory. But the notion of 'morally hazardous' or opportunistic behaviour is almost by definition related to interest formation, and the calculation and minimisation of transaction costs necessarily implies some idea of agency. Market failure can occur as a consequence of the purposive action of parties whose interests diverge, yet the hierarchical solution proposed does not deal with this divergence.

This problem achieves no salience in the MH framework because the reduction of transaction costs in the employment relation is desirable over and above the sectional interests of the transactional participants. Hence:

It is in the interest of each party to seek terms most favourable to him, which encourages opportunistic representations and haggling. The interests of the *system* by contrast, are promoted if the parties can be joined in such a way as to avoid both the bargaining costs and the indirect costs (mainly maladaptation costs) which are generated in the process. (Williamson 1975, p. 127).

and, subsequently:

Systems rationality entails global optimisation, whereas rational sub-group behaviour is that which enhances the individual and collective objectives of those parties who effectively control the transaction, or related sets of transactions in question. (Williamson 1975, p. 119).

The possibility thus exists that sectional agency which aims at a reduction of transaction costs will serve system goals. This may well be unsatisfactory generally since, given the nature of the MH approach, it appears as a presumption in favour of takeover and merger. But it is particularly unsatisfactory given the way in which Williamson applies the organisational failures framework to the employment relation.

For Williamson, it is primarily the *employees'* goals which are problematic: managerial and employer goals are less so. This follows more or less directly from the focus on buyers' problems. Buyers are boundedly rational: by contrast, the principal characteristic of sellers is opportunism, which becomes acute where uncertainty and small-numbers bargaining prevail. The failure of (managerial) buyers of labour is predominantly their limited capacity to further unproblematic goals: the failure of (employee) sellers of labour is their tendency to 'morally hazardous' behaviour. Consider the following:

Although it is in the interest of each worker, bargaining individually or as part of a small team, to acquire and exploit monopoly positions, it is plainly not in the interests of the *system* that employees should behave in this way. (Williamson 1975, p. 73).

On the one hand, 'system' and management goals, on the other, worker opportunism. Williamson implies a correct 'standard' or datum of behaviour from which opportunistic behaviour diverges. But opportunism, though by assumption a universal tendency, arises in practice as predominantly a worker habit.

The problem as I see it can be illustrated by shifting the focus of Williamson's framework. Assume a situation where *sellers* are boundedly rational, and structural features generate small-numbers bargaining over purchase in a situation of uncertainty. In this situation, *buyers* could be opportunistic. The preconditions for this would include the requirement that buyers achieved first-mover or learning-by-doing advantages. One example might be where buyers distribute sellers' products to a market to which sellers do not have access. Another is clearly the situation where sellers of labour power are unaware of the nature of product demand from which the demand for their labour is derived.[1] Given that buyer opportunism arises, then, the seller's solution to the transaction cost problem would be internal organisation by takeover. This raises two sets of problems.

Firstly, the improbability of a single labour seller controlling a labour buyer is not dealt with. This is symptomatic of a more general failure to deal with power relations which is also a feature of the orthodox 'seller-opportunism' variant. Internal organisation may be an appropriate solution, but the *processes* by which hierarchy supplants market are less central to the MH framework than the logic of why it should do so. Hierarchies may have a basis in consensus or constraint, it is not clear, yet atmospheric considerations and the nature of co-operation are important.

Secondly, the 'reversal' of the model gives a completely different complexion to 'moral hazards'. Obviously questions must be asked about the previously unproblematic relationship between buyer interests and system goals; if buyers can be opportunistic, what are system goals? The answer to this involves a discussion of the ethical basis of the MH approach, and of the notion of 'atmosphere'. For Williamson, opportunism consists essentially in the generation of an 'unfair' imbalance in the performance reward relationship in the preferred direction. But reversal does encourage a concern with other problems, because power disparities between buyers and sellers of labour power are implied. A shift of the concern with moral hazard away from the supply side towards that of demand encourages a focus on the decisions about the nature of demand for labour that buyers make. In the 'orthodox' version, sellers resort to opportunism as the immediately available hazardous tactic. Buyers can be much more radical: they may not only under-reward performance, but may bolster this opportunism by taking strategic decisions about what sort of performance is required. In Williamson's discussion, the nature of labour demand appears almost as a given where buyers are system agents, and efficiency considerations are the basis of such strategic decisions. If one suggests that buyers are 'flawed' one simultaneously evaluates their decisions while implying that *sellers* could be system agents in a way which alters the whole emphasis of the analysis.

Furthermore, the assumption of bilateral opportunism severely jeopardises the logic for Williamson's preferred mode of contracting for labour, for two reasons. Firstly, because it undermines the notion of atmosphere, at least in the form in which it is presented. Secondly, because it exposes the normative basis of Williamson's preference for internal labour markets.

Atmosphere and Internal Labour Markets

Reflecting his more general concerns, Williamson's focus on the employment relation seeks to outline the 'transactional attributes' of alternative modes of contracting for labour, and to interpret 'evolving institutional practices with respect to idiosyncratic production tasks, principally in efficiency terms, (Williamson 1975, p.57). He argues that transaction costs, rather than technological inseparabilities, explain the form of the employment relationship. Hence:

conventional arguments which rely on indivisibilities to explain the employment relation do not, without more, go through. Recourse to transactional considerations is ultimately necessary (1975, p. 61).

The substitution of hierarchy for market exchange follows from the joining of non-separability with information impactedness and opportunism. And the latter factors are clearly the most important: non-separability itself would not occasion hierarchy but information impactedness plus opportunism clearly would, indivisibilities aside. Consequently, not only is the growth of industrial organisation a consequence of transactional rather than technological considerations, but subordination of the latter implies that certain types of technology may be too idiosyncratic for transactional efficiency. Technological choice clearly follows from efficiency considerations and

Although least-cost production technologies are sacrificed in the process, pecuniary gains may nevertheless result since incumbents realise little strategic advantage over otherwise qualified but inexperienced outsiders. (Williamson 1975, p. 68).

Furthermore, these transactional considerations are clearly to the fore in Williamson's later suggestion that, under the 'internal labour market' mode of contracting 'systems concerns are made more fully to prevail' (1975, p. 73). It becomes clear that the minimisation of 'transactional costs' is predominantly a 'man-management' problem. Internal labour market structures lower bargaining costs and defuse some of the potential problems with 'investments of idiosyncratic types'. Their emphasis on due process results in 'a greater sense of justice' and 'consummate' rather than 'perfunctory' co-operation is encouraged: these are 'atmospheric' advantages. Williamson's concerns here clearly overlap with some of the traditional concerns of industrial sociology: in particular we are concerned here with the nature of industrial conflict and the values and morale of employees under different institutional conditions. The appropriate questions concern how well Williamson discusses such issues.

Williamson argues that, where the environmental conditions of uncertainty/complexity and small numbers bargaining are ensured by job idiosyncracies, individualistic bargaining models are inviable. Sequential spot contracting is chronically prone to opportunism: contingent claims contracts fail to economise on bounded rationality. Simon's 'authority relation' similarly does not solve the problems of opportunism. Moreover, 'intensive metering' to ensure that opportunism does not arise is unwelcome for atmospheric reasons: the requisite contractual mode is the internal labour market.

This form of reasoning is sociologically extremely interesting, since the comparative advantage of internal labour market structures stems from attitudinal considerations. The argument against intensive metering runs as follows:

efforts to divide the employment relation into parts and assess each separately in strictly calculative, instrumental terms can have, for some individuals at least, counterproductive consequences. . . . Rather than regard transactions in strictly *quid pro quo* terms, with each account to be settled separately, they [individuals] look instead for a favourable balance among a related set of transactions. (Williamson 1975, p. 256).

The control measures to be adopted to prevent opportunism need to be devised in such a way as to encourage worker involvement. Since individuals may look for a favourable balance among a related set of transactions, instrumental assessment of the employment relationship by management may be counterproductive because of the 'influence of metering intensity on work attitudes' (Williamson 1975, p. 257).

The form of involvement to be encouraged is termed 'consummate co-operation'. The distinction from 'perfunctory co-operation' is as follows:

Consummate co-operation is an affirmative job attitude – to include the use of judgement, filling gaps, and taking initiative in an instrumental way. Perfunctory co-operation, by contrast, involves job performance of a minimally acceptable sort – where minimally acceptable means that incumbents, who through experience have acquired task-specific skills, need merely to maintain a slight margin over the best available inexperienced candidate. (Williamson 1975, p. 69).

By shifting to a perfunctory 'mode' workers may 'destroy' idiosyncratic efficiency gains where they cannot 'retain' them for any reason. But the object of the managerial exercise is to appropriate such gains.

Consummate co-operation and maintained efficiency are compatible, given the correct managerial strategy. This strategy must account for employees' affective tendencies to prefer 'involvement' relations and to allow interaction effects between transactions. A 'requisite mixture of structures' must be provided 'to allow individuals to match themselves to organisations in accordance with their involvement–productivity trade-offs' and the interaction effects must be accommodated by avoiding dysfunctional transaction-specific metering. Internal labour markets fit the bill quite well.

There are a number of major problems with this. For example, it is difficult to identify the determinants of balance between involvement and productivity, or to say why this point of balance differs between individuals. Hence the precise basis of a strategy for encouraging consummate co-operation is obscure. Moreover, to the extent this is so, it is not possible to identify any social structural basis for disaffection, and consequently the nature of co-operation appears as a tractable human relations problem awaiting only the appropriate metering or involvement-generating solution: this is clearly consistent with a focus on remediable failure. The residual nature of 'atmosphere' is evident: it is used in an *ad hoc* manner to deal with clearly salient problems, but is theoretically poorly articulated. However, the principal problem is that in saying that the atmospheric consequences of internal labour market structures are such as to remove the threat of opportunism, Williamson is suggesting that there are definite conceptions of equity which can be enshrined in particular institutional arrangements: workers co-operate in consummate fashion because they are satisfied with internal labour market structures. This is worth closer analysis.

In presenting his idea of an internal labour market, Williamson relies heavily on Doeringer and Piore's idea of an 'enterprise market' (Doeringer and Piore 1971). He chooses to emphasise four key elements:

1. Wage rates are attached to jobs rather than workers: incentives to opportunism typical of individual bargaining are attenuated, and group disciplinary disincentives are also deployed.
2. Agreements are reached through collective bargaining, and unforeseeable contingencies are referred to arbitration machinery.
3. Grievance procedures allow changing conditions to be dealt with in a non-litigious manner.
4. Internal promotion ladders are established which encourage a positive worker attitude towards on-the-job training and enable the firm to reward co-operative behaviour.

Since the efficiency implications of such a structure are almost entirely derived from its capacity to encourage consummate co-operation by offering security and advancement prospects, so reducing labour turn-over, opportunism or the destruction of 'idiosyncratic gains', it is of some interest to look at what is implied for the pattern of workers' values.

It is assumed that social actors are generally agreed that rewards should be based on some measure of performance: given consistently applied rules and procedures and prospects for advancement, 'atmos-pheric' conditions will preclude opportunism. These ideas are closely related to clearly articulated ideas on Williamson's part about the equity of rewards. The idea of 'morally hazardous' behaviour implies that workers may pursue advantages that they 'deserve' and ones that they do not. Advantages that follow from 'pre-existing and fully disclosed productive conditions (for example, a unique location or differential skill)' are in some sense morally 'correct'; ones which follow from 'self-disbelieved promises regarding future conduct' are not. In the former instance 'parties are simply realising returns to which their pre-existing position entitles them' (Williamson 1975, p. 26).

Williamson expresses a wish to devise

a contractual relation that promises fair [competitive] returns, promotes adaptive efficiency and is relatively satisfying in terms of the involvement experience (1975, p. 99).

Actors compete in terms of their available contributions, and fairness consists in the appropriate differential reward of (differential) relative contribution. The superiority of internal organisation over the market lies in its greater ability to distinguish meritorious performance and assign rewards to deeds. Hence

the firm offers managers job security and an internal equity system in return for which managers agree to being evaluated in terms of their contribution to the system as a whole. (Williamson 1975, p. 99).

Elsewhere in the hierarchy disaffected groups may indulge in 'deviant conduct' including the allocation of rewards 'in a perverse fashion' (1975, p. 129). Intensive metering can prevent this, but trans-action-specific settling of accounts can be unsatisfactory in 'atmos-pheric' terms. The presumption appears to be not only that social actors generally agree that reward should be based on some measure of performance, but that the decisions structuring the demand side are unproblematic. Reward is to be based on contribution but, explicitly, the decision on the structure of contribution is to be made by management seeking to minimise transaction costs. The determinants of contribution are thus separate from the determinants of individual propensity to contribute, yet the ethical focus is on the supply side. The difficulties presented by this are overcome by the conflation of managerial and system goals. Although failures may occur and organisations may develop slack, indicating that management can get it wrong, when they get it right and minimise their own transaction costs, they are merely agents of the system.

Williamson is thus operating with an heroic set of assumptions about workers' views of equity and sources of attachment to particular institutional forms. Moreover, these assumptions are highly implausible in terms both of the model of internal labour markets which Williamson adapts and of his own organisational failures framework.

The circumstances under which workers will favour internal labour markets are contingent. As Doeringer and Piore note, their role is primarily defensive

Because skills are not transferable among enterprises, because employers seek to induce stability through economic incentives, and because mobility is frustrated by actions taken in other internal labour markets, workers become increasingly protective of such markets and the privileges which they confer. (1971, p. 40).

Moreover, their value to the workforce is premised upon the absence of alternative arrangements for ensuring future income: as these have improved, the relative economic value of internal labour markets is reduced (1971, p. 38). Conflict may be an endemic feature of such markets – over seniority vs. ability in promotions, over the size of mobility districts and the like – such that haggling and perfunctory co-operation may persist (Doeringer and Piore 1971; Herding 1972). Consequently, although Williamson stresses the selectivity of his focus on the benefits rather than the costs of internal labour markets, these costs need to be noted, since they arise directly from instances running counter to Williamson's general assumptions about 'attitudinal considerations'.

But Williamson's assumptions about workers' values are implausible in a more fundamental sense: they conflict with the assumptions of the organisational failures framework. I have already noted that the emphasis on employer opportunism is extremely muted in Williamson's discussion. If one takes it into consideration it is plainly unlikely that the internal labour market structure will have the effects he claims. Why should workers be encouraged to consummate co-operation by a device which restricts their own scope for opportunism but places no similar restraints on the employer? It is true that the consistent operation of bureaucratic rules would mitigate what one might term *capricious* opportunism which discriminated between worker and worker. But there are no devices within the proposed institutional mode to correct *systematic* opportunism on the part of the employer wherein all labour is consistently underpaid. Workers might be expected, under the organisational failures assumptions, to offer extremely perfunctory co-operation to internal labour markets just as to intensive metering.

In emphasising only *seller* opportunism, Williamson's discussion of the employment relationship tends to be one-sided. A concern with both buyer *and* seller opportunism shifts the emphasis away from the remedies for industrial inefficiency to a focus on the basis of endemic interest conflict. It may be useful, therefore, to look at other approaches to the problems with which Williamson is concerned which emphasise conflict, before returning specifically to MH later on.

Some Alternative Approaches

As noted above, Williamson clearly feels that the growth of industrial organisations follows from the attempt to minimise transaction costs rather than being determined in any unproblematic way by technology. Moreover, Williamson explicitly suggests a closely related idea; that considerations other than cost-minimisation might inform technological choice for reasons closely connected with the management of labour. In proposing these two ideas, Williamson gains some unlikely bed-fellows.

From the MH perspective the possibility arises that certain idiosyncratic production technologies might be avoided by employers where the possibility of job incumbents realising untoward strategic advantages at the contract renewal stage persists. In Williamson's terms, equipment, process and communication idiosyncrasies, together with 'informal team accommodations' may be the basis of an opportunistic worker strategy. Given the critique of opportunism above, clearly one would prefer to say here that what is at issue at contract renewal (which is largely an abstraction in employment contracts in any event) is the resolution of a shift in control over work from employer to incumbents which gives the latter enhanced bargaining power. *Ceteris paribus* then, the employer selects a technology (and presumably a pattern of work organisation) which is as cost-efficient as possible while impeding this shift of control.

David Gordon discusses such a strategy from a very different perspective, one which regards as given the 'opposition between the ruling class and direct producers'. He is concerned with the same trade-off between efficiency and control which is implicit in MH as the trade-off between least-cost technology and transactional efficiency. He distinguishes 'quantitative' and 'qualitative' efficiency as follows:

a production process is *quantitatively* (most) efficient if it effects the greatest possible useful physical output from a given set of physical inputs (or if it generates a given physical output with the fewest possible inputs). . .
a production process is *qualitatively* (most) efficient if it maximises the ability of

a ruling class to reproduce its domination of the social process of production and minimises producers' resistance to ruling class domination of the production process (1976, p. 22).

The pursuit of qualitative efficiency is more important in explaining capitalist development: capitalists do not simply select the qualitatively most efficient technology from a range of quantitatively efficient variants among which they are otherwise indifferent, rather they resolve quantitative–qualitative conflicts in favour of the latter.

Clearly, this set of ideas is no substitute for Williamson's analysis. In Gordon's short paper the empirical basis of his qualitative–quantitative distinction remains elusive, but it is clearly linked to a notion of 'real interests' represented in the concept of 'socialist efficiency' and in Marxist notions about class domination. Nevertheless Gordon emphasises two points which are largely ignored by Williamson.

1. The endemic and fundamental opposition of interests in industrial organisations, and
2. that technological change and choice are consequently inherently problematical for workers in such organisations.

As he notes, the

imperatives of qualitative efficiency continually force capitalists to substitute machines for workers in pursuit of greater control over production (1976, p. 25).

While this simple Marxist 'deskilling' approach is probably over-simplified, one needs to problematise the implications of technological choice by divorcing – on the lines indicated above – the goals of employers from those of 'the system'.

This is clearly Marglin's intention. He too sees the growth of industrial organisations as following from non-technical processes. But the parallels are limited: Williamson's 'system agents' are, for Marglin, parasites who *generate* a role for themselves in the productive process. Marglin views the developments in factory organisation and of the 'minute division of labour' as effecting distributional shifts in favour of capitalists rather than as 'technically superior' to previous methods of production. He contends that

innovations in work organisation were introduced so that the capitalist got himself a larger share of the pie at the expense of the worker (1975, p. 22).

Whereas, then, Williamson approaches Adam Smith's classic pin-making example of work fragmentation with a concern simply to show how internal organisation avoids excessive transaction costs between individual producers, regarding the economies of fragmentation as given, Marglin contests the existence of such economies. The 'minute' division of labour was the result of a search not for a technologically superior organisation of work, but for an organisation which guaranteed to the entrepreneur an essential role in the production process (1975, p. 20).

In effect, Marglin is reversing the MH approach in a simpler and more radical fashion than that proposed above. He goes beyond the mere recognition of endemic conflict in industry to a reversal of Williamson's unitary focus of organisations. From Marglin's *marxisant* perspective, workers are system agents, and capitalists become the opportunists: there are parallels in Marglin's work to the mechanisms discussed in MH.

In particular Marglin describes buyer-opportunism features such as small numbers purchasing and information impactedness. In the capitalist division of labour, the workman's task became so specialised that 'he had no product to sell, or at least none for which there was a wide market'. A small number of intermediaries purchased from a mass of workers where individual products were unmarketable unless deployed by the intermediary to produce a final product: allow minimal product differentiation and this becomes virtual monopsony. Clearly producers have severely bounded rationality and information is heavily impacted in favour of the intermediary (1975, pp. 16, 22) Admit Williamson's assumption of universal tendencies to opportunism and the reversal of the model is complete. Indeed, historically, subsequent developments in factory organisation, such as scientific management, can be seen as opportunistic attempts to maintain information impactedness (Nelson 1975).

The extent to which Marglin's views can be presented as a mirror image of the MH analysis is limited, since reversal of the conceptual apparatus does nothing for the actual state of affairs: Williamson's system agents own industry and Marglin's do not, yet internal organisation controls are always implemented by the organisation's dominant groups under the MH framework and one's approach to such groups colours one's diagnosis of the effect of such controls. Nevertheless, in both instances, the combination of an idea about 'real' system interests and a unitary view of organisations which allows only opportunistic deviance leads to unnecessarily radical diagnoses.

I am not, therefore, suggesting that Gordon and Marglin's perspective is inherently preferable to that of Williamson, but rather that untestable assumptions about the existence and legitimacy of specific real interests of social actors are present in both types of analysis, allied to some vaguely articulated conception of system interests. In MH, these interests are those of neoclassical economics. In the alternative conception, they have to do with a concern to achieve some non-exploitative historical datum point. Adoption of either conception influences the use of the market failure framework detrimentally: the powerful tools Williamson develops for analysing small numbers bargaining under uncertainty are used with clear normative implications.

Some of the general arguments for this are detailed above. In what follows, I want to look more closely at Williamson's detailed analysis of the employment contract, and at sociological work directed at the same issues which would fault it. To recap, Williamson is arguing that internal organisation allows the intensive metering which prevents opportunistic accumulation of rewards disproportionate to performance. But the sensible approach avoids bad 'atmosphere' and prevents 'perfunctory' co-operation by slackening transaction-specific metering in the adoption of less rigorous modes of labour contracting: the appropriate institutional form is the 'internal labour market'. The sociological shorthand term 'atmosphere' has a crucial role to play in generating efficiency via consummate co-operation. Now this distinction between perfunctory and consummate co-operation has certain parallels with sociological work not directly concerned with efficiency implications; in particular with Alan Fox's distinction between high and low trust relations (Fox 1974).

I propose to focus on these similarities rather than summarise Fox's work here. At a general level, it is clear that Fox shares certain premises with the MH framework. For Fox, a purely contractual social order cannot exist, nor can economic exchange be characterised by totally prescribed terms. All contracting – and particularly contracting for labour – is pervaded by affective 'diffuse' relations involving some degree of trust. Moreover, these extra-economic elements of contract behave similarly to Williamson's 'attitudinal considerations'. So, for example, one element in the 'high discretion syndrome' associated with high-trust roles is an absence of close supervision or detailed regulation. And high-trust reciprocation by the occupants of high-trust work roles is created

by promoting a given individual through a series of posts each vested with greater discretion than the one before. It is usual for an individual moving thus up the hierarchy to display an increasing intensity of commitment to, and identification with, the organisation and its imputed interests. (Fox 1974, p. 114).

These similarities should not, however, be allowed to obscure the fact that Fox is offering a comprehensive theory of the construction of work roles in industrial organisations while Williamson merely discusses a rule-of-thumb solution to labour disaffection under intensive metering. Consider Table 6.1. Fox distinguishes work roles in terms of their discretionary content: high discretion roles are associated

Table 6.1   Fox's high and low discretion syndrome

Low	High
1. Incumbent subjected to close supervision, hedged by impersonal rules	1. Close supervision seen as inappropriate
2. Incumbent perceives supervision as not trusting him	2. Role occupants have moral commitment to organisation
3. Close co-ordination of work roles established by routines	3. Problem-solving relations not externally unposed routines
4. Inadequacies of incumbent seen to result from carelessness, indifference/insubordination	4. Inadequacies due to substandard exercise of discretion
5. Conflict handled through collective bargaining	5. Conflict resolution a problem-solving exercise

with high vertical trust relations between sub and superordinates, and low discretion with low trust to such an extent that one can speak of distinct 'syndromes'. At the extreme, the lowest trust situation probably corresponds to Williamson's transaction-specific intensive metering, but it is clear that the changes Williamson proposes to such metering constitute a very limited move in the direction of high-trust. So, while adoption of the internal labour market would relax supervision, and increase some forms of commitment, the remaining items of the low trust syndrome are likely to remain, particularly the handling of conflict through collective bargaining which is central to Williamson's conception of an internal labour market.

For Williamson, metering relaxation is essentially a human relations device assisting productive efficiency. Atmospheric considerations militate against an extreme low-trust syndrome, but do not encourage high-trust relations. Indeed at one point Williamson (1975) dismisses a clearly high-trust approach to labour contracting as 'utopian'.[2] Fox's analysis of trust relations indicates just how marginal such a metering change is. The fundamental dimension of institutionalised trust is the degree of discretion invested in a role (discretionary trust): a secondary dimension is prescriptive trust, which may be variable at one level of discretionary trust.

Not only can it be asked how far a subordinate is trusted to exercise discretion: it can also be asked how far he is trusted to obey, conform and honour the prescribed rules which limit his discretion. There is scope for great variations in the frequency, rigour and punitiveness with which those rules are policed and infractions penalised. (Fox 1974, p. 69).

Williamson's atmospheric improvements are seen to follow from less intensive metering – the policing of prescribed rules. But the discretionary content of jobs might increase as one goes up the labour hierarchy, implying that the internal labour market is a significant move in the direction of high trust relations. Unfortunately, such changes are likely to be marginal, given the low skill range of manual jobs (Blackburn and Mann 1979).

In two further respects, Fox's analysis has more explanatory power than the MH framework. Williamson recognises, but cannot explain, the incidence of 'attitudinal interaction effects among sets of trans-actions' rendering intensive metering dysfunctional. Fox's use of discretionary content as a device for distinguishing work roles is a powerful tool for explaining where and when such attitudinal effects might be important. Similarly his trust analysis indicates how individuals in work roles subjected to low vertical trust may respond by establishing high lateral-trust relations. Williamson recognises – again without explanation – how individuals vary in their 'involvement–productivity' trade-offs: but, again, this is not seen to follow from particular structures of work roles. The problem is rather

> to supply the requisite mixture of structures which vary in the intensity of metering, thereby to allow individuals to match themselves to organisations in accordance with their involvement–productivity trade-offs (Williamson 1975, p. 55).

which are taken as given.[3] In the event, the 'requisite mixture of structures' turns out to be the adoption of internal labour market structures of a specific type, which presumably accommodate all 'involvement–productivity' trade-offs.

But, while the precise nature of individual trade-offs remains un-clear, one can envisage – on the basis of Fox's framework – situations where groups of individuals might not be encouraged to consummate co-operation by the adoption of an internal labour market mode. The difficulties involved here may be brought out by discussing three particular cases. Assume a situation where a group of workers are employed on piecework, i.e. 'incentive payments on a transaction-specific basis'. In this situation,

> The employment relations would . . . revert to a series of haggling encounters over the nature of the *quid pro quo* . . . and would hardly be distinguishable from a sequential spot contract. (Williamson 1975, p. 77).

But the principal disadvantage of sequential spot contracting is the scope for opportunism and, given any characterisation of opportunism as interest conflict, it is difficult to see how or why a shift away from transaction-specific to long-term promotion incentives should encourage consummate co-operation. Much of the British evidence shows 'opportunism' under piecework to be both widespread and popular (NBPI 1968; OPCS 1975; Brown 1973; Batstone, Boraston and Frenkel 1977). A shift to some form of internal labour market might well be resisted and, if imposed, resented to the extent that perfunctory co-operation would be provoked.

The other two cases are related. The first has to do with Fox's concept of lateral trust. It may not simply be the case that workers used to low vertical trust who have developed high lateral trust relations will be slow to adapt to internal labour markets which raise the vertical trust level. Rather, the implementation of such a market may be foisted upon a workforce by an employer keen to dislocate solidary lateral relations: his concern may be less the promotion of good atmosphere than the dispersal of countervailing power.

The second has to do with the planning of the internal job structure, independent of external market conditions. This will be done with productive efficiency in mind as well as consummate co-operation. Doeringer and Piore note:

Most engineers appear to favour job simplification and the substitution of capital for labour wherever decision making processes permit them to exercise discretion in these matters . . . [which] implies a general bias towards 'labor-saving' or 'skill-saving' technologies. . . . (1971, p. 99).

This disposition may encourage such a de-skilling of jobs that the internal hierarchy ceases to be a useful way of utilising on-the-job training and becomes a simple personnel device. But its usefulness in the latter respect – in the promotion of consummate co-operation – may be severely limited. Slight increases in prescriptive trust are unlikely to have positive atmospheric effects where discretionary trust is being withdrawn.

A comparison with more detailed sociological work thus reveals a number of problems with the MH framework. Williamson laudably seeks to deal with 'extra-economic' attitudinal factors. To do this, he makes a small number of assumptions about universals of human behaviour, just as those who practise 'received micro theory' do. And, just as conventional assumptions about economic behaviour seek to outline the universal motivations of all social actors – which are assumed to operate at constant strength irrespective of context – so Williamson's 'attitudinal considerations' are presented as the universal elements of normative consensus in such a way that social structural influences on attitudes and preferences in specific contexts can be difficult to explore.

Conclusion
This point deserves some development both because it is of funda-

mental importance to the relationship between sociology and economic micro theory and because it may appear that I have ultimately adopted the position I criticised at the outset as a glib treatment of the value problem in social theory. In fact, I want to stress that the value problem with which I am concerned here is more specific to the organisational failures framework.

What Williamson calls 'received micro theory' operates with a set of assumptions about human behaviour. So, for example, social actors are universally rational and maximising in undifferentiated degree. Now, this is problematic for sociologists who would argue that social actors are universally neither, that one could offer sociological reasons why such assumptions were invalid for certain social groups, and that certain consequences follow from these realisations in terms of the way one conceptualises the social order. But the 'value problem' in MH is of a different order. Williamson goes beyond the simple assumption that there are universal motivating elements of personality to offer a 'unitary' perspective involving *value* consensus. Only self-disbelief can be the basis of a divergence from system interests: in Fox's terms, management is in conflict with 'deviants' rather than 'non-conformists' (Fox 1974, p. 248). Opportunists are involved in behaviour which is not simply divergent from what would be rational from a 'global' perspective: it is also *'morally* hazardous'.

To achieve a consensus of this sort, one needs to assume more than behavioural universals: the Hobbesian pre-contract situation is premised on behavioural universals. Social consensus only becomes unproblematic where it is assumed that these motivating elements of personality are introjected versions of the values which compose some more thorough-going consensus about the 'rules of the game'. Under such assumptions, the problem of social order is collapsed into a problem of individual integration: all 'deviant' behaviour is characterised as a psychological problem. As Giddens notes,

conflict of interest in this conception never becomes anything more than a clash between the purposes of individual actors and the 'interests' of the collectivity (Giddens 1976).

It is such a Parsonian conception of social order which enables Williamson to start out with a set of assumptions about human nature differing from 'conventional micro theory', but still stressing universals, and end up with a problem of sectional behaviour. Opportunism in his framework is a feature predominantly of individual *worker* behaviour. It is simple 'moral hazard' because, given value consensus, it cannot be anything else but individual deviance. And it is a feature mainly of worker behaviour because Williamson tends to present buyers of labour as associated with system interests, imputing illegitimate motives elsewhere.

The movement from universal behavioural tendencies to a concern primarily with sectional behaviour is a *tour de force* accomplished by the importation of a notion of managerial legitimacy and of value consensus. In this sense, Williamson's organisations are 'unitary'.[4] The usefulness of the organisational failures framework for sociologists depends on the shedding of such notions: the universalistic behavioural assumptions, particularly the universal disposition to opportunism, may be unwelcome to purist sociologists, but pose no great problem in the adaptation of the framework.

This adaptation would include a number of elements.

1. A recognition of buyer as well as seller opportunism in the labour market.
2. A recognition of the potential for imbalance in employment contracts, yielding greater advantages to the employer, *ceteris paribus*.
3. An examination of the implications of the organisational failures framework for collective bargaining.

Given the modifications (which would imply also the shedding for all practical purposes of the idea of a notionally 'correct' relationship to be distorted by opportunistic behaviour), one could examine different contractual modes, imputing the desire to minimise transaction costs to each side – management and workers. Different modes may display context-specific patterns of costs and benefits to either party.

To give only one example, sequential spot contracting might yield considerable benefits to workers while raising transaction costs for managers: a change to an internal labour market mode might lower managerial costs while raising those of workers. Indeed, maximising 'opportunistic' behaviour might be a generally preferred strategy for workers where the advantage of small numbers bargaining generally and continuously accrue to management. Different contractual modes must then be seen as different means of institutionalising authority and power relations rather than as differentially efficient solutions to a single unequivocally defined problem.

Notes

[1] This is no fundamental change. Williamson acknowledges buyer opportunism at one point (1975, p. 66ff), but does not elaborate. I would argue such elaboration makes his emphasis on internal labour markets mistaken.
[2] This high-trust solution would involve extracting 'a promise from each willing bidder at the outset that he will not use his idiosyncratic knowledge and experience in a monopolistic way at the contract renewal interval' (Williamson 1975, p. 68).
[3] Fox is sensitive to the problems of change in these areas where Williamson appears not to be. Although individual differences in involvement preference are allowed, the general utility of internal labour markets in atmospheric improvement is implied: intensively metered individuals will respond favourably to change.

But low-trust attitudes may not be reversible (Fox 1974, p. 116). Increasingly prescriptive trust – minimal shift though this is – might simply allow slacker work behaviour with no atmospheric improvement. 'This will be hailed by the sceptics as evidence of original sin which justified the low-discretion work design in the first place'. (Fox 1974, p. 117).

[4] Fox (1974, p. 249) defines a unitary perspective in the following terms:

> Emphasis is placed on the common objectives and values said to unite all participants. Arising logically from this firm foundation is said to be the need for a unified structure of authority, leadership and loyalty, with full managerial prerogative legitimised by all members of the organisation. From this view, the failure of some groups of lower and sometimes even of middle rank participants fully to acknowledge management's prerogative and its call for obedience, loyalty and trust is seen as springing from responses of doubtful validity and legitimacy.

PART IV

7 Control through Markets, Hierarchies and Communes: A transactional approach to organisational analysis
R. J. Butler

Markets, Hierarchies and Communes

Social science theories and concepts are inextricably rooted in the political economy of their time. Since Adam Smith and Karl Marx lively debate has centred upon the relative merits of markets and bureaucracy as appropriate means of distributing goods and services in complex industrial societies (Boulding 1968; Crosland 1959). As a counterweight to the ravishing effects of nineteenth century capitalism the first half of the twentieth century saw increasing intervention of state bureaucracies into decisions previously reserved for individuals resulting in associated planning and welfare state mechanisms.

Inadequacies of marketplaces as a means of distributing goods and services acquired saliency in men's minds. The inadequacies described have ranged from the inhumanity associated with casting off labour in depressions, to the manipulation of the 'technostructure' by large corporations (Galbraith 1967), to the inability of markets to provide adequate provision of basic needs, such as health and education, to the poor. Bureaucracies, or organisations, were the mechanisms by which some of these evils were to be ameliorated. 'The organisation' was almost affectionately accepted as a dominant social institution of our time and, as a matter of course, the quasi-discipline of organisation theory was born (Pugh 1966).

Underlying the bureaucracy v. market argument is the recognition of two fundamentally different methods of controlling transactions within a society. Bureaucracy co-ordinates the activities of a number of actors by means of a hierarchy in which the superordinate level directs a number of subordinates concerning what they should do and how to do it. Market co-ordinates the activities of economically motivated actors by allowing them to produce products in the greatest demand, but with the least supply, because this is the activity in which the most profit is to be made.

Revival of this always latent market v. hierarchy debate occurred in the 1970s. Bureaucracy became associated with inefficiency, debilitating effects upon humans, and loss of personal freedom (Hayek 1959). 'Bureaucrat', 'Organisation Man' became terms of scorn and to be replaced by a new freer man in a forthcoming 'entrepreneurial revolution' (*The Economist* 1976).

Old debates take on a new form as, apparently buried, they are resurrected wearing a new shroud. Williamson's (1975) recent discussion of organisational v. market failures within a single theoretical framework draws particular attention to the effect of transactional complexity upon selection of the most appropriate mode for conducting transactions. In a different vein Hirschman (1970) has recently argued in favour of the use of 'voice' as a means of consumers pressuring delinquent providers of public services for improvement, rather than the alternative 'exit' procedure of the marketplace.

But a remarkable feature about the market v. hierarchy debate is the apparent total lack of interest shown on the part of organisation theorists and the apparently complete monopolisation by economists and political scientists. Markets do not seem to exist for organisation theorists as the subject is still floundering in a systems approach, albeit updated by ecology (Aldrich 1979), which starts from the assumption 'in the beginning there were organisations'. It is a contention of this paper that the alternative starting point 'in the beginning there were markets' (Williamson 1975) needs also to be considered. It is suggested that the notion of the transaction is useful as the fundamental building block of a theory of organisation, and that it is possible to consider transactions in the aggregate and hence consider also overall characteristics of organisational control.

Our enthusiasm to pursue the images of markets and hierarchies, of transactions governed either by blind economic motivation, or by direction, should not obscure for us the possibility of transactions conducted within self-governing communities in which the main source of control is the meeting of beliefs and values to produce a congruence of interests. The idea of peer groups, or communes, as appropriate mechanisms for controlling transactions summarily dismissed by Williamson (1975, p. 45) as 'vulnerable to free rider abuses' and 'collective decision-making processes are often relatively costly'.

Mauss's (1954) essay on the gift in which he reveals complex systems of obligations to give, receive and return in archaic societies suggests that transactions may be conducted by means other than by direction from above on one hand, or by the search for maximum objective gain. Titmuss (1970) has extended the idea of the 'Gift Relationship' further into Western life in his comparison of the American market blood donor system and British voluntary blood donor system. He argues that the voluntary method, by invoking an altruistic and caring streak in people, leads to a more efficient blood donor system, both in terms of cost and by minimising the incidence of disease in the receivers of blood.

This paper aims to develop a framework to allow a fertilisation between the ideas of economics and existing organisation theory. Specifically it develops an approach to organisations owing much to Williamson's seminal book which builds upon the concept of transaction, but sees three rather than two fundamental ideal types of modes for controlling transactions, namely market, hierarchy and the third, as yet relatively undeveloped type, commune or peer group. The emphasis is on the various ways in which transactions can be controlled. No special magic should be assigned to the limitation of possible modes to two, nor should undue significance be associated with the number three. Rather, other discoveries can always be made.

Especially interesting in Titmuss's argument for the gift relationship is the idea that a mode of controlling transactions is not just preferable because it invokes higher sentiments in men but also because it is more efficient as measured by certain well-defined indicators. The possibility that people can act altruistically and that altruism and efficiency might coincide in modern industrial society must surely be an even greater revelation, locked as we are into concerns for simplistic economic efficiency, than the rediscovery of the marketplace. Organisations based in part on the idea of commitment and service to an ideal in which a person gives himself in return for care have been very significant historically. Even though practice has been far from perfect, the list of attempts must be long, ranging from Mauss's tribes of Polynesia, Melanesia and North America to the Communes of Paris, from English public schools to the collectives of China, from the Red Cross to the Peace Corps. From these examples the reader will protest that they are also hierarchical, and in some cases market organisations. This is true and it has been shown how organisations started on the highest of ideals develop hierarchies. But just in the same way that pure markets and pure hierarchies never exist, neither will pure communes. Each will contain a trace of the other. In this paper the market, hierarchy and commune are seen as three dominant ideal types, in the Weberian sense, of modes of transacting which provide analytical anchorage points from which real transactions, transactional systems and organisations can be examined.

Nevertheless, it must be admitted that attempts to organise in the mode of a commune appear to be particularly unstable but that this is probably to do with the dominant values in society. The trend in industrial society away from community was pointed to by Weber with the foreseen consequences of over-bureaucratisation. Similarly Tonnies (1951) in contrasting *Gemeinschaft* to *Gesellschaft*, and in describing the move in industrial society towards the latter, was discussing the tension between the rational will inherent in extrinsic economic transactions in which goods are separate from owners and profit as the end, and *Gesellschaft*, in which there is a community of feeling and shared life experience. Taken to the limit, if all transactions were conducted through markets everybody would be isolated, there would be no marriage, families, groups, firms or nations. Durkheim (1933) also described a move from the mechanical solidarity of strict hierarchical order towards the more fluid arrangements of organic solidarity.

I would extend this argument and suggest that if all were arranged in orderly fashion around hierarchies there would be no room for change. Hierarchies are universal in nature and are even rooted in the biological necessity of kinship. Markets are also universal and are rooted in the need for humans to conduct exchanges and in the evolutionary notion of 'survival of the fittest'. Communes are universal and are rooted in the need for humans to associate with other humans without concern for extrinsic exchange. This paper's principal concern is not to advocate the dominance of one or the other of the three principal modes over the others but to develop an analytical framework for examining the modes used to conduct transactions within organisations and to examine the conditions under which each, or a mixture of each might be used.

Organisations as Transactional Arenas

The parable of the three modes

To help create an image of the three modes of transacting imagine, first, a jamboree in which three groups, Calculus, Maximus and Socius are to demonstrate their constructional prowess. For the moment you are asked only to observe the arena of activity and to withhold judgement about preferable performances and forms of organisation.

First, Calculus enters and it is noted that a central instructor details precise tasks, which are sub-tasks of the whole task, to others. Some of these others then detail sub sub-tasks to other-others. What each person does is determined by his instructor who observes and co-ordinates the activities of all those he instructs. Closer acquaintance with the group indicates a concern of each participant with the technical details of his task but no concern with others' tasks. Participants are given resources which have been calculated by their instructor as appropriate for the task in hand. In return for these resources they duly complete the task in hand. Sometimes activities appear unco-ordinated and the response of the group is an attempt to define in even finer detail the precise nature of the task each is supposed to be doing. Task duly completed Calculus leaves the arena; we have been watching a hierarchy at work.

Now the Maximus group enters and the initial impression is of disorganisation with participants coming and going in and out of the arena, apparently waiting for things to happen. At this point we become aware of adjacent arenas in which other similar displays are occurring. Closer acquaintance shows one participant signalling to others and what is best described as an auction occurs, with tenders and bids. The 'winners' of these tenders set to work on a task while others, some disgruntled, depart to corners of the arena or to apparently lusher pastures in other arenas. There is still a constant coming and going with contracts made and re-made, with new arrivals from neighbouring arenas joining in, some leaving the arena after completing a job and failing to win another contract. Participants receive a currency for their tasks which they can exchange for materials needed with other participants in other arenas. The amount received varies from participant to participant and is not only proportional to the time spent but also to the demand for their services. Some participants successfully bid for further tasks, others fall by the wayside and are discarded. The construction emerges from the activities of participants co-ordinated not by instructions but by an apparent concern to maximise the value of currency held. Task duly completed, Maximus leaves the arena; we have been watching a market at work.

The third group, Socius, enters the arena and we see a quite different form of organisation. The most noticeable feature is the lack of explicit commands and exchanges. And yet the participants seem to be giving their whole being to provide a successful display. If one shows signs of weakening others gather around and take his burden until he is sufficiently recovered to rejoin the task. But there is no malingering even after hurt or injury. Participants are plunging straight back into the fray. It is difficult to see how these participants know what to do and why they do what they do with such enthusiasm. They seemed to carry something with them into the arena and every so often they form into a huddle to emerge with reinforced vigour. These participants are neither controlled by command nor by the pursuit of an extrinsic reward but rather by an inner conviction as to the rightness of what they do and a willingness to join with others in pursuit of a worthy goal. Task duly completed, Socius leaves the arena; we have been watching a commune at work.

An image of organisation

Unlike Simon's (1962) parable of Hora and Tempus, the hierarchical and non-hierarchical watchmakers, my parable of the groups Calculus, Maximus and Socius must remain without a moral for a while. Possibilities about the appropriateness of the Calculus, Maximus or Socius way of going about the tasks have yet to be explored. Some obvious factors, however, which might enter into such considerations would be the nature of the task, the commitment, motivation and skills of individuals.

If we now consider the image of an organisation as an arena in which transactions with various elements are conducted with a corporate body, we can see that these transactions can be conducted within a market, hierarchy or commune mode. There are two kinds of actors in this arena, elements and the corporate body.

Elements   The elements with which the transactions are conducted comprise a constellation of interests (Astley et al. 1980), which may be departments, divisions, individuals or external organisations such as suppliers, customers, or government agencies providing grants.

The corporate body   Often the corporate body is legally defined, as in the case of a firm, the corporate body represents the actor conducting transactions and in the case of the market is typified by a firm. In the case of the hierarchy the corporate body is typified by the governing body of a public agency which acts as an employer. In the case of the commune the corporate body is typified by the membership and all transactions are conducted in the name of the membership.

Need and denial

In some way all elements contribute to the operation of the organisation in a functional sense. In other words the idea of *need* has to be satisfied before control even has to be considered. In a sense the ultimate form of control is denial of a need but we must assume that this does not happen.

This helps us to deal with the particular elements identified above such as government agencies which are acting in a regulatory rather than a functional sense. They may, for instance, be governing the way in which transactions occur between other elements and the organisation but not contributing anything in a functional sense. In this case the organisation does not *need* such elements and its means of control is *denial*. Usually agencies of this nature can muster significant coercive forces and such denial may not be possible. If denial is not possible then control of such elements can still be in any one of the three modes. Foreshadowing the discussion below, options may be available (market), it may be possible to increase the visibility of the agencies activities by routinisation (hierarchy), or to increase congruence of the agency with the organisation by indoctrination.

Arenas   The arena is that sphere of activity within which transactions take place between elements and the corporate body and may be compared to the notion of a decision-making arena (Astley et al. 1980).

Transactions   An element has a relationship with the corporate body. Each element performs activities; there are carryings-on between an element and the corporate body which comprise the transaction between that element and the corporate body. The notion of a transaction has its origins more in economics (this is especially associated with Commons 1934), but has an obvious affinity to exchange theory in sociology (Blau 1967).

Blau (1967, pp. 91–2) sees social exchange as the 'voluntary actions of individuals that are motivated by the returns they are expected to bring . . . from others'. But Commons (1934) would add that this free exchange is only described by what he called the bargaining transaction. The bargaining transaction corresponds to transactions conducted within a market. Two other kinds of transactions are included by Commons; the rationing, typified by budgets in organisations and taxes in a nation; and the managerial, typified by the transactions between hierarchically superior and inferior individuals. Both the managerial and rationing transactions I would see as transactions conducted within a hierarchy, the kinds of transactions performed within a peer group being omitted from Commons's discussion.

However, the concept of transaction appears to have considerable merit in forming a fundamental building block for a theory of organisation. The notion of organisation abstracts exchanges within a transactional arena into exchanges between elements and the corporate body. When interdependence is pure pooled (Thompson 1967) all exchanges are with the corporate body. With sequential or reciprocal interdependence exchanges between elements become also transactions with the corporate body, but of varying complexity.

Transactions can involve exchange of goods and services, information or money. What is exchanged will depend upon the definition of the element and the needs of the corporate body.

What is physically exchanged is unimportant. The nature of the transaction is the kind of relationship between elements and the corporate body. If corporate body C buys from element E, an exchange of goods for money has occurred within a market. The marketplace offers specific *controls* to guide that transaction through to completion. If C now employs E, E exchanges part of his life for considerations from C, thus giving C specific rights to *control* E's actions. A hierarchy with its inherent manager–managed relationship provides a means for guiding that transaction. If C now cares for E and expects in return compliance with its wishes, if C is a group that also includes E then the peer group relationship has specific inbuilt *controls* for that transaction.

From the viewpoint of building a theory of organisation what becomes important, therefore, are the characteristics of these three different ways of controlling transactions.

Controlling Transactions

If the image of organisation is of a transactional arena within which transactions are conducted the question to be considered is how a corporate body can control the various transactions that it conducts. In order to examine this question we need concepts of control applicable across the three modes. Essentially the question comes down to how the corporate body can exert sufficient influence over the various elements in order to ensure that they provide satisfactory services or products. This is the question of the power that the corporate body has over elements.

Three sets of variables are seen to be appropriate to examining this question. These are the *predilections*, *bases*, and *activation* of control and are shown in *Figure* 7.1. Predilections are to do with the orientation of involved actors, bases are to do with the conditions that enable activation, the process of actually influencing, to occur. In other words, control has to take account of an ability to harness the minds of men, an ability to muster resources and an ability to take action to utilise those resources and to provide corrective action when matters get out of hand.

Predilections

Predilection of control governs the orientation of people and task elements involved in the organisation and also governs the relationships between individuals. The variables are to do with the characteristics that actors in the transactional arena bring with them and define the favourable prepossession of mind necessary for a particular control mode to operate. Each mode is characterised by the existence of two variables of predilection.

Maximisation–reciprocity   In a market, task elements, people and social groupings, will conform to the notion of the searching, instrumental rational economic man (March and Simon 1958). Without this proneness to maximise outcomes the corporate body could not rely upon elements to direct their activities towards the most profitable products and services. This is not to say there are not limits, that is bounded rationality (Simon 1957), on this instrumental behaviour but as an ideal type of orientation maximisation will be met in the ideal market. Behaviour will be searching, adventurous and entrepreneurial under conditions of bounded rationality with decision-making under conditions of limited information.

Hand in hand with maximisation goes the principle of reciprocity which must rule the relationship between individuals in a market. We noted in the Maximus group how participants waited on the sidelines to join the fray if an opportunity for profit presented itself. These fleeting

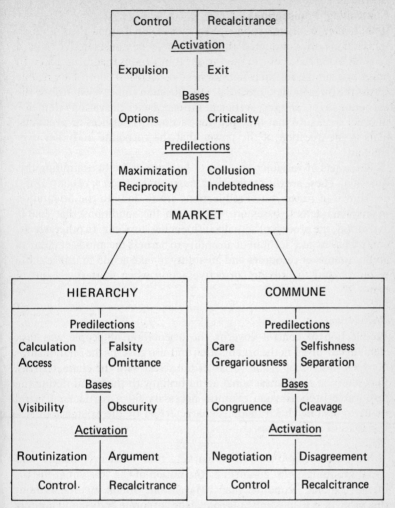

Figure 7.1   Salient features of market, hierarchy and commune at modes of control

excursions into the market are to provide a precise good or service in return for a reward. Elements wait on the threshold for opportunities. Services rendered demand a direct return on a quid pro quo basis. Recriprocity thus governs relationships in a market and aiding this reciprocity is the use of a generalisable currency which permits transactions then to be conducted with third parties, hence assisting the entry of competitors, necessary for the availability of options and expulsion, the bases and activation appropriate in a market. Direct payment is given for services given or received as opposed to a lump payment in the budget or grant of a hierarchy, or the deferred return of the gift in the commune.

Calculation–access   In the parable of the Three Modes we noted how participants in the Calculus group were concerned with technical details of the job in applying calculative methods to determine the best way to do the task. A mechanistic application of procedures to achieve task proficiency, rather than efficiency, distinguishes bureaucratic man from economic man or social man. To an outsider such behaviour within hierarchies can appear stupid and leads to some traditional dysfunctions of bureaucracy such as buck-passing and red tape, which are simply keeping to the rules. A hierarchy in its ideal form will consist of beavers who follow the instructions and do not concern themselves with the activities of others or indeed with pressures, perhaps from Maximus or Socius group types of individuals, towards non-calculative behaviour.

Paired with the calculative motive of individuals is the principle of access governing relationships between elements and the corporate body. In a hierarchy superordinate levels, in principle, have access to the decision-making and task activities of elements. The most obvious mechanism for implementing the idea of accessibility to task elements activities is the employment relationship which legitimises the corporate body's ability to prescribe the activities of elements. Neither the precise reciprocity associated with a transaction in the market mode, nor the concern for the wholeness of an individual in the commune where high access would be considered a trespass of an individual's integrity can reach this level of access. Access granted to higher authorities in a hierarchy will be accompanied by appropriate subordinate deference and a willingness to obey instructions.

Gregariousness – care   The Socius group was marked by an enthusiasm to join together in an enjoyment of each other's company. This gregariousness is a necessary condition for the formation of a commune or peer group. Instead of the instrumental maximising behaviour of economic man, or the mechanical–calculative behaviour of bureaucratic man, communes will be noted for an instinctive altruism in which there is caring for others in hardship. Whereas the market would automatically reject the runts of the litter, it was no accident that the Socius group gathered around individuals who were finding the going tough.

It is in this sense of caring that Titmuss (1970) regards the gift relationship as exemplified in the British voluntary blood donor system. Membership and permanence becomes the essence of the relationships between elements and the corporate body instead of the fleeting in-and-out relationship of market sub-contracting, or the deferent succumbing of employees to superordinates in a hierarchy. Membership becomes the essence of the relationship rather than the sub-contracting in the market, or employment in the hierarchy.

Bases and activation

Whereas the predilections necessary for control have laid down the orientation individuals must bring with them into the transactional arena, both in terms of their primary goals towards which they are motivated and their behaviour in social relationships, bases of control lay down the conditions that must exist within the arena for a control mode to operate. Bases form a springboard from which, in conjunction with the appropriate predilection, appropriate activation can occur.

Activation defines the type of activity that the corporate body has to engage in to obtain satisfactory service from a task element. Activation is an acknowledgment that predilections and bases are not enough in themselves for adequate control. The controlling body has to do something. Again, variables of bases and activation especially appropriate to each mode of control are identified.

Options and expulsion   Protagonists of the market as a means of controlling the distribution of products and services in society will point to the freedom inherent in the availability of choice of supplier and the efficiency that such choice can give through the ability to dismiss a delinquent provider. For this to work as a method of control options have to be available, the base, and expulsion has to be understood by the task element as a possible way of dealing with unsatisfactory performance, that is, activation.

With elements coming to the relationship with a strong tendency towards maximisation and reciprocity, hand in hand with options and expulsion the corporate body can exert effective control. Expulsion, the reverse of the exit (Hirschman 1970) that dissatisfied consumers can exert in a market, for unsatisfactory performance is efficient from the corporate body's viewpoint. There need be no concern with the aftermath for the elements as in a commune. However, as we shall see, the possibility of recalcitrant elements exiting and leaving the corporate body in the lurch now becomes a distinct possibility and quite legitimate, according to the rules of the game of the marketplace.

The market relationship amongst all social relationships exhibits a tolerance of all other frailties providing the service is satisfactory. There is no concern here on the part of the corporate body for the 'whole man' or the right attitudes as in a commune. Whether the task element is of a high moral or low standing, or of high or low proficiency in any other sphere of activity is irrelevant. Unsatisfactory performance for the specific required service must be immediately punished by expulsion.

Ruthless expulsion of individuals in the past regardless of other needs is the source of a major criticism of markets. This however is largely a matter of the options available to the provider. A balanced market in which people are not exploited would require not only options available to the corporate body but also to task elements.

We can also see the need for well-informed decisions concerning options. The corporate body will need to keep itself continuously informed of options available. In manufacturing firms this is often called dual sourcing where more than one supplier of a vital commodity or component is deliberately fostered. This ties in with the maximising reciprocal predilection. Rational economic man will be constantly searching for alternative ways of satisfying a particular need. Thus, for the market to operate as a mode of control not only must elements exhibit the maximising and reciprocating predilections, so too must the corporate body.

Visibility and routinisation   It was seen how, in the Calculus group, tasks were defined in great detail and the response to any lack of co-ordination and control was to attempt to specify to an even finer precision the appropriate methods to be used in a task. Thus, the base of control in a hierarchy is the visibility of the tasks in the sense that the more the task can be defined both in terms of outputs and in terms of methods the easier it is for superordinates to exert influence over subordinates. Visibility thereby provides the base for activation.

Putting into effect this base of control is a process of routinisation. Activating visibility will require setting up programmes (March and Simon 1958), or specialisation, formalisation and standardisation (Pugh et al. 1968) which are the familiar paraphernalia of bureaucracy. Courses of action which follow a regular, unvarying and mechanical round fit well with a proneness to calculation on the part of the actors involved, and require a high degree of access to the task element by the corporate body in order to be able to understand the technical points concerned with the job.

Congruence and negotiation   As already mentioned congruence between individuals and the corporate body is perhaps rare. It is after all difficult to have, on the one hand encouragement of self-gain and maximisation inherent in the market, or on the other hand a proclivity towards mechanical calculations and a concern for technical precision, and a oneness with the overall aims of the corporate body.

Encouragement of congruence between task elements and the corporate body is the main source of control in a commune. This can be activated by a number of precise techniques, such as making the corporate body and the task elements one and the same through the notion of membership. Pursuing the same approach to activation as above in which it was noted that the predominant course of activation is to be seen when things get out of control. In our Socius group we saw how the supportive caring attitudes of individuals had to be reinforced on such occasions by periodic bouts of group meetings and get-togethers. Values have to be overhauled and refitted in a process of indoctrination to provide the necessary congruence.

Huddles of this nature also have a function of allowing discussion of task matters as problems unfold. This toing and froing provides the fundamental activation process of negotiation in a commune.

Negotiation in a commune is included in Hirschman's (1970) idea of voice as an alternative means to exit for exerting influence over deficient suppliers. But negotiation is a more precise idea than simply complaining. Negotiation specifically means a two-way flow of views and information between parties and excludes the general noise that an unhappy customer makes in the hope that some improvement will occur.

Modes of control

It is with the variables of predilections, bases and activation outlined (see Table 7.1) that a picture can be painted of the three modes of control typified by the groups Calculus, Maximus and Socius. The picture does not pretend to capture every aspect of markets, hierarchies and communes but includes only those landmarks necessary to portray these as modes of organisational control. Within a kaleidoscope of a changing landscape, as an organisation moves from one mode to another, we will see landmarks varying in density according to the mode. In any one snapshot there will be dominant landmarks, as represented by the appropriate variables for that mode, but always visible will be a ghost of all other features.

Prominent features for each mode of control are shown in Table 7.1 denoted by III as already described above. Single Is against all other variables indicate that a minimal amount of the other variables is necessary for a particular mode to operate. Whereas, for instance, the market specifically requires elements to direct their energies towards maximisation and reciprocity and for options to provide opportunities for expulsion of unwanted or naughty elements, elements have to show some proclivity towards joining, albeit for only fleeting moments, others to conduct business transactions. Such minimal gregariousness must be associated with a minimal ability to calculate outcomes of transactions. Likewise access for elements to the transactional arena has to be granted, their activities have to be observable, and therefore sufficiently visible, and no market can exist without some commonness of aims (congruence), and negotiation between parties is almost inevitable but played out within a set of, at the least, informal rules and routines. Similar arguments can be forwarded for other variables in connection with other modes. In this way no one variable is a sufficient condition but is a necessary condition for control to be exerted over transactions between elements and the corporate body.

A mode forms a kind of factor in the factor analytic sense of the word as summarised in Table 7.1 and contained within these factors are a number of hypotheses of the form:

in the main, maximisation and reciprocity predilections of individuals will be associated with the use of expulsion, when things go wrong, which can only happen when options are available. This we shall call a market.

This is an empirical statement concerning expectations about the real world but it also allows for contradictions, in that for instance expulsion might be found as the primary method of activating control, but the appropriate predilections are not present. But on the whole we expect certain variables to 'hang together'.

Table 7.1   *Variables of control in markets, hierarchies and communes*

	Market	Hierarchy	Commune
Predelections			
Governing motivation of elements and corporate body			
Maximisation	III	I	I
Calculation	I	III	I
Caring	I	I	III
Governing element/corporate body relationships			
Reciprocity	III	I	I
Access	I	III	I
Gregariousness	I	I	III
Bases			
Options	III	I	I
Visability	I	III	I
Congruence	I	I	III
Activation			
Expulsion	III	I	I
Routinisation	I	III	I
Negotiation	I	I	III

Tactics of recalcitrance

The view of control presented so far has been, in some respects, one-sided. Partly, this is intentional because the main concern in this paper is with the question of how a corporate body can maintain control over task elements. The perspective has been that of the corporate body and not of the elements being controlled. Partly also the one-sidedness is only a result of the necessity of presenting ideas in linear fashion. We must not lose sight of the fact that task elements, people or social groupings, are also social actors and capable of indulging in tactics to avoid control. This I call the tactics of recalcitrance.

Recalcitrant elements will attack the foundations upon which organisational control is built that is, upon the predilections, bases and activation. An additional tactic of recalcitrance is possible, and may in many ways be the most effective, that is, the tactic of denial. As already mentioned it has been assumed that the provisions provided by the task elements are essential to the organisation, although the provisions need not come from that particular element. The converse of this is denial of the need of the organisation on the part of an element. Certain non-violent protest movements, for instance as used by Gandhi against the British rule in India, using fasts and hunger strikes demonstrate a lack of need on the part of elements for the captors. Control can only be re-exerted by coercion in these circumstances. Intriguing though this avenue of enquiry is, it is not explored in this paper, but we will see that recalcitrant elements who decide to exit from the organisation are in fact denying the usefulness of that particular organisation to them.

Recalcitrance in a market　The easiest way for a recalcitrant element to kick back against the hand that controls it is to exit from the relationship. Exit is the privilege of dissatisfied customers in a market (Hirschman 1970) and is supposed to act as a message to the corporate body that all is not well.

A form of recalcitrance that incurs a greater cost on the part of the element in question is to increase its criticality to the organisation either by reducing the number of options available to the corporate body or by increasing the need of the organisation for the element. This requires a rejection of the reciprocity and maximisation predilections of economic man and a tendency towards collusive behaviour in which indebtedness, rather than fulfilling the obligation for quick repayment, becomes the norm.

Figure 7.1 summarised the variables of recalcitrance against each appropriate variable of control.

Recalcitrance in a hierarchy　As routinisation in a hierarchy is the predominant form of activation the brand of recalcitrance aimed at destroying the ability of the organisation to utilise this form of activation will be to indulge in incessant argument over ways and means thereby creating a kind of mystique surrounding an element's activities. A good example of this is the maintenance engineers described by Crozier who successfully managed to resist control by management and maintain their control over production workers by resisting routinisation of their activities. Argument may also be part of the rather ill-defined notion of voice forwarded by Hirschman (1970). But argument was only possible because of low visibility of the maintenance engineers' activities and a strategy to obscure activities was also part of their perversity.

Also to be noted in Crozier's case of the maintenance engineers was a rejection of calculative means which can also extend, although not necessarily in that case, to falsification of information. Similarly, an ability to omit the corporate body from an element's activities adds to the bag of tricks for recalcitrance in a hierarchy which will go hand in hand with falsification of information and a denial of the legitimacy of superordinates to oversee work.

Recalcitrance in a commune   If argument as a tactic of recalcitrance in a hierarchy is one aspect of the voice mechanism referred to by Hirschman (1970), disagreement is another aspect of voice and is a tactic of recalcitrance in a commune. Argument as a logical statement of reasons for not doing what is required by the superordinate in a hierarchy can thrive on the ambiguity contained in complex transactions, as we shall see later. Communes will activate control based upon congruence by an indoctrination, a process which is impermeable to logic but outright disagreement with the underlying beliefs contained within indoctrination will breed disaffection amongst elements which can spread as does a disease.

Such refractoriness will be added to by subverting the congruence base of control in a commune, and further still by breaking down the gregariousness tendencies by techniques of separation. The recipe to make a commune fly apart is, then, to disagree and subvert the underlying congruence of beliefs, and to separate and liquidate members to break down the permanent gregariousness nature of a commune.

Complexity

To leave matters at this point might be interesting and even useful in the sense that contradictions within a mode of control can be pinpointed and perhaps corrected. But the image of organisation presented has seen organisations as nothing but control, and as having no task. If, for the moment we return to the Calculus, Maximus and Socius groups of our parable there might be things we could say about the nature of the task and the corresponding appropriateness of a particular control mode to fit the nature of that task.

Using still the image of organisation as an arena in which transactions are conducted the complexity of those transactions and the amount of feedback between the corporate body and task element required over the transaction's duration are seen to be of crucial importance in determining the appropriate mode of control.

Complexity of a transaction is defined as the multiplicity of contingencies that the corporate body is likely to encounter in relation to a specific transaction and is a result of three factors. First is the uncertainty that arises in a transaction in terms of a lack of ability to predict outcomes. Second is the interdependence of the element making a transaction with other elements in the organisation. Third is the vagueness of the output of the element. These will be returned to later.

But in order to control transactions, control of recalcitrant elements is required. Thus, control involves both the technical requirement of synchronising transactions, that is feedback, but also coping with the propensity of elements to indulge in self-seeking behaviour against the interests of the corporate body. Control of recalcitrance contains, therefore, Williamson's idea of opportunism, 'self-seeking behaviour with guile' but includes also any propensity towards throwing off the yoke of corporate control. This may include opportunism but may include many other factors as already seen.

The thrust of the argument can now be seen outlined in Figure 7.2.

Feedback
If a transaction is complex the need increases for synchronisation of activities as a transaction proceeds. This kind of mutual adjustment (Thompson 1967) by the parties involved results from new information as new conditions reveal themselves. Complexity therefore leads to a need for feedback.

Feedback is a result of the technical characteristics of the transaction, and impacts especially upon control activation. Thus, expulsion as a form of activation represents a low degree of mutual adjustment. The outcome is either satisfactory, or not: if not, expel. Routinisation represents more feedback, the mutual adjustment having occurred in the defining of the routines some time previously. Negotiation is the form of activation allowing the highest degree of feedback.

There is a suggestion that expulsion is the least costly form of activation, negotiation the most costly, with routinisation as involving a medium amount of cost. This is assuming that recalcitrance is under control and also ignores the cost of setting up bases and predilections of

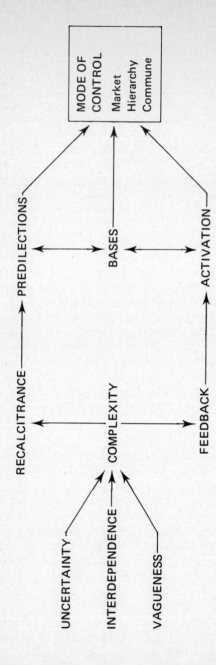

Figure 7.2 Factors leading to control mode

control. Expulsion may be the least costly activation but to create the options needed for a true market may be costly. It is at this point that consideration needs to be given to the notion of economies of scale.

Recalcitrance

Whilst complexity impacts upon the control variables through the feedback process, complexity also impacts, as we will see in more detail, directly upon the control bases. Although markets are not confounded by a degree of complexity derived from uncertainty caused by an inability to cope with the required feedback, there is a danger that market conditions may break down particularly because of recalcitrant tendencies by elements. Similarly complexity of transactions emanating in particular from the multiplier effect of interdependence can reduce visibility as a base of control sufficiently to confound hierarchies, or complexity of transactions emanating from the addition of vagueness can reduce congruence sufficiently to confound communes.

Uncertainty, interdependence and vagueness

Uncertainty Complete certainty as to outcomes of a transaction or as to the circumstance under which a transaction is needed renders the control problem trivial. As Simon (1957, pp. 240–41) comments:

if there were no limits to human rationality administrative theory would be barren. It would consist of a single precept: always select that alternative, among those available, which will lead to the most complete achievement of your goals.

If there was no uncertainty surrounding a transaction no feedback would be required over its duration. The actors concerned would be perfectly informed; hence viewed from the perspective of the market hierarchy and commune modes the single precept would equally hold. For the market the image follows the perfectly informed economic man, for the hierarchy the image follows the perfectly calculating man, from the commune the image follows the perfectly socialised man. In fact the distinction between the modes with certainty disappears; all present an equally trivial problem of control.

As uncertainty comes into play some feedback is required between the corporate body and an element as the transaction proceeds. As Williamson (1975) suggests markets are not necessarily flawed by uncertainty providing small numbers do not exist, that is, options are available. With uncertainty, although circumstances leading to the transaction and outcomes are not predictable before the transaction, there is no doubt as to whether outcomes are satisfactory upon completion of the transaction. Unsatisfactory performance can be punished and providing options are available an alternative element found, assuming, of course that the predilection conditions of maximising and reciprocity are satisfied.

Examination of the possible tactics of recalcitrance shows the possibility of the organisation being left in the lurch by premature exit by the element, which can only happen with criticality, and by collusion with others in the market. Given proper vigilance by the corporate body against such breakdown in the market mechanism the market mode can provide adequate control.

Interdependence Thompson (1967) pointed out the connection between interdependence and the complexity of co-ordinating organisational sub units. However, interdependence without uncertainty also renders the co-ordination problem trivial. The significant thing about Thompson's reciprocal interdependence as the most complex is that the failure of any one element has greater effect upon the whole organisation than the failure of an element with pooled interdependence. Complexity of transactional control by the corporate body, then, arises out of the number of linkages an element has within the transactional arena combined with the uncertainty of the outcomes of the transactions. Any hiccups in the transactions with a highly interconnected element will reverberate throughout the organisation. The need for feedback for a given level of uncertainty thereby increases with interdependence, but so too does the opportunity for recalcitrance.

Uncertainty combined with interdependence is likely to prove too much for the market. When failure is isolated, even though critical in other respects such as in absolute cost, expulsion can occur without any further recriminations.

Even though the conditions for expulsion may be satisfied the prevention rather than the cure of failure becomes paramount if an element is highly interconnected. The access and visibility afforded by a hierarchy is better able to deal with this problem. Feedback can occur as the transaction proceeds through routinisation of activities provided that outcomes required from the element, although uncertain, can be specified in sufficient detail, that is, when vagueness is absent.

Interdependence also can lead to recalcitrance. Random exit by an element and collusion with others in the market or with other elements with which an element is interdependent will reverberate throughout the organisation.

Given the predilections of calculation and access a hierarchy is better able to cope with this situation by increasing visibility and allowing routinisation. The move from a buyer/seller relationship to an employment relationship increases access as Williamson (1975) indicates.

Vagueness   In general I agree with Niskanen (1973) when he says:

In the contemporary environment, when most goods and services that are augmented by collective action are supplied by bureaus, it is often difficult to understand the functional and historical bases for choosing bureaus, rather than profit-seeking organisations, to supply these services. The primary functional reason is the difficulty of defining their characteristics (i.e. the goods and services) sufficiently to contract for their supply. (pp. 10–11).

Thus, vague, imprecise statements about required outcomes from an element further complicate control of transactions. Vagueness may derive from a vagueness of the overall aims of the organisation as propounded by the corporate body, or from the nature of the task given to an element.

Perhaps difficult to imagine and almost certainly difficult to find in reality, vagueness of outcomes without uncertainty would have little consequence for complexity of controlling transactions. But vagueness of the internal processes of an element combined with certainty of outcomes is imaginable and again would still be a trivial problem from the viewpoint of controlling transactions between the element and the corporate body. Likewise an isolated and independent element with vagueness would have little effect upon the organisation as a whole if failure presented itself, and hence control would not present a major headache to the corporate body. A market or hierarchy could still be adequate.

But present the corporate body with transactions that are uncertain, interdependent and vague and neither markets nor hierarchies will be adequate. Expulsion of a delinquent element will cause reverberations throughout the organisation because of interdependence, and routinisation is not possible because of vagueness. It is therefore under the combination of uncertainty, interdependence and vagueness that communes are needed to control transactions. Fostering of congruence with corporate aims involves nurturing gregariousness and caring commitment towards an ideal which, nevertheless, is difficult to define. Consequently negotiation will constantly occur over the aims of the organisation.

Complexity and modes of control

Complexity of transactions can now be seen as a kind of scale in the Guttman sense with the least (trivial) complex transactions of zero uncertainty, then uncertainty only, then uncertainty combined with interdependence, and the most complex as combining uncertainty, interdependence and vagueness. We can see now how each mode of control has associated with it a variable of complexity, representing the maximum degree of complexity that a specific mode can cope with.

Thus, markets can cope with uncertainty, hierarchies with inter-dependence and communes with vagueness.

Conclusion

The missing moral of the parable of the three modes, Socius, Calculus and Maximus can now emerge. Maximus the Market is most likely to be successful when the multiplicity of contingencies likely to occur during transactions is low. Maximus can deal with complexity to the extent of uncertainty without any appreciable interdependence or vagueness. Calculus the Hierarchy is able to cope with uncertainty and inter-dependence but requires that the ends towards which each transaction is aimed are clear. When vagueness of ends enters the scene Socius the Commune is more likely to be successful. For this simple moral to hold, however, we would require that all the conditions of the specific control mode are present. That is, the predilections, bases and activation of control have to be able to operate for each of the modes to function satisfactorily.

This paper shows that consideration of the markets and hierarchies theme needs to take into account two questions. First, is the question of detailing and examining the dimensions of the market, hierarchy, and the third and missing control mode of the commune, to allow direct comparison of these ideal types of control. Variables of the type out-lined are required before comparative empirical research can be under-taken into the conditions under which one mode rather than another might be used.

Hence, the second question is that of identifying these conditions. Complexity is seen as the key concept, which is constituted, in par-ticular, from the uncertainty and vagueness of transaction outcomes, and from the interdependence of an element with other elements.

8 Market, Hierarchy and Technology: some implications of economic internationalism for labour
A. Braendgaard

I. Introduction

According to C.B. Macpherson (1973, 1977), 'The outstanding models in political science, at least from Hobbes on, have been both explanatory and justificatory or advocatory.' The two latter terms presumably correspond closely to the Mannheimian distinction between 'ideology and utopia', and as Macpherson is more concerned with the analysis of the former, that is with theoretical structures which *justify* existing arrangements rather than with those which *advocate* their complete or partial replacement, he uses the term 'justify' or its derivatives most of the time. In the present context I shall do likewise because most of the positions or theorists examined are chiefly concerned with justifying institutional arrangements which have some claim to existence.

Macpherson also emphasises that 'Those who start from the tacit assumption that whatever is, is right, are apt to deny that they are making any value judgement. Those who start from the tacit assumptions that whatever is, is wrong, give great weight to their ethical case (while trying to show that it is practicable).' The argument made by Macpherson with respect to political science applies equally well to most other branches of social knowledge dealing with contemporary institutional arrangements although many economists consider themselves beyond the reach of such 'soft stuff' as value judgements and justifications. Milton Friedman, the advocate of 'positive economics', certainly also advocates a number of other things, some of which have substantial political consequences, to say the least.

The presence of justificatory arguments is not a problem in itself. In moderate amounts justification is probably a necessary and insistent ingredient also in scientific discourse, where it may serve as an indicator of the importance or relevance of the questions at issue. The adequacy of a theoretical position may thus depend on both explanatory and justificatory performance. Both Hirschman and Williamson, whose work will be central to the discussion here, take exception to some elements of received theory on both counts. However, it is possible to argue – at least that is what I intend to do – that they do not go far enough in adjusting theory to explain some real-world developments, such as the internalisation of economic life and the technological factors making it possible, or made possibly by it, and the failure to 'explain' also result in a failure to 'justify' the existing institutional arrangement and its outcomes (Hirschman 1970 and Williamson 1975; referred to as EVL and MH respectively in the remainder of the paper).

This paper proposes to examine some persistent problems in a tradition of thought which originates in classical political economy, and which has institutional and neoclassical economics as its most recent progeny. In this context focus is on the consequences of the orderly, or disorderly, as the case may be, operation of the capitalist economic system for the working class (labour) and its (level of) reproduction.

First the theoretical background, joining classical and institutional (organisational) economics, will be outlined, emphasising more or less acknowledged structural failings and responses to them. Secondly, some of the problems caused by the development of an international economy (division of labour) for this justificatory theory will be summarised. That summary will be followed by an outline of an alternative theoretical position, a political economy of organisations, which provides a more accurate and adequate explanation of actual phenomena and points to the limitations of current justificational efforts. Both MH and EVL contain an abundance of what Stinchcombe has referred to as 'conservative rhetorical opportunities'. In fact Charles Perrow, acting as rapporteur at a seminar on 'Organisations in their Societal Context',[1] suggested renaming EVL 'Monopoly, Repression, and Propaganda'.

Perrow is no doubt overstating his case here, if only for rhetorical purposes. A wholesale rejection of the approach represented by people such as Hirschman and Williamson is hardly justified. Some of the pitfalls of their analytical frameworks may be avoided. Failure to exercise the formal options of 'exit' and 'voice' is not sufficient evidence that all is well with the world, but concepts from the EVL and MH frameworks may be combined with elements of a political economy of organisation to achieve a more coherent theoretical structure, which is both critical and operational. This will, however, entail abandoning some of the assumptions entertained in EVL and MH and possibly adding some new ones.

II. Theoretical Background

Classical political economy
In his preface to the second edition of *Capital* Marx made a distinction between the position of classical political economy which reflected a

genuine scientific effort to come to grips with a changing economic order and its social implications, and a position which he referred to as 'vulgar political economy'. The latter replaced serious scientific enquiry with 'the bad conscience and the evil intent of apologetic'. John Stuart Mill presumably represented a middle position by attempting to retain scientific standing and bring into harmony with 'the political economy of capital the claims, no longer to be ignored, of the proletariat'. Historians of nineteenth-century England call the presence of an impoverished working class the most significant historical fact of the period. The 'vulgar political economists' attempted to reconcile this fact with the expectations of harmony held out by their theory and to make the masses accept their fate.

Macpherson has suggested that the problems of liberal democratic theory have to do with inconsistencies between concepts of 'freedom' employed in the dual realms of economics and politics. The claims to equal self-fulfilment of everybody located in the political realm are frequently used to justify or legitimise the system, while these very values are violated by the freedom of the stronger in the economic realm (the market).

Most of the argument here about the theoretical position, explanatory as well as justificatory, of classical political economy is based upon the exposition of it by Adam Smith. The interesting point about it in this context is his quite explicit admission of some of the structural problems, which give rise to justificatory deficiencies in his theory or at least should occasion much more reluctance to celebrate the 'invisible hand' and its marvellous potential for creating and/or restoring a socially optimal equilibrium.

Analytically the economic system of liberalism can be divided into two separate networks. One of these assembles the productive resources required to manufacture a specific product, and the other establishes relations between the consumers and producers of different products. These networks are linked by the entrepreneurial function, which Adam Smith vested in concrete persons referred to as 'masters', a term suggestive of a mode of production where roughly equal parties contracted about the exchange of goods and services, including labour power.

This mode of production, however, was coming to an end already when Smith was writing. The master increasingly performed functions outside the immediate production process, but by virtue of his ownership to the means of production he (the master) retained control over the production process itself as well as its final product. Competition between individual masters in the labour and product markets as well as competition between suppliers of goods and services in other markets was to be the theoretical warranty of the optimising properties of the system, its ability to ward off exploitation and inefficiency, in short to achieve a just and equitable balance, even if nobody sought anything but his own interests. Smith, however, was aware of some difficulties with his formal model, even allowing for the retention of the term 'master' as an appropriate label for the one party to the exchange in both networks.

The masters clearly are at an advantage over both consumers and workers in a number of formal respects. The market is generally more transparent to them, and they generally, by virtue of their control over the production process, know better than consumers and workers, in the pre-contract stage at least, what purchase of a product and acceptance of employment may entail in terms of advantages and risk. 'Let the buyer beware' is therefore not an adequate precept when it comes to retaining or restoring equilibrium in more than a formal sense.

In addition to the information aspect referred to in the preceding paragraph the 'masters' also enjoy a formal advantange when it comes to setting the terms of the exchange as exhibited in the *Wealth of Nations*:

The masters, being fewer in number, can combine much more easily, and the law, besides, authorises, or at least does not prohibit their combinations, while it prohibits those of workmen. We have no act of parliament against combining to lower the price of work, but many against combining to raise it. (p. 169).

Masters are always and everywhere in a sort of tacit, but constant and uniform combination not to raise the wages of labour above their actual rate. (p. 169).

People of the same trade seldom meet together, even for merriment and conversion, but their conversation ends in a conspiracy against the public, or in some contrivance to raise prices. (p. 232).

Awareness of problems of this kind should have conditioned more restraint in the celebration of the 'invisible hand'. Mancur Olson has recently formalised more or less the same point in his *The Logic of Collective Action* (1968), but without citing Smith for an early recognition of some of the problems caused by the formal properties of market relations.

To be sure most legislative restrictions in the right of labour to organise, when the inertia of the rational economic man model in the field of collective action has been overcome, have been removed now, at least temporarily, in the so-called advanced industrial societies. There are, however, also trends working for a reversal. For instance the implications of some of the recommendations of the OECD Inter-futures Study Group Report (1979), which advocates the abolition of 'rigidities' and a return to market forces, might be of that kind. A contributory factor here undoubtedly is the ability of business to travel in time by travelling in space.

The last remark referred to the transnationalisation of economic relations in the post-war period, which has made it possible for firms in the 'advanced industrialised countries' to reveal their preferences for labour-repressive, low-wage systems when they choose locations for certain industries. This remark, however, was merely an aside arising out of the explanatory completeness, but justificatory deficiency, of classical political economy *vis-à-vis* the social implications of unfolding capitalist relations of production. (New) institutional economics also attempts to make up for the justificatory shortcomings of received theory, and in doing so it also makes an effort to correct some of its more obvious explanatory deficiencies. The complexity of current socio-economic relations, however, makes it appreciably harder to distinguish between the two main functions of theory.

The institutional paradigm

Kenneth J. Arrow (1973, 1974) bridges the gap between the classical and the institutional position, at least a point of departure of his, bargaining costs and their unequal distribution among system members ties in directly with the justificatory worries voiced by Adam Smith. Misallocations of resources and social costs may result from these structural failings of the market model, which Arrow proposes to correct by way of three major mechanisms:

- state action (coercive and collective);
- firms of any 'complexity' may bring about a public good; and
- norms of social behaviour (ethical and moral codes).

In view of the difficulties encountered in creating political or collective action, which Arrow also admits to, this solution is not particularly reassuring from a justificatory perspective, although the general political process holds more promise than either collective action by 'monopoly', which must be what the second mechanism really is all about, or collective action by ideology. Collective action by monopoly as an optimising device must require some additional assumptions. Under what conditions, to suggest an outrageous, but not entirely inappropriate analogy, might the 'big bad wolf' optimise for the 'three little pigs'?

I used the term 'ideology' to refer to Arrow's concept of 'social norms', but that does not mean that I want to deny that social norms may be relevant in a context like this. However, one should not forget – as Arrow seems to do – that these norms arise out of the very social arrangements, which they purport to regulate. A change in social norms therefore presupposes institutional change of some sort to be effective, and that comes about slowly in critically important regulatory areas. Hirschman and Williamson are more useful in dealing with some of these problems because they develop the institutional framework in greater detail, although still at a fairly high level of abstraction. Whereas Arrow, in discussing the types of collective action, borders on apologetics, explanation and justification are more equally represented in both Hirschman and Williamson.

Both appear to proceed from the assumption that in the beginning there was competition. They at least do not seem to speculate so much about whether competition was ever a solution to societal co-ordination problems. In present-day society, however, the assumption for instance of a frictionless chain or process of transactions is no longer warranted. The costs are simply exorbitant. Rather than reverting to a nostalgia for the markets of yesteryear, which may also have been mirages, efforts are made to analyse the implications of changing environmental conditions. Any analytical innovation considering these which is incorporated into explanatory frameworks will in all probability be out of tune with core tenets of conventional theory of wisdom and will therefore create a legitimisation deficiency.

By way of a first comparison EVL emphasises processes where MH, at least judging by the title, seems more concerned with structure, but the prominent place occupied by the concept of 'transaction' in Williamson's discussion modifies this impression somewhat. So to some extent both frameworks are dynamic, but neither of them makes much allowance for the effect of such real-world dynamic concepts or variables as power, control, conflict and the like. In fact they barely occur in the text or the indices, although the concept of 'exploitation' is used by Hirschman in a more technical sense. Williamson's revealed preference for terminological innovations makes it harder to survey his discussion in this respect.

The problem really is to come up with a functional alternative to competition, which holds some promise, at least theoretically, either of harnessing the mighty energy of self-seeking economic actors and enlisting it in the services of the common good, or of neutralising its problematic consequences. Hirschman in a sense is more radical by questioning the appropriateness of competition as a control mechanism in some areas where Williamson merely suggests that in some areas and settings competition is no longer a feasible mode of transacting business.

A functional alternative to competition should have the desirable properties of ensuring efficient utilisation of productive resources and of preventing exploitation of one social grouping by another. Hirschman is particularly eager to emphasise that inefficiency rather than exploitation is the more serious of the two types of systematic malfunctioning, or maybe rather malfunctioning of systems, because

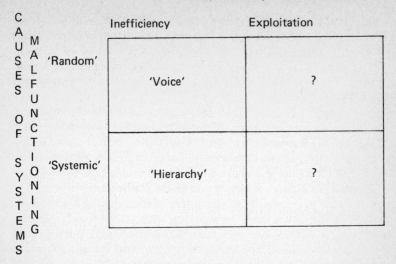

Figure 8.1   Types of 'malfunctioning' of systems

also random decline in the functioning of firms, organisations, and states is covered by his theory. The fourfold table in Figure 8.1 provides a basis for illustrating some of these connections.

An obvious difficulty with this scheme, which Hirschman does not admit to, is the fact that the boundary between inefficiency and exploitation is not well-established. He contrasts the concepts of 'slack' and 'taut economy' and suggests that 'voice' can be used to restore 'taut economy' after a temporary relapse into 'slack' of one kind or the other. However, a tightening up of slack, which may take place by both 'carrot and whip', will become problematic after a point in systems with human components. Taylor to the contrary there is no scientific way of deciding what the appropriate work intensity is. After a point, further progress towards a taut economy will be the straw that breaks the 'camel's back', and some break more easily than others. The location of the break-even point relative to the breaking point will at any particular time be decided by the distribution of power within existing institutional frameworks, whether economic or political.

Here the vertical dimension, random v. systemic factors, takes on added importance. Hirschman may avoid some of these difficulties by focusing chiefly on decline due to 'random causes'. In the introduction he talks about the ubiquity of decline, 'if only for all kinds of accidental reasons'. Received micro theory accepts this 'organisational condition'. It tends to view the economic process as a biological succession struggle, where the young and vigorous continuously replace the old and feeble in an essentially unproblematic fashion. Hirschman recognises that it no longer is acceptable 'to let nature take its course'. Even very sizeable organisations (firms) catch this disease, and although orthodox economists would tend to argue that efforts to save the patient would be ineffective at best, and harmful at worst, Hirschman is no doubt right in arguing that saving the patient, that is restoring a firm to productive life, will entail other (social) savings as well. 'Voice' may here be viewed as an early warning system, and when the patient is informed of a diagnosis in no uncertain terms, self-interest should be a sufficient incentive to correct the deficiencies.

The reference to self-interest still implies that other sanctions must ultimately be available to those 'voicing discontent', but in the case of randomly induced decline consensus about the goals between sender and receiver of 'voice' are more plausible *a priori*. If differences of interests and power exist between sets of actors, something more than 'voice' is required to produce a socially optimal outcome, unless power is assumed to be distributed roughly proportionate with relevant interest and/or value categories, that is effective demand and socially optimal demand is congruous. A considerable amount of constitutional engineering would be necessary to bring this state of affairs about in economic life, and the impetus will have to come from a different social arena. Politics is the most likely candidate, but the formal barriers to collective action referred to above, which are still real, reduce the possibility of change in institutional arrangements of this nature. The groups interested in, that is standing to gain from, institutional change, workers and consumers, at least only have former excess power available in the political arena, but structural change in the economy is up against all sorts of ideological defences. The problem is how to convert power in one arena into power usable in another. Economic internationalisation may prove to be the most serious obstacle to the democratisation of the economy, though, because it has not been accompanied by a similar or correspondent build-up of political institutions. Political power is wielded mainly at the national level it seems.

Hirschman is probably right in saying that economic theory has neglected 'inefficiencies' of the kind covered by his category of 'voice', but its treatment of 'exploitation', an as yet undefined concept, has not been adequate either, dealing mainly with the phenomenon in 'markets' where monopoly or oligopoly conditions obtain, and not in systems-level settings. Referring back to Figure 8.1 I would argue that most of Hirschman's reasoning applies only to the combination random-inefficient, at the micro-level at least. It may be added here that the combination random-exploitation probably is an empty category, that is if a phenomenon is not somehow 'systemic' it does not make sense to talk about 'exploitation'. Given some additional elaborations the Hirschman framework could conceivably be extended to the two lower cells of the box. The distinction between 'inefficiency' and 'exploitation' will also be exceedingly hard to draw when dealing with 'systemic factors'. Williamson, as I see it, deals almost exclusively with systemic inefficiencies resulting from high transaction costs. But the factors giving rise to extreme transaction costs can also, as Williamson recognises – at the micro-level at least – give rise to exploitation.

The concept of exploitation is in need of further specification. Both major established paradigms in economics, Marxism and neoclassicism, have fairly well-defined concepts of 'exploitation', neither of which is entirely satisfactory in a broader context.

I shall refrain from an extended discussion of either concept of exploitation here. Suffice it to say that the most abstract version of the Marxist concept seems too preoccupied with the formalities of property relations. Under favourable conditions, such as reasonably full-employment levels, proper institutional 'checks and balances' should be able to remove the worst abuses arising out of the operation of a private system of production. Also nominally socialist systems, i.e. where private property has been formally abolished, may experience problems reminiscent of exploitation because some groups have preferred access to important social resources without proper controls. The literature on these problems is too extensive to quote, but I shall return to a smaller segment of it after discussing some of the amendments to received theory put forth by Williamson.

The discussion of Williamson is based only on MH, which is a presentation of a theoretical framework with some applications. It is not possible to discuss the applications of the MH theory in detail here. Williamson apparently intends his conceptual framework to be general in scope. However, it seems more appropriate for smaller subsets of transactions, such as intermediate products, than for labour-market or consumer-goods transactions.

Williamson, like Hirschman and most other economists, seems to proceed from the assumption that in the beginning there were markets. However, as Polanyi (1957) and others have shown, markets often had to be, if not invented, then at least implemented. The transition from market to hierarchy does therefore not necessarily constitute the fall suggested by many economists, but not Williamson, who sets out to explain this transition.

Two major types of factors, referred to as environmental and human factors, are used in the MH framework. In MH Williamson reveals a very distinct preference for 'terminological innovation'. 'Small numbers' and 'uncertainty', which refer to the number of actors involved in a particular transactional arena and its complexity or opacity respectively, are the subdivisions employed by Williamson on the 'environmental' dimension. The other major dimension is divided into 'bounded rationality' and 'opportunism' as two major species of human frailty. The last of these neologisms seems particularly euphemistic in design.

To Williamson 'opportunism' is the conventional assumption that economic actors are self-interested, extended to allow for strategic behaviour. The more complete description of the term reads 'self-interest seeking with guile'. Two major etymological paths meet in 'guile': one with the root meaning of 'cunning' and the other with the root meaning of deceit. It may have come as a surprise to some economic theorists that deceit, law-breaking, and more generally strategic behaviour are part and parcel of economic life, but economic historians have always been keenly aware that W.C. Fields's quip 'a thing worth having is worth cheating for' reflects an important insight into economic life.

Now Williamson has chosen the slightly euphemistic term 'opportunism', but he stays fairly close to the root meaning 'deceit' in most of his discussion. Distortion and misrepresentation are key descriptors of the information-exchange and exchange process (bargaining) in transactions between market actors. Both social and individual losses are likely to occur as the outcome of this process. Williamson's solution to the problem is 'hierarchy', i.e. to let the same economic actor span both sides of the exchange process as a way of getting around the condition of 'information impactedness', another neologism, which he defines as follows:

a derivative condition that arises mainly because of *uncertainty* and *opportunism*, though *bounded rationality* is involved as well. It exists when true underlying circumstances relevant to the transaction, or related sets of transactions, are known to one or more parties but cannot be discerned by or displayed for others. ((1975, p. 31) emphasis added to point to Williamson's core elements or types).

The human factors 'bounded rationality' and 'opportunism' presumably must be considered historical constants although the increasing complexity of the environment of exchange is likely to confer a more relative status on the capabilities of human rationality. Williamson emphasises transactional factors at the expense of technology in his explanation of the transition to hierarchy, it seems. However, technology must be an important contributory factor in any account of the complexity/uncertainty component of 'information impactedness' which lies at the heart of the problem of high transaction costs.

Under conditions of 'information impactedness', exchange is, by definition almost, costly to all parties to a transaction, who will devote considerable resources to finding out – or concealing as the case may be – the true underlying circumstances of a contemplated transaction. The transaction costs, however, are not necessarily distributed equally among all parties to a particular transaction or set of transactions. Williamson is largely silent on this aspect of the transactional process, which nevertheless is a very crucial one for understanding both the emergence of hierarchy and its character, e.g. its quality of being more or less exploitative. The Hirschman framework of 'exit' and 'voice' seems to open up for this aspect a little more directly.

Williamson does not appear to use the term 'exploitation' at all in MH although related concepts occur in conjunction with his discussion of differences of interests and power. Because Williamson steers clear of transactional problems involving larger social segments or classes, for instance workers v. capitalists or consumers v. producers, it is harder to relate his discussion to the fourfold typology of Figure 8.1. The transactional framework explicitly aims at settings where everybody stands to gain from the creation of an authoritative decision structure (hierarchy), but some of the core components of the model, notably 'opportunism' and 'complexity/uncertainty' and differences in the distribution of the latter would seem to make the perspective applicable also to the 'systematic/exploitation' cell of the typology of Figure 8.1.

Williamson, however, appears unwilling to go this far. He seems to be of the opinion that 'a little hierarchy is a dangerous thing', and also that hierarchy is particularly dangerous if it implies the imposition of public power over private power, that is political over economic power. At least he does not seem to be equally concerned about the creation of hierarchy as the vertical integration of particular fields of production, although this must also cause a legitimation deficiency as it accumulates. Williamson is only prepared to measure state action out sparingly, for instance as antitrust regulation, but it is not quite clear how state intervention fits into his general model of environmental and human factors which is derived mainly from transactions at a sub-systemic level. The MH model does not account for the emergence of the state as a systems-level actor, the ultimate hierarchy, and it does not describe the extent and direction of state action.

Williamson shares this rather flimsy conception of the state with many other economists. One of the three externality reduction mechanisms in the Arrow scheme referred to on p. 163 was state action. There is also considerable congruence between another of Arrow's categories, 'social norms', and what Williamson refers to as 'atmosphere', a 'super environment' in which the transactional model of MH is embedded.

The two concepts may not be entirely synonymous, but 'atmosphere' must also be constituted by 'social norms' and expectations, which facilitate exchange because they internalise social controls and thereby create or reinforce expectations about the quality of interpersonal and social relations. I do not want to argue that social norms and values are irrelevant as determinants of behaviour, but certainly more attention needs to be devoted to exploring their limitations and potential before they come to occupy such a central position. In terms of the initial dichotomy I would suggest that 'atmosphere' is high in justificatory value, but low in explanatory power.

Constructs of this nature always seem to turn up as a lame afterthought to elaborate theoretical schemes whose authors have come to doubt the closure of their systems. After all, if atmosphere and social norms carry the weight attributed to them, it would not be necessary to create the complex and ingenious institutional checks and balances which these writers spend most of their time deducing. Values and norms moreover are themselves products of the very institutions they purport to regulate. Change in 'atmosphere' will therefore in all probability be an extremely slow process, which will have to be initiated by forces outside the narrow transactional process itself.

The problem is how we, given initial 'information impactedness', may create an 'atmosphere' which will 'loosen' the flow of transactions. If hierarchy is involved, it will have to be tempered by the consent and participation of the 'lower echelons'. Williamson appears to think that the prospects for a benign hierarchy are bleaker where the state is engaged in the organisation of production. It is not intuitively obvious, though, why organisations designed to further social ends should be more likely to succumb to such abuses as 'exploitation' and 'inefficiency' than organisations premised on the pursuit of self-interest, when either holds a position of monopoly in their respective 'markets'. In democratic capitalist societies all citizens have the formal option of 'voice' in political matters, but these democratic rights are for the most part not valid at work where property rights take precedence. To be sure voice can be exercised through state and trade union activity, but apart from that influence can be exerted only indirectly, by voting with one's feet (exit). Hierarchy moreover implies that this option either disappears or becomes prohibitively expensive for most individuals.

Hierarchy has been on the rise in most subdivisions of the economy. The preceding paragraph used the labour market to illustrate the implications of hierarchy in terms of a reduction in the availability of 'exit' without any compensatory increase in 'voice'. I slipped into EVL terminology at this point because it lends itself more directly to the formulation of questions linking structure and performance than the MH framework does. The two approaches are very similar in some respects, but Williamson seems more committed to the structure-conduct paradigm whereas Hirschman allows for both the existence of functional equivalents and for the existence of complementarity between the two, i.e. that 'voice', theoretically at least, may make up for 'failure of exit' by restoring responsiveness and responsibility and thus halting organisational decline whether in the form of 'exploitation' or 'inefficiency'. Williamson, however, seems only to accept the concept of 'exploitation' in a much more particularistic meaning, and Hirschman for his part is also reluctant to admit to the possibility of exploitation more generally.

Neither Hirschman nor Williamson are, it seems, able to establish satisfactory correspondence between the categories of their analytical frameworks and those of the real world, which is inhabited by social classes and groups struggling over the distribution of scarce resources. Therefore both are unable to account for the existence of conspicuous differences in access to systems outcomes, whether in the sphere of production or in the sphere of consumption, other than in terms of functional requirements for systems performance. That is closer to justification than to explanation, it seems.

The shared interests of similarly situated individuals may provide the basis for collective action (politics) to overcome disadvantages sustained in the marketplace (economics). Above I pointed to some factors, which have long been recognised to make collective action a scarce resource for some of those groups who need it most. To be sure collective action has occurred. It is difficult to create organisations around interests in the sphere of consumption, but trade unions and political parties, whose claim to existence is the protection of wage earner/worker interests, have come into being and can point to some accomplishments.

The primary locus of these organisations or forms of collective action, however, is the nation state, but recent developments in the organisation of production, that is, its internationalisation, has reduced congruence between the two realms of decision-making. Economic power in the form of control over investment decisions at all levels is a very versatile and mobile source of influence. At the national level there is already substantial opportunity to contain it, but if decisions are regionalised (decentralised), it may be harder to consider these interests because a new structure may have to be built to articulate them at this level. This difficulty is compounded if practically the entire world is opened up to the pursuit of private economic interests without a correspondent growth of 'countervailing power'. At the international level only fragments of state authority exist, and international trade unions are at the moment rather rudimentary, at least compared to the TNCs. The next section will explore some consequences and implications of economic internationalisation.

III. Economic Internationalisation, Labour, and Technology

The simple model of capitalism is a closed system consisting of two classes, one owning only its labour power and another owning the implements needed to make that labour power productive. Either part needs the property of the other, and the price at which exchange will take place is determined by the ability of one to do without the other, given some demand and supply conditions. Historically labour has tended to procreate at a rate, which, along with the not entirely un-related tendency of the capitalist (firm) to innovate and develop labour-saving technology, has systematically depressed its (labour's), terms of trade in the labour market. Unions were formed to counteract this market bias which pertained to qualitative as well as quantitative aspects of the labour contract. In this context 'quantitative' and 'qualitative' refer to wages and working conditions respectively. In terms of the EVL framework, unions might both perform the function of *exit* and that of *voice*, and with respect to the latter, both directly *vis-à-vis* the capitalist owner and indirectly *vis-à-vis* the state. Unions were both economic and political organisations. Capitalism and liberal society claimed the credit for freeing labour from its feudal bonds. The freedom gained was a rather formal one, though, because even if labour was no longer under any obligation to work for a particular capitalist, it was still mandatory for labour to sell its labour power to somebody. This condition might be described as a transition from a state of individual to a state of collective serfdom. Labour, in a sense, now belonged to the capitalist class rather than to particular individual capitalists, and the market became the mediating factor.

This description of a theoretical system was approximated to varying degrees by various historical systems. Departures from the theoretical norm occurred as a result of the repeal of anti-union laws, the enact-ment of health and safety laws, etc., which might have been necessary reforms to halt the movement of the system towards self-destruction. Many of these reforms, which were enacted against the vehement opposition of most capitalists, may nevertheless have been in their best interest. In many cases opposition was not voiced against particular measures to modify the operation of the system. Rather the stand against it was framed as opposition to its deplorable effects on the competitive standing of a firm, an industry, or a country. Exit has always been a more feasible option for capitalists than for workers, it seems, and opposition to specific laws was often garnished with state-ments to the effect that these adverse consequences would eventually force the firm or the industry to relocate its activity to 'greener pastures'. Some of these threats were carried out, but others were no doubt only strategic cries of 'wolf'.

Some locational factors made it difficult for specific industries and firms to move. World trade was not nearly as liberalised as is the case today. Relocating production therefore might mean moving away from established markets. Also contemporary communications and travel technology is much more conducive to internationalisation than that of yesteryear.

Some writers (see Fröbel et al. 1977) argue that we now have an international market for production locations. As noted above, this means that the firm can move in time in terms of, for instance, the standard of working conditions and environmental control applicable, if it moves in space by relocating its production to industrial free zones in third world countries. Some Asian and Latin American countries can supply labour at costs that may be competitive with those obtaining during the industrial revolution. Labour repression becomes a comparative advantage for some of these countries. Careful production planning helps the transnational corporations to split up their production processes to take maximum advantage of the international division of labour originating in these 'comparative advantages'. The option of 'careful location planning' is also made available to smaller companies by international business consultants. Rising standards in a number of regulatory fields during the 1960s and 1970s had accentuated these trends. An exodus of dangerous and dirty industries to third world countries is reported to be in progress (Settle 1976 and Castleman 1978).

Different interpretations of recent economic internationalisation are possible, but the transnational corporations (TNCs) indisputably play a major part in it. Does the new international division of labour create sustainable growth in the countries where the TNCs locate production facilities? Is this growth 'stolen' from the older industrialised countries, and has a process of de-industrialisation been set in motion in them? How does this affect overall systems stability? Is the tendency of the TNCs to produce in low-wage countries and take out their profits in low-tax countries compatible with efforts to manage aggregate demand?

Certainly as far as the developing countries goes, a sizeable literature raising questions about the beneficial nature of the kind of development generated by these forms of economic relations has emerged in recent years. Above, suggestions about the kind of productive activity likely to converge upon the developing countries were cited. Newer forms of dependence may supplant the old colonial variety, such as dependence on food supplies from abroad, on access to the markets for mass products in the developed countries, on imported technology, on foreign sources of finance (while indigenous savings are likely to be managed by international finance capital), and finally more generally on the role assigned to a particular country in the international division of labour by international capital.[2]

It is difficult to determine whether the developed industrial countries as a geographical block have benefited from the development of what has been called dependence or underdevelopment by some writers. The relation of this chain of events to the current economic crisis is not absolutely clear. On theoretical grounds it might be argued that the incorporation of these developing countries into the international division of labour has afforded international capital, in particular the TNCs, new opportunities for control through the options of 'voice' and 'exit', which may be complementary strategies for these economic actors when dealing with nations or national working classes.

Internationalisation of the market for production locations is more or less equal to the creation of an international labour market. At least it makes it possible to let labour in the developing and the developed countries compete with each other for employment opportunities. It means the creation of an international reserve army of labour which can be called into service at the discretion of international capital, that is the TNCs. They are now able to play working classes in different nations off against one another. If a strategy of 'voice' *vis-à-vis* a nation or an organised national working class does not work on a particular occasion, a TNC may choose to exercise its 'exit option' and relocate its production facilities. The exit option may also be activated to punish recalcitrant countries or national working classes.

As a consequence of this abundance of 'exits' available to the TNCs and the absence of the requisite 'countervailing power', whether in the form of transnational unions or state-like structures or functions, the balance of class power appears to have tipped decidedly in favour of (international) capital. They, the TNCs that is, are able to determine labour conditions through the choice of location so to speak. Exit thus becomes a way of integrating different levels or of creating hierarchy, but it must be considered a highly questionable one from the perspective of a social optimum. Choice of location, or rather the latitude provided by the many different national locations of most TNCs, enables them to realise or take out their profits where tax laws and similar rule sets are most lenient. The TNCs are thus in practice able to avoid contributing directly to defraying the social expenditures arising out of their activity. Admittedly I have focused on the gloomier consequences of internationalisation in this brief account. Hirschman, in a recent article (1978), shows concern about the advantages accruing to capital from this vastly increased opportunity for exit whereas Williamson still appears to operate under the assumptions of a closed system with a state that may intervene and prevent excesses as in the case of antitrust regulation. But TNCs are not vulnerable to such measures except in a few of the bigger countries. A different model is called for to explain this situation.

IV. A Political Economy of Organisations: Markets, Hierarchies, and the 'International Connection'

Section II was both a discussion and an exposition of the EVL and the MH frameworks of analysis. Some of the issues raised in this section may therefore have been touched upon before.

My main difficulty with both Hirschman and Williamson is their common failure to accept the existence of antagonistic interests more openly as a fact of life, and consequently as the starting point for analytical endeavours like their own. In terms of Figure 8.1 both Hirschman and Williamson deal almost exclusively with problems of 'inefficiency', which may also originate in conflicts of interests, but where the achievement of consensus and harmony is nevertheless possible.

I have employed the rather abstract concepts of 'class' and 'interest' in the preceding discussion. The real-life counterparts of these analytical categories are admittedly somewhat subtler and less clear-cut. However, the abstraction of these concepts seems preferable to the vacuity of the likes of 'complexity', 'rationality', and 'transaction', to name just a few such theoretical jokers, which are completely without predictive content in some of the most important areas of practical and theoretical concern.

In spite of this reservation I think that EVL and MH expresses important insights into the socioeconomic process, which may make it possible to extend their applications into the realm of 'exploitation' represented by the other half of Figure 8.1. Absence of 'exit' and 'voice' may signify unavailability of these options rather than the satisfied quiet and snug acceptance of organisational performance which justificatory theories are likely to come up with as explanations of this fact.

As far as the working class goes, availability of 'exit' has been the exception rather than the rule, and 'voice' is strictly circumscribed by the ideological defences of systems' characteristics. Union action and working class articulation of demands to the political system represent 'voice', but it has been extremely difficult to gain acceptance for interventions into what some refer to as the orderly operation of the market. There is no agreement about what an externality is, though, and what is an acceptable level of externalities. Those who gain by imposing externalities on other actors will 'cheat' when they fight change. International competitiveness can take its place alongside other time-honoured 'economic constraints' called into service from time to time to prevent the introduction of structural reforms in the system. During periods of high growth systems managers have become increasingly confident that they cater to all interests while retaining the identity of the system. Internationalisation has helped belie this.

From the perspective of capital, on the other hand, 'exit' has generally been plentiful – and increasingly, a result of international-isation – although some problems were encountered during the late 1960s and early 1970s when high employment levels enabled labour to be more 'choosy' by increasing the availability of exit within nations as an individual response to experienced decline within firms. Recent statements to the effect that both investment and labour are now mobile at the international level must be carefully qualified with respect to the latter. During periods of almost full employment it is perfectly possible to set into movement great masses of people – as witnessed by the immigrant workers of both Europe and the US. The disparity of living conditions between centre and periphery has been sufficient to bring this about. If hope for betterment is to power the migratory process, reversing its direction for the indigenous working classes is hardly a feasible solution in anything but a fraction of the cases. In effect the 'import' of labour served to reduce the availability of 'exits' to indigenous labour and was therefore primarily beneficial to capital.

Another, and probably the most important, way of influencing the availability of 'exit', the market balance of power, which is available to capital in a closed system as well, is technology, which is forever changing, almost exclusively at the instigation of capital. New products and production processes are the two main divisions of the pheno-menon of technology in this context. The conflict mainly arises over the development and introduction of labour-saving process technology, which in terms of scale at least is also related to the size of markets.

At the moment prospects for democratic reforms of the economy seem rather bleak, both at the national and at the international level. The new international division of labour is not the 'new international economic order' hoped for in UN circles. It is not a 'new deal'. In fact it is probably the same 'old game', except that it is even harder to figure out now who is with or against whom.

The TNCs are hierarchies with an extra level. They may reduce transaction costs somewhat, but the boundaries between transaction costs (or inefficiencies) and exploitation are often hard to draw. TNCs may be an illustration of the second mechanism in Arrow's scheme (see p. 163 above) that 'firms of any complexity may bring about a public good'. This is essentially collective action by monopoly, and without additional, very stringent and not particularly plausible, assumptions about the harmony of interests or the wisdom and benevolence of the managers of monopoly, it is not possible to have much confidence in this solution.

The consequences of production are social, but its planning and execution, and most importantly, the appropriation of its results remain private. To refer back to the parable brought up in conjunction with the introduction of Arrow's views above, 'the big bad wolf' has not turned vegetarian, and all 'little pigs' should therefore be careful and not too trusting. Social dislocation and exploitation are still part and parcel of the capitalist mode of production. That is what it feeds on. In fact the argument here has emphasised that internationalisation has provided additional opportunities for the pursuit of private economic goals. International competition has emerged as the great new 'economic constraint', which is utilised in most defences against demands for improvement, also by industries not exposed to foreign competition. The logic of international competition and economic crisis is nibbling away at social defences created at the national level during decades of struggle.

Theories of international trade explain the new international division of labour as the realisation of comparative advantages made possible by the progressive removal of trade barriers. I do not wish to argue that 'natural endowment' in the sense suggested by the theory of comparative advantage is totally non-existent. However, also 'historical accidents' of one kind or another, for instance 'first-mover advantages', are significant. A more problematic sub-set of 'comparative advantages' alluded to a number of times above, also man-made, are low-wage, labour-repressive systems, absent or non-consequential regulation of health and safety at work and of emission of pollutants into the environment. In this theory nations, no less than people, have to accept the 'station in life' accorded them by self-regulating market. Some countries are industrialised, and others are de-industrialised, and nothing much can be done about it.

Maybe this note is too pessimistic to conclude on. Some of these problems are only tendential, and the process of internationalisation has not been carried through to its logical conclusion. The TNCs are not equally powerful everywhere, and the process may be halted or reversed, if a non-fatalistic approach is adopted which does not consider economic processes as inexorable, extra-historical forces. At a very general level we may distinguish among three main types of strategies:

- compensating the victims of the process;
- prevention without fundamental change, adaptation; or
- fundamental structural change, hierarchy with voice or socialisation of production.

The first of these is likely to be of little interest in dealing with some of these issues. It is part of the problem that those who gain cannot be taxed to compensate the losers. The dividing line between efforts to adapt to systems failures and efforts to transform the system is of course hard to draw. The agents of change may differ with the level of change.

One obvious failing which is located in the twilight zone between adaptation and structural change is the absence of anything but fragmentary channels for the exercise of 'popular voice' at the international level whether in the form of supranational political institutions or international unions. A serious difficulty, even if such channels were available, would be the formal impediments to the creation of collective action on the part of the most numerous social categories referred to above. Some well-organised international unions exist, but their penetration and scope is often limited. Any supranational political structure may also be taken over by well-organised capital fractions and used as sounding boards for ideological messages and political defences. The OECD, and particularly the Interfutures Group, provides an instructive illustration of this. There are also entirely unofficial bodies, such as the Trilateral Commission, which have considerable potential power.

The Interfutures Report envisages periods of stepped-up competition between the major industrial countries. It advocates adaptation as the main strategy. Protectionism is the spectre of one scenario. The report, however, gives no satisfactory explanation why protectionism of all possible 'beggar-my-neighbour' policies should be dreaded most. Why is it to be feared more than low wages, dangerous production processes, and depleted environments? These questions are analogous to one suggested by one of the quotations on p. 162 from *The Wealth of Nations*, namely why there are so many laws against combining to raise the price of labour, but none against combining to lower it. It has something to do with the interests which the larger social structures are programmed to promote. A reprogramming, to the extent it is possible, is likely to be a slow and protracted process. Some may want to argue, to continue the metaphor, that the old system has to be scrapped in its entirety before a new one can be implemented. This requirement would all but make change impossible.

The purpose of any new system would have to be the improved co-ordination between individual and social goals. This is obviously not the place to start a comprehensive discussion of these matters, and I shall merely point to a body of literature which seems pertinent, and which is mainly available in German.[3] The starting point is the so-called 'socialisation debate' in Weimar Germany. It is the most ambitious and comprehensive effort to confront the question of structural transformation of the economy.

The question of socialisation is relevant in this context because it is what hierarchy is all about. Should societal transaction costs be minimised by letting private capital fill out the space available, much in the fashion foreseen by Schumpeter (1942)? Will the end state then be socialism, corporatism or some unknown mutation, and more importantly will it be benign? Occasional arguments are heard again from the representatives of international capital that capitalism and democracy now have come to the parting way. Certainly the revealed preferences of some TNCs in Latin America and Asia do not give much reason for optimism. This aspect should also be considered when the internationalisation of the economy is being discussed.

Notes

[1] DMC and EIASM Seminar on 'Organisations in their Societal Context', 5–7 December 1977, Copenhagen.
[2] See for instance Chapter XVII, 'Le Procés Inachevé d'Internationalisation de l'Economie', in de Berris, G. and Bye 1977. They point to the above sources of dependence, but emphasise that the process of integration has not been concluded yet.
[3] Korsch (1969) contains a classic statement while Novy (1978) surveys the more general debate.

9 Markets and Hierarchies: a suitable framework for an evaluation of organisational change?
T. McGuinness

I. Introduction
This paper examines the apparent paradox that, whilst *Markets and Hierarchies* is one of the few recent economics books to have attracted much attention from other social sciences, there are aspects of its analysis that attract strong criticism from those quarters. The aim is to identity the factors of an 'economic' approach to organisational evolution that might be objectionable to non-economists. Two main factors are suggested: firstly, optimism that no new organisational form will survive that makes some members of the organisation worse off; secondly, that a person's revealed preferences are a satisfactory indicator of true welfare. Identification of issues that divide different social sciences is a necessary step towards progress in interdisciplinary work.

II. New Institutional Economics
Williamson (1975) has made a stimulating contribution to the rapidly-growing area of 'new institutional economics', whose aim is the comparative analysis of economic systems. In *Markets and Hierarchies* alternative forms of organisation, market and non-market, are compared in terms of the difficulties they would encounter in effecting various kinds of transactions (labour, product, and financial) in a variety of environmental circumstances. Testable implications are derived by assuming that competitive processes in society work in such a way that the organisational forms that actually emerge and survive do so because they incur lower transactions costs than known alternative forms.[1] In this sense, Williamson has an efficiency explanation of the evolution of organisational forms in society. Other comments in the book suggest that a narrow efficiency theory is not enough to explain organisational developments in all circumstances. Firstly, the quote reported in note 1 is qualified by stating that a presumption of market failure when transactions are shifted out of a market 'is merely a presumption. Transactions are sometimes shifted out of a market into a firm because the firm thereby realises a strategic advantage over actual

and potential rivals and in relation to customers' (Williamson 1975, footnote 1, 20). However, in the same place, it is also stated that such monopoly incentives 'by no means constitute the main reason for supplanting market mediated transactions'. Secondly, references to the concept of 'atmosphere' take the discussion beyond a narrow efficiency explanation of actual organisational forms. For example

Recognition that alternative modes of economic organisation give rise to differing exchange relations, and that these relations themselves are valued, requires that organisational effectiveness be viewed more broadly than the usual efficiency calculus would dictate. . . . Preferences for atmosphere may induce individuals to forgo material gains for non-pecuniary satisfactions if the modes or practices are regarded as oppressive or otherwise repugnant. . . . A full discussion of atmosphere and its ramifications raises a wider set of sociopolitical issues than can be addressed here. (Williamson 1975, pp. 38–39).

Nevertheless, the fact that the book does not address this wider set of sociopolitical issues suggests that, despite awareness of their existence, the intention is to relegate them to a secondary level of importance. The bulk of the explanatory power is attributed to comparative transactional efficiency in the narrow (material) sense of the word 'efficiency'.

To anticipate later discussion one might note at this point that, even if 'atmosphere' were given a central role in the analysis, so that alternative organisational forms could be compared in terms of their 'psychic' efficiency, which only partly depended on material efficiency, Williamson would still have an efficiency explanation of actual organisation: those that emerged and survived would be attributed with comparative 'psychic', if not material, efficiency.

To summarise, Williamson attributes the occurrence of one organisational form instead of another to some combination of three things: superior material productivity (lower transactions costs); to gain a strategic advantage over individuals outside the organisation (rivals or customers); or superior psychic productivity, despite inferior material productivity. The second reason is explicitly given a minor role in the explanation of markets being supplanted by firms. The third reason is given a minor role by default. It seems justifiable, therefore, to claim that the spirit of Williamson's analysis is to attribute the emergence and survival of actual organisational forms to the material gains that result from their superiority in effecting a given set of transactions.

III. The Interdisciplinary Appeal of New Institutional Economics
To a far greater extent than most books by economists *Markets and Hierarchies* has attracted the interest of other disciplines in the social sciences.[2] Such genuine interdisciplinary interest is a rare enough occurrence to merit seeking an explanation. I feel that the attraction of

Markets and Hierarchies to several of the social sciences is derived from its attempt to deal directly with problems posed by the existence of historical time. Analysis of these problems inevitably assigns a key role to features of the human condition that have been ignored for a long time in mainstream economics but have held the centre of the stage in other social sciences. For example: it is the existence of time that thrusts bounded rationality to the fore in the analysis of decision-making; it is the irreversibility of time, and the inability to 'buy' time in any real sense, which are responsible for the emergence and persistence of 'first-mover' advantages, hence for idiosyncratic exchanges, and hence for the appearance of those organisational problems that arise from the joining of opportunism with small-numbers exchange conditions. Features of the human condition such as bounded rationality and opportunism have been far more the stuff of other social sciences than of mainstream economics. The latter has made pervasive use of notions of equilibrium. When imposed at any level of analysis higher than that of the individual decision-maker it is arguable that the equilibrium concept precludes a complete appreciation of the essence of time,[3] and leaves one to infer an image of the individual that is merely a functional link in a chain of theoretical argument rather than a representation of a real person. The absence of human characteristics from the image of the individual in mainstream economic theory, 'economic man', perhaps goes a long way to explain the alienation of other social sciences from that theory.[4] Conversely, the crucial role assigned to human characteristics in *Markets and Hierarchies* helps to explain its appeal beyond the narrow confines of economics. Despite introducing elements that, compared to mainstream economics, make its analysis more palatable to other social sciences, *Markets and Hierarchies* can hardly be said to have received unqualified approval from exponents of these disciplines.[5] The final section of this paper suggests a number of reasons why one might criticise the analytical framework used in *Markets and Hierarchies*.

IV. A Critique of New Institutional Economics

In section II it was argued that the testable implications of *Markets and Hierarchies* are based on the assumption that the organisational forms that emerge and survive do so because of the material gains they generate in effecting a given set of transactions. In addition to using this assumption as the basis for positive analysis, there is a strong sense of approval of circumstances in which such organisational forms emerge: in other words, the framework contains normative overtones. The following discussion deals with three points on which the framework might be criticised: its narrow, material concept of efficiency; its neglect of distributional issues; and its willingness to accept the revealed preference of people as indicators of their true welfare.[6]

Williamson's comments on 'atmosphere' (for example, the quote on p. 181) indicates his willingness, in some circumstances, to attribute the emergence of one organisational form rather than another to non-pecuniary advantages. This possibility suggests one could work with a broader concept of efficiency, 'psychic' efficiency, wherein satisfactions are attributed partly to pecuniary and partly to non-pecuniary sources. A move from one organisational form to another might lead to a net improvement or a net worsening of each source of satisfaction, pecuniary or non-pecuniary.[7] To simplify the discussion, imagine an organisational change that leads to a net improvement in the total amount of pecuniary gains available to members of the organisation. If there is also a net improvement in the total amount of non-pecuniary gains available, one might claim that the change is unambiguously beneficial. Call this Case I. If there is a decrease in the total amount of non-pecuniary gains available this might (Case II) or might not (Case III) be more than compensated for by the pecuniary advantages of the organisational change. Given the welfare criteria implicitly being used, the change is beneficial in Case II, but not in Case III. Whilst one might criticise these welfare criteria on other grounds, as below, there is little substance to the claim that the framework in *Markets and Hierarchies* is deficient because it is necessarily restricted to a consideration of only material sources of welfare.

One aspect of Williamson's approach that might provoke a more substantial basis for concern about its normative overtones is the absence of any consideration of whose plans are the source of organisational changes observed in the real world. Without such consideration it is impossible to hypothesise the typical intention of a plan whose pursuit gives rise to observed developments in organisational form, and this might preclude a complete understanding of the processes by which organisations evolve. Moreover, the neglect precludes discussion of how any change in total (pecuniary and non-pecuniary) gains or losses are distributed amongst members of the organisation. One then might object to the normative overtones of the approach adopted in *Markets and Hierarchies* because it focuses on total systems efficiency, and ignores distributional issues. As a first step towards taking these issues into account, each case identified above might be categorised further according to the way in which the total gains or losses from an organisational change are distributed amongst members of the organisation. To simplify the discussion, assume we can focus on the welfares of just two groups: 'workers' and 'capitalists'. Assuming it is the plans of capitalists which give rise to organisational changes, one can assume that their welfare is increased by emergent organisational forms that survive in the long run. Overall evaluation of a change then depends on

Table 9.1   Effect of an organisational change on total (pecuniary and non-pecuniary) gains available, and on the welfares of 'capitalists' and 'workers'

	Case					
	I		II		III	
Total gains	+		+		−	
	IA	IB	IIA	IIB	IIIA	IIIB
Capitalists	+	+	+	+	+	+
Workers	+	−	+	−	*	−

(+) Increase; (−) Decrease) (*) Not applicable

its impact on the welfare of workers. The cases identified earlier can be classified further on the basis of an increase (sub-case A) or a decrease (sub-case B) in the welfare of workers (sub-case A of case III logically cannot exist), given their prevailing preference structures. (The possibility that preferences are endogenous is discussed below.) This welfare taxonomy is summarised in Table 9.1.

This classification scheme can be used to try to identify the positions taken by different people who have discussed the normative consequences of organisational changes. The discussion in *Markets and Hierarchies* suggests that typical instances of vertical or conglomerate internalisation fall into Case I or Case II. Moreover, although distributional issues are not treated explicitly, there is a strong implication that Cases IA or IIA occur rather than IB or IIB: in other words, no new organisational form can survive in the long run if some group within it is left worse off than before the change.

Marglin (1975) discusses the historical replacement of the putting-out system by the factory system, and takes a clear welfare position when evaluating this change. He suggests that the appearance of this new organisational form had little to do with increasing the size of the 'pie' to the advantage of all, but much to do with ' "the capitalist" (getting) himself a larger share of the pie at the expense of the worker'. For Marglin the success of the factory system

had little or nothing to do with the technological superiority of large-scale machinery. The key to the success of the factory, as well as its inspiration, was the substitution of capitalists' for workers' control and the production process: discipline and supervision could and did reduce costs *without* being technologically superior. (Marglin 1975, p. 34).

The discussion in Marglin's paper makes it obvious that the distributional effects of any organisational change play a prominent role in his welfare framework, and that, whatever other consequences the change to the factory system had, capitalists were left better off than under the putting-out system. He quotes evidence from Bythell (1969) that factory wages for handloom weaving were higher than wages earned for the same work performed in the worker's cottage. Marglin interprets these higher wages as 'reward for submitting to factory supervision and discipline', which is here taken to imply that the factory system provided workers with less non-pecuniary satisfaction than the putting-out system. The location of Marglin in the above classification scheme then depends on whether the higher wages more than compensated for the 'atmospheric' losses suffered by workers. If they did, then his evaluation of this organisational change is in category IIA. If they didn't, it is in either IIB or IIIB.[8] The tones of his discussion suggest that he believes workers were left worse off after the change, so that categories IIB and IIIB are the relevant ones.

Therefore, if the interpretations developed above are correct, the approach in *Market and Hierarchies* implies a different welfare evaluation of the emergence of the factory system than does the approach in Marglin's paper. Why does this difference arise? On our interpretation, Williamson presumes that no new organisational form can survive in the long run if some group within it is made worse off than before the change. This position is perhaps based on a belief that a solution is always attainable to the problem of '[supplying] the requisite mixture of structures, which vary in the intensity of metering, thereby [allowing] individuals to match themselves in accordance with their involvement–productivity trade-offs' (Williamson 1975, p. 55).

The crucial question here is whether a dynamic capitalist economy can support a rich enough variety of organisational forms to satisfy a wide range of tastes for 'atmosphere' and at the same time enable individuals who would prefer to be in a 'high leisure/low productivity' organisation to satisfy their material needs. If so, then the stance taken in *Markets and Hierarchies* seems justifiable. The explanation of the different stance taken by Marglin is based, perhaps, on his belief that 'high leisure/low productivity' options may cease to be available as developments in 'low leisure/high productivity' parts of the economy make it impossible for members to subsist in the former type of organisation.[9]

Workers may have had no option to move out of factories, even though they were worse off there, because preferred organisational forms (cottage industry) ceased to be available. Consider, for example, the scenario suggested by Marglin:

Where alternatives to factory employment were available, there is evidence that workers flocked to them. Cottage weaving was one of the few, perhaps the only important, ready alternative to factory work for those lacking special skills. . . . However, the bias of technological change towards improvements consistent with factory organisation sooner or later took its toll of alternatives, weaving included. . . . Where this alternative was not available, the worker's freedom to refuse factory employment was the freedom to starve. (Marglin 1975, pp. 51–2).

The process of capitalist development implied here is one capable of rejecting Williamson's optimism about the mutual advantages of organisational evolution: workers, initially worse off in factories, try to return to cottage industry. But the factory system gives capitalists more incentive for technological innovation, and ensuing technological progress increases productivity in factories. If the factory wages are unchanged, factory prices can fall and the return to capitalists increase. To enable cottage products to remain competitive, the wages of cottage weavers must fall; but once they fall below subsistence level, cottage industry disappears, and workers are forced back to factories to avoid starvation. In terms of our classification scheme, the technological progress in factories implies that any IIIB outcomes are eventually replaced by outcomes in category I or II. If Williamson's optimism is to be rejected by this argument, however, one finally needs the assumption that collective bargaining does not allow factory workers to appropriate enough of the higher productivity gains for their pecuniary rewards finally to outweigh their non-pecuniary losses. (For this would cause IA and IIA outcomes to prevail over IB and IIB outcomes.)

We have tried to identify the kinds of claims one must make as a basis for rejecting the assumption in *Markets and Hierarchies* that organisational evolution leaves everyone better off. The argument involved two crucial steps: firstly, that organisations differ in the growth rate of their material productivity, so that low-productivity forms cease to offer their members a subsistence wage and thus disappear from the scene; secondly that workers (or some other group in the organisation) are unable to get a sufficiently large share of the material gains to compensate for any non-pecuniary losses they incur. If claims such as these seem historically inaccurate, are there no grounds for opposing the normative evaluation of organisational development implied in *Markets and Hierarchies*? The final criticism of Williamson's framework considered in this paper is its willingness to accept the revealed preferences of individuals as indicators of their true welfare.

Even if all parties to an organisational change eventually express a preference for the new state of affairs over the old, a welfare analyst might criticise the change if he is not prepared to accept that all individuals are the best judge of their own welfare. This type of paternalism seems to apply to a number of 'new left' critics of capitalist economies and orthodox economic theory. For example, Gintis (1972) suggests that the notions of individual welfare employed in neoclassical economy theory are unsatisfactory because they fail to recognise that welfare depends on characteristics ('capacities') of the individual that are themselves the product of the actual social and economic environment of that person. He suggests that the institutions of capitalist societies might be conducive to the development of capacities required for adequate role performance in the capitalist system, rather than capacities compatible with individual welfare. For example, the nature of technology (by which he means not just physical technology but also the organisational forms that govern relations between those entering into production) influences the available set of work activities and, thereby, the pattern of preference structures and the paths of individual development actually followed (Gintis 1972, pp. 591–3). Until we know more about how alternative institutions affect individual development, and how various types of individual development affect individual welfare this extended kind of welfare framework is, as Gintis admits, unoperational. But if the aim is to address questions of long-term institutional change (which new institutional economics does) one can hardly deny the existence of channels of influence between the environment and the individual. The fact that this influence is complex in nature does not justify an assumption that institutional changes influence individual development in ways that always are conducive to greater individual welfare. That this assumption is implicitly made in *Markets and Hierarchies* is perhaps the main reason for doubting Ouchi's claim that the book kindles hope that 'a unified social science may be possible during our lifetime' (see note 2).

V. Conclusion

The type of question addressed in *Markets and Hierarchies* and in 'new institutional economics' in general, is of interest to any social scientist. Moreover, the approach used therein seems more palatable to other social sciences than the approach of mainstream economic theory: this paper suggests the explanation for this is the key role assigned to human characteristics which mainstream economics has ignored. Despite this, the analysis in *Markets and Hierarchies* and its apparent approval of any organisational change that increases total pecuniary (net) gains, seem unacceptable to some people, especially some members of what Lindbeck has called the 'new left'. Two possible reasons for the disagreement are: firstly, a belief in the long-term viability of new organisational forms that leave some members of the organisation worse off than before the change; secondly, the feeling that the welfare framework implicit in *Markets and Hierarchies* neglects the effect of society on individual capacities and preferences, and thus is too narrow as a basis for evaluating long-run institutional changes. These are the sorts of issues on which interdisciplinary work should focus if we are to progress towards a unified social science.

Notes

[1] For example

> [My] concern throughout the book is with comparative institutional choices. Only to the extent that frictions associated with one mode of organisation are prospectively attenuated by shifting the transaction, or a related set of transactions, to an alternative mode can a failure be said to exist. Remediable frictions thus constitute the conditions of interest. . . . (A) presumption of market failure is warranted where it is observed that transactions are shifted out of a market and into a firm. (A) presumption of internal organisational failure is warranted for transactions that are unshifted (continue to be market-mediated). (Williamson 1975, p. 20).

[2] For example 'With *Markets and Hierarchies*, the promise first made by Chester Barnard and given impetus by the genius of Herbert Simon can truly be said to be reaching fruition. At times, one is tempted to believe, while reading this book, that a unified social science may be possible during our lifetime.' (Ouchi 1977, p. 542).

[3] 'A state of equilibrium, by definition, is a state in which something, something relevant is *not* changing; so the use of an equilibrium concept is a signal that time, in some respect at least, has been put to one side.' (Hicks 1976).

[4] The nature of 'economic man' is discussed in Machlup (1972). For example: 'It is probably agreed that *homo oeconomicus* is not supposed to be a real man, but rather a man-made man, an artificial device for use in economic theorising. Thus, he is not a *homo* but a *homunculus*.' (Machlup 1977 p. 114).

[5] This was apparent at the Imperial Conference itself, in some of the papers and the accompanying discussion. The remainder of this paper is a substantial re-drafting of the one circulated at the Conference, with the aim of interpreting the sense of the critical comments made there.

[6] These points correspond closely to the set of five points identified by Lindbeck (1977) as the thrust of the 'new left' critique of traditional economics.

[7] One reason why 'atmosphere' is accorded only a secondary level of importance in *Markets and Hierarchies* probably is the peculiar difficulty of analysing the effect of organisational changes on non-pecuniary satisfaction.

[8] Both IA and IB are precluded by Marglin's assumption that the organisational change did not increase the size of the 'pie' to the advantage of all.

[9] At a more macro level than the issues discussed in this paper the same question appears: can 'high leisure/low productivity' economies survive competition from 'low leisure/high productivity' ones? If not, the renowned characteristics of Japanese workers may have dramatic long-run consequences for other capitalist economies. For a characterisation of the 'workaholic' Japanese, see Whymant (1980).

10 Conclusion: Power, Efficiency and Institutions: some implications of the debate for the scope of economics*
J. Turk

There can be no economy where there is no efficiency.

> Benjamin Disraeli, *Letters to Constituents*

All the papers in this volume have examined the possibility of explaining the existence and form of organisations by means of arguments which derive from Oliver Williamson's analysis of the role of transactions costs. Some of the papers have been exploratory, indicating how influential such essentially economic ideas can be in organisational studies. Others have been critical, questioning the hegemonic tendencies of economics. Most of the critiques have been developed directly from clear foundations in sociological theory. There has therefore been a direct opposition between economic and sociological arguments in many instances, and this was particularly evident in the discussion of the papers when they were presented at the EGOS Conference. Economists (and some organisation theorists) tended to contend that organisations are all about efficiency; sociologists (and other organisation theorists) retorted that organisations are all about power.

A question which has not been so clearly addressed in this volume is the extent to which this sociological critique has more general implications for economics, particularly institutional economics. In view of the similar way in which economic reasoning has recently begun to colonise other areas outside its traditional domain (as was pointed out in the introduction) this is a particularly important issue *for economics*. A triangle is therefore completed: transactional economics seems conceptually useful in organisation theory, but its use here has stimulated a sociological critique which not only questions the value of economics in organisation studies but has evident ramifications in the discipline from which the original impulse came. The effect of 'completing the triangle' on economics might suggest that Williamson's particular form of trans-

* This paper represents a response to the debate about the relative usefulness of power-based and efficiency-based models of organisations at the European Group on Organisational Studies Conference on 'Markets and Hierarchies' held at Imperial College, London in January 1980. I would like to thank Willy Brown, Sandra Dawson and Arthur Francis for comments on earlier versions of this paper.

actional analysis may be less penetrating than he supposed; or that the idea of 'economic man', and mainstream economics in general, may have more limited possibilities in extending the realm of economics; or that there may be reasons to doubt some of mainstream economics' central tenets. This paper is addressed mainly at the second issue, at the conceptual level. Empirical evidence is of course crucial in deciding the importance of Williamson's particular contribution, and some papers in this volume seek to provide such evidence. However, within organisational studies, insufficient empirical work has been carried out to enable a balanced judgement to be reached at this stage. In addition, there are considerable methodological difficulties in deciding how to assess a position which relies so openly on its originator's presentations on ecological survival tests and a Friedmanite positivism. The third issue, which lies behind some of the previous papers, particularly that of Bauer and Cohen (Chapter 4 of this volume) stems primarily from a through-going and largely independent critique of both economics *and* mainstream sociology which cannot with justice be dealt with in a paper of this length.

This concluding paper, then, seeks to summarise some of the issues debated in previous papers by 'completing the triangle' and examining the opposition between economic and sociological ideas in the form which suggests that economists are most interested in efficiency, while sociologists concentrate on relations of power. Although framed in this way, the opposition at once stimulates all kinds of moral and emotional responses, and will polarise even those who have never heard of Pareto or Machiavelli, there are some fairly uncontroversial elements of the debate. For example, some of the differences in the conclusions of economics and sociology reflect a distinction between the theory of the firm and the theory of bureaucracy: in practice economists are too readily assumed that all productive institutions are located in a broadly competitive environment, and sociologists have sometimes thrown together the results of investigations into 'profit-making', and 'non-profit-making' institutions.[1] Even so, different people have chosen to look at essentially similar problems in very different ways and with very different empirical techniques, and the traditions of established academic professions have inevitably been a polarising influence.

Economic and Sociological Themes

The distinctive theme of the economist is his concern with efficiency. In this, Williamson is a faithful representative of the economic tradition. The corresponding hallmark of the sociological interest in organisational theory has been identified by Williamson, and he is certainly not alone in this, as the use of 'power' as the principle explanatory concept. The meaning of 'power', and the role which various forms of power play in organisational design and operation have been two of the more lively issues of debate. For example, Peter Abell has written:

A strongly rooted tradition in the sociological theory of organisations (particularly the theory of Bureaucracy) insists that the distribution of tasks within an organisation (including decision-making) is ultimately determined by top management and its various aids. So the power of management – including the power to delegate responsibilities – is largely taken for granted. . . . There has, of course, been a counter-tradition emphasising intra-organisational conflict and the problems of handling non-routine situations. (Abell 1975, p. 1).

In other words, one aspect of the debate within sociology is between those who see power as a relatively unilateral dimension of organisations and those who stress that the sources of power are diverse and contribute to collective decisions in a very complex way. Going beyond this, other more radical writers have disputed the assumption of legitimated rational–legal authority made by those in the tradition of the theory of bureaucracy (Francis, Chapter 5 of this volume).

It is very easy to assume that there is no conflict between the activities of the sociologist and the economist in organisational analysis. But it may not be true. Williamson himself takes up a very clear position:

The neglect of power by the M & H is not to suggest that power is either uninteresting or unimportant. We submit however, that power considerations will usually give way to efficiency – at least in profit-making enterprises, if observations are taken at sufficiently long intervals, say a decade . . . our position is that those parts of the enterprise that are most critical to organisational viability will be *assigned* possession of control over critical resources, will *have* preferential access to information, and will be *dealing* with critical organisational uncertainties. . . . Failure to assign control to that part of the organisation would contradict the efficiency hypothesis but would presumably be explained as a power outcome. (Williamson and Ouchi, Chapter 1 of this volume).

Williamson is therefore arguing that efficiency is a more important idea than power in explaining organisational structure. He also believes that it is methodologically more expeditious:

Inasmuch as power is very vague and has resisted successive efforts to make it operational, whereas efficiency is much more clearly specified and the plausibility of an efficiency hypothesis is buttressed by ecological survival tests, we urge that efficiency analysis be made the centrepiece of the study of organisational design . . . power explains results when the organisation sacrifices efficiency to serve special interests. (Williamson and Ouchi, Chapter 1 of this volume).

Is Williamson justified in these two claims? Or is operationality achieved only in return for explanatory vacuity? And the apparent dominance of efficiency over power only the result of an unsubtle simplification of the two ideas?

Efficiency as an Undercontested Concept

Neither power nor efficiency is a simple concept. The complexity and elusiveness of power is always recognised. Gallie has referred to power as an 'essentially contested concept' (Gallie, quoted in Lukes 1974, p. 9). And although it may be true, as Giddens has argued (Giddens 1979, pp. 89–91), that there are very few concepts that are not, it is certainly difficult, if not impossible, to pin down an essence of power which pervades all reasonable uses of the term. The three strata of power unearthed by Steven Lukes, though perhaps not an uncontestably definitive interpretation, show how difficult it is to make a simple opposition of 'power' to anything else at all (Lukes 1974). The first, and most transparent, dimension of power which Lukes describes involves 'a successful attempt by A to get B to do something he would not otherwise do' in cases where there is actual and observable conflict of subjective interests in decision-making. In the 'two-dimensional' view of power, allowance is made

for consideration of the ways in which *decisions* are prevented from being taken on *potential issues* over which there is an observable *conflict* of (subjective) *interests* (Lukes 1974, p. 20).

The fully 'three-dimensional' view of power, which Lukes advocates, extends the notion away from a narrow 'behavioural' focus on actual decisions to include the latent conflict which

consists in the contradiction of interests of those exercising power and the *real interests* of those they exclude (Lukes 1974, p. 24–5).

In this last conception, power becomes more nearly a structural property, although the incorporation of 'real interests' is in itself ambiguous about the nature of those interests. The relationship between structure and voluntary action is presently the subject of a good deal of controversy in social theory, although perhaps most of the protagonists would accept that power is a property of human agency. These debates have not generally involved or captured the imagination of economists. But in the present debate about the explanation of organisational structure they are of considerable relevance. Arguments of the kind advanced by Williamson take very strong positions on the relative importance of the structural determinants of organisational form.

It is perhaps not too far-fetched to describe efficiency as an 'under-contested concept'. Efficiency too is multi-dimensional. In a general sense, efficiency involves the maximisation of the ratio of outputs to inputs. The ideas of technical and allocative efficiency based on the Pareto criterion have in recent years been supplemented by more sophisticated aspects of efficiency. For example, Harvey Leibenstein, in his investigation into 'X-efficiency', has examined the way motivational inefficiency may arise because the relationship between inputs and outputs is not a determinate one: there is more to 'technical efficiency' or the achievement of the transformation frontier than a simple cause and effect relationship between input magnitudes and output magnitudes (Leibenstein 1976). Both allocative efficiency and X-efficiency are static concepts. Efficiency relates to a fixed amount of resources and fixed preferences. Recent work in the 'Austrian' tradition has turned attention to the way in which individuals 'make' the world and respond to changes in the economic environment that surrounds them (Kirzner 1973; Rizzo 1979). The essential ingredient for the analysis of dynamic efficiency is an ability to deal with uncertainty in the Knightian sense (that is in contrast to calculable risk). It is by no means certain that an organisation that is optimally adjusted to its current environment will be the one which is most able to respond to changes in that environment, and a number of trade-offs may be involved: Klein describes the trade-offs between progress and specialisation; between efficiency and durability; and between dynamic efficiency and excess capacity (Klein 1977, Chapter 3). But there is not only efficiency in response to environmental change, but also efficiency in moulding the environment to serve the purposes of the organisation. Not only may environment and behaviour change, but structure may also be a variable. The ability of an organisation to adapt its structure to changing circumstances has been labelled 'adaptive efficiency' by Marris and Mueller in a recent review article (Marris and Mueller 1980). Lastly, McGuinness distinguishes between 'material' and 'psychic' efficiency, depending on whether or not there is efficiency in the allocation of non-monetary advantages and disadvantages (McGuinness, Chapter 9 of this volume).

These various pairs of dichotomies are not all mutually exclusive, and they all add valuable points of complexity to the idea of efficiency, even when that term is interpreted in a narrowly economic way. What kind of efficiency is Williamson concerned with? Or, more correctly, what kind of efficiency is implicit in his analysis, since it may be that he has taken a less comprehensive view than other aspects of his argument require? Williamson is first and foremost concerned with real cost minimisation, and therefore with attainment of positions on the transformation frontier. In the long run, competition will ensure that this is the case. Therefore, it is adaptation of the structure to a static environment which is stressed: if the environment is constantly varying, then the Williamson method of testing his theory is impossible. In principle, then, Williamson's conception of efficiency is inclusive of all forms of material static efficiency. In the first place, the claimed advantage over power analysis is lessened: most of the elements of psychic efficiency are intrinsically subjective, and not 'operational'. If the further assumption of perfect competition in factor markets is made so that it can be assumed that psychic costs and benefits can be taken as being reflected in factor rewards, then the explanatory power of the approach is weakened, since the attainment of psychic efficiency is tautological, given material efficiency. Once the concept of efficiency is elaborated, the methodological simplicity of Williamson's approach is considerably diminished. And in particular the extent to which it relies on the selective properties of competition in factor and product markets is highlighted. Here there is always the danger of circularity: if it is competition which defines the qualities of efficient organisations, then we cannot argue that competition is or is not effective in taking into account subjective costs. In fact, the elements of psychic efficiency are 'culturally determined' in a way which consumes much societal energy, and are the object of much governmental influence. There is a natural tendency to wish to extend the idea of efficiency into this area, so that we may be able to say something about the effectiveness of cultural characteristics and governments in attaining 'higher ends' by this means.[2]

Both power *and* efficiency are complex multi-dimensional concepts. The operationality criterion is not simple, unless we restrict the idea of efficiency to one which is not satisfactory even to many economists. The alleged dominance of economic theories of structure is by the same token in doubt, and it may be interesting to look in more detail at the relative positions of the efficiency-based economic and power-based sociological contributions to organisational theory.

The Relationship between Power and Efficiency
There is a sense in which power is more conspicuous than efficiency in firms and other organisations. The order to close a factory, whether for 'good reason' or not, contrasts to the many small decisions that lead a firm to attain a position on the boundary of its feasible production set. In addition, the exercise of power, at least in the commonplace usage of the phrase, implies an element of voluntariness – the decision-maker could have done otherwise. In the Williamson model, on the other hand, in the long term the individual firm, and the head of that firm are closely, at the limit completely, constrained by the parametric behaviour of others: the Williamson model aims at complete structural determination of long-term outcomes, and any content of 'power' must be largely a structural form of power.[3] As in any general equilibrium economic model, the tendency is for economic power to be fully dif-

fused, and in fact this is a definitional requirement for the kind of perfectly competitive market in which all Williamsonian firms find themselves to be operating in the long term. The power of each actor depends on his or her resources, and these are distributed so widely that none holds any quantity sufficient to affect the final outcome by his or herself. The economy as a whole decides what is a valuable resource, in relation to the technical requirements of production and the preferences of individuals. The amount of effective resources the individual holds initially is largely a matter of social luck, and the use he makes of them the outcome of his own judgement. This is the extent of his or her personal power: it is power only over nature or the infinitely resilient economic environment.

There is, of course, another element to this story: it is necessary to determine what represents acceptable competition – the nature of the process by which efficiency is obtained. This will affect the final distribution of outcomes (the meek will inherit the earth only when aggression is outlawed, or atrophies). Power can clearly be exercised in determining the rules for the measurement of efficiency.[4] But at what level are these rules so determined? Williamson, and *a fortiori* such writers as North and Thomas who seek to explain institutional changes during economic growth, are concerned to drive back this frontier by seeing rules as determined by efficiency considerations and not imposed exogenously (North and Thomas 1973). However, explanations of this kind cannot be the final answer (as Field has argued) and it is certainly feasible that a power analysis of these 'rules of competition' could be illuminating, even if their operation, once they were decided upon, were perfectly 'automatic' (Field 1979).

It is deeply embedded in the traditional economic view of the world that, except in a few well-defined cases, the problem of power is a problem of the relationship between individual action and structural constraints. In any economic model which is predicated to a significant degree on some kind of competition mechanism, the power of any individual over any other tends to insignificance. In the Williamson model, the constraints determining outcomes are traditionally economic and external constraints, given the model of man which he employs. It is not surprising, therefore, that he is uninterested in power in terms of individuals and groups, and only interested in the diffused yet collective 'power of efficiency'. This mode of thought is taken as read by many economists. In many ways it is similar to that taken by the extreme structuralist sociologist or social theorist, though it is not as thorough-going – to an Althusserian the individual is close to a cypher, at least to the economist he has preferences that are honourably his own.

The relationship between action and structure provides us with one clue to the differences in 'flavour' between the approaches of the economist and the sociologist to organisations. We shall take up below the fact that the constraints which are operative may be more numerous than those typically included by the economist or sociologist alone. Lukes has a nice example of the complexity of the issues:

Compare the case of an employer who declares some of his workers redundant, in pursuance of a strategy to cut his costs, with that of an official government liquidator who declares an insolvent company bankrupt, thereby throwing its workers out of work. The first case is a simple case of power exercise on almost any definition; the second is not, just because we assume that the liquidator has no alternative (as liquidator – we may argue otherwise if we separate the man from his role). (Lukes 1977, p. 7).

The first case may seem an obvious case of power to the sociologist, but is it so to the economist? For the economist, any such categorical assertion would certainly have to be prefaced by an analysis of the competitiveness of the markets in which the firm operates.

A second general difference between the lay conceptions of power and efficiency which carries over confusingly into some of the academic discussions between sociologists and economists (and here perhaps the economists are the more guilty of misconception) is the balance between the explanatory and normative aspects of the two ideas. After all, power corrupts, but efficiency improves the balance of payments. Cost reduction has a very strong deterministic explanatory ability in a traditionally constructed economic system, whereas power is not so clearly determining because it has an element of potentiality – it is dangerously versatile. Efficiency is only versatile when a firm has market power, an inferior state of affairs to perfect competition in welfare economics. It is no coincidence that in the sort of economics where the nature of competition is not seen to be static, but is a process of dynamic research for quasi-rents and temporary economic power (such as the Austrian economics of Kirzner), the concept of efficiency is less well-defined and the certainties of normal welfare economics dissolve, usually into a kind of conservative pragmatism (Kirzner 1973, Chapter 6).

This initial, very impressionistic, comparison between power and efficiency does seem to suggest that power is the more *general* concept: efficiency is more likely to be a special case of power than power a special case of, or dominated by, efficiency. Power is wider in its scope; the sources of power are much broader than the sources of efficiency. Efficiency itself needs interpretation in the light of its 'power content', and this may be less neutral, and more deeply buried in the rules for measuring efficiency, than it seems to be at first sight. *This* may seem obvious to the sociologist, but is it so to the economist?

The Role of Economic Power

The tentative inclusion of efficiency within a broad conception of power immediately raises the question about whether the debate can be settled by a recourse to the idea of *economic power*. The notion of economic power is only slightly less complex than that of power in general. In the light of our previous discussion of power, we would expect that we may be able to describe alternative conceptions of economic power which either imply voluntary action by an individual (or a group) on the basis of 'subjective interests' or which interpret power in a more structurally orientated way, including some idea of 'real interests'.

The normal characterisation of economic power involves the existence of market imperfections, which enable sellers, or less often purchasers, to obtain more than merely the relevant marginal valuation. In this sense, and in the context of standard welfare economics, the very existence of economic power leads *prima facie* to an undesirable outcome for the economy as a whole.[5] Economic power lies fundamentally in the ability to withhold what others want, and the economic model of man supplies actors with an incentive to do so. This form of economic power may be traded off against non-economic goals or the exercise of non-economic power. A worker may accept a lower wage for the job in exchange for greater control over the production process; or an industrialist may use profits made in his business to finance political activity. It is for this reason, at least primarily, that economic power is sometimes seen by economists as the most fundamental source of power, perhaps even a necessary condition for the exercise of other forms of power. Complementary to the notion of 'monopoly power' is the 'power of competition'. The competitive firm, that is the real cost minimising organisation, will in the long run survive as the typical market participant. The power of competition may be actual or potential, as when monopolists charge entry-deterring prices. In equilibrium, the power of competition is the 'potential' power of all against one, and is by that token de-personalised; out of equilibrium, producers are motivated by the possibility of quasi-rents, and the power of competition is manifested in *temporary* monopoly power.

In equilibrium, rewards will not generally be equally distributed. The amounts of resources available to each participant in a generally competitive economy will vary, what constitutes a valuable resource being defined by the overall abilities and preferences of the community (so that the *ab initio* equalisation of resource endowments would not be logically possible unless the final state of the economy arising from the alternative distributions were also known *ab initio*). If power is seen as arising from such unequal resources and rewards (and this may be especially plausible when it is possible to trade off economic r-

against other, more direct, forms of power), *even if* those rewards
are obtained in perfectly competitive markets, then power is highly
unlikely to be diffused completely in an economy which aims for and
achieves efficiency. Such power derives from decisions of individual
insignificance, but does not itself have that property.

A particularly interesting case of the existence of economic power in
the monopolistic sense is, in fact, one of the theoretical underpinnings
of Williamson's analysis of organisational efficiency. The transaction
costs which Williamson is able to identify as important in determining
the character of the employment relation arise from the existence of
specific skills in the labour market, and from sources of information
which are monopolised by workers and management. In these circumstances, there is a multitude of cases of bilateral monopoly, the simplest
being where the employer and the worker have jointly invested in the
acquisition of a skill which is only of use in the particular firm where it
was acquired, and therefore both have an interest in maintaining the
relationship. In cases of bilateral monopoly, both sides of the relationship have some degree of power over the other: Williamson describes
such relationships as 'idiosyncratic' because the identities of the people
involved really do matter. The extension of the assumption of economic
man to that of opportunistic economic man then does become necessary
to ensure that his model is fully determining.

Nevertheless, we do still have the possibility of different tastes for
work habits and organisational forms, so that while the existence of an
organisational form that will allow the development and 'governance' of
such idiosyncratic relationships is dictated by efficiency considerations
reinforced by selective competition, the form which that organisation
takes is not fully determined. As long as the money costs of producing
its real output are minimised, it is possible that workers may accept a
lower wage in return for less onerous supervision, and more
importantly that they may trade some of their monopoly rents for such
an outcome. At a given wage, work patterns and work organisations
may be different in two organisations, depending firstly on the
preferences of the two sets of workers and managements, and secondly,
on the abilities of both pairs of participants to divert rents in their
directions: comparisons may be made, but there is no direct competitive mechanism to enforce those comparisons within the 'rent
band'. All organisations in a Williamson world are agglomerations of
small but not insignificant power sources. Economic power does, therefore, 'allow' one to take the view, as Abell docs, that:

organisations are . . . complex mechanisms for arriving at '*collective decisions* '
through bargaining and influence processes amongst a set of power and influence holding units. (Abell 1975, p. 1).

This kind of organisational sociology at least is feasible in a world of complex economic relationships.

Economic Autonomy and the Role of Economic Power

As Williamson recognises in admitting his concept of atmosphere, his system is not completely determining, without some very strong assumptions about the 'psychology' of workers and managers. Although an individual has a degree of 'economic autonomy' in a Williamsonian organisation, that autonomy may be closed out to the extent that rules and norms determine his use of that latitude. One is reminded of James Duesenbery's caricatures:

Economics is all about how people make choices. Sociology is about why people don't have any choices to make. (Duesenbery 1960, quoted in Heath 1976, p. 3).

Rules and norms not only help to determine the outcomes of internal choices in the realm of organisational structure, but also affect the nature of competitive processes. The content of the process of compétition has been unreasonably neglected in welfare economics. The distribution of goods and services is no longer determined by a shoot-out at noon. There are good traditional economic reasons for this, in that it is a method of distribution that is wasteful of real resources (in the long-run, economies which choose to distribute goods by means of the market mechanism would survive those which chose more self-destructive methods – as perhaps they have done) but clearly there are also social and moral norms which constrain the competitive process in ways that *need* not be narrowly utilitarian. In this way the province of sociology surrounds the domain of economics as well as occupying the interstices in structures whose determination is in general terms 'economic'. In such aspects, the orientations of economics and sociology are clearly complementary, although in specific instances they may be competing explanations.

There are, then, two main kinds of economic power. One is derived from the system characteristics, and the other from the way in which particular elements of the system can separate themselves from the system. Within this second class, it is possible to distinguish ideal types of power-ridden economy: in the 'monopoly capitalist' variety, power is polarised on a small number of individuals in a small number of organisations, who make decisions which may be to the disadvantage of some members of, or all, the rest of the economy; in the 'efficient organisational' variety, many individuals will have a small amount of economic power, but the actions of these organisations will be pretty closely constrained by general competitiveness of markets (individual power would arise from individual, not organisational, circumstances). Williamson is of the second persuasion.

How far can this idea of power as 'bargaining power', which becomes in the limit 'competitive power', take us? It does not seem to exhaust all that the organisational sociologist has in mind. Nor is the extension of economic power to include the potential realm of action provided by the mere possession of economic resources a sufficient modification. At least one other ingredient, the Weberian conception of authority, is required, as Francis argues (Francis, Chapter 5 of this volume). One 'economic' way of incorporating this into organisational analysis is to relax the assumption that preferences are independent of organisational form, and additionally that actions are directly valued by the actor in the way that goods are valued by the consumer: this latter modification is a first move away from the consequentialism which pervades almost all work in welfare economics. There has, however, been almost no economic work along these lines: it seems pretty clear, on the other hand, that its elaboration would provide further ways in which economic and sociological analysis can be made complementary (from an econo-centric point of view, how more 'space' can be made for sociological explanations in organisational studies). This is one clear way in which the sociological critique of Williamson organisation theory can provide useful clues to fruitful progress in the economic theory of institutions.

The question as to whether organisations with different structures will have different corresponding economic characteristics (such as different distributions of earnings or different total wage bills) remains an open one. There are certainly a number of sources of diversity. Features of organisational form that are especially highly regarded by workers or managers may be traded off against wages if they have efficiency implications, especially if factor markets are competitive: or there may be different degrees of rent extraction by either party; or different norms of action within 'Williamsonian spaces' may apply in different industrial circumstances; or there may simply be differences in product or factor market structure. A great degree of variety is possible under all sources of economic power, and its existence is not sufficient by itself to confirm any particular relationship between economic power and organisational structure.

Conflicts between Economic and Sociological Approaches

Thus far it seems reasonable to conclude that the notion of power which the sociologists bring to the study of organisations is not equivalent to, nor wholly dependent upon, either the standard or an extended version of 'economic power'. Here is another sense, therefore, in which the two disciplines can be complementary rather than competitive. But there are certain issues on which the two approaches do represent genuinely contradictory explanations, especially in areas where economics is seeking to extend its traditional domain.

We have seen that one way in which power may be incorporated into efficiency analysis is by recognising that elements of monopoly may enable performances to be modified. Abell puts it thus:

Gone are the days when we can uncritically accept a set of preferences and search for the most appropriate allocation of resources to maximise their satisfaction. Is it too much to hope that, with theories (and this with adequate conceptualisation) of the generation of preferences that we might reasonably hope to see a 'rapprochement' between economic and social theory? (Abell 1975, p. 7).

This view of the relative roles of economics and sociology sees them then as having distinct provinces which may be separately developed and then brought together to complete any particular examination of an actual distribution of economic goods and services. This project could never, in my view, suffice as a final reconciliation of economics and sociology for a number of reasons. To start with, the idea of preferences is too narrow to encompass all the possible contributions of the sociological mode of thought. In economics, preferences are typically thought of as relating to the distribution of consequences of events and actions rather than anything in the nature of those actions and events themselves. To incorporate as expansion of preferences would be possible up to a point: one could, for example, plug such valuations into a utility function, though, as the arguments of Sen and Georgescu-Roegen have demonstrated, this is unlikely fully to capture the intention of such an extension (Sen 1979; Georgescu-Roegen 1971, pp. 344–5). It is quite certain, also, that a true sociological account of preferences would require them to be interdependent both intertemporally and interpersonally. These issues have been discussed in an illuminating way by John Elster: there is a great deal of scope for joint enterprise between economists and sociologists in this area, but the technical problems of incorporating complex preferences into the corpus of standard general equilibrium and welfare economics are formidable. For the present argument, the important point is that there is a distinctively economic way of forming preferences, so that they may satisfy all the traditional conditions of economic rationality. A typical economic treatment of preferences, according to Elster, would suggest that

consistency requirements should be imposed both upon the actor's *choice of successions* and upon his succession of *choices*. Non-fulfilment of the first requirement is exemplified by inconsistent time preferences, of the second by endogenous changes of preference. (Elster 1979, p. 66).

But this is not the only way of generating preferences. It is not implausible that typical differences between economists and sociologists should concern their approaches to the formation of preferences.[6] And one way in which these differences arise is as a result of their different conceptions of rationality.

Economics is traditionally associated with the notion of rationality in terms of the achievement of predetermined goals. Economic rationality is nearly always instrumental rationality. Economic man, the model of man associated with that concept of rationality, is selfish, parsimonious and utility-maximising: he makes choices in line with this concept of rationality. There is less agreement about the nature of sociological man, but one common conception sees him as a social individual constrained by the norms and expectations of the role which he occupies in the system as a whole. His existence is therefore intrinsically normative. The sociologist may study the norms to which he or she implicitly or explicitly subscribes without making any normative judgements. As a rule, the economist is not especially interested in the basis of those judgements unless they are made as decisions of economic or social policy: under normal circumstances, they have no implications intermediate between their personal import to the particular actor concerned and their contribution to aggregate social valuation.

Economic rationality, therefore, is a matter of the efficient achievement of ends, regardless of what those ends are. But, as Martin Hollis has cogently argued, there is an obfuscation here. How is it that economic man is interested only in means in the economic realm? More specifically, why is it rational for him to *maximise* utility or anything else? The answer which Hollis provides is:

These assumptions [about the rationality of ends] did not obtrude . . . because they were dressed up as assumptions about human nature. It is the idea of rational economic man, the selfish maximiser, which underpins the instrumental rationaliser, and without that model of man this concept of rationality cannot easily be sustained. (Hollis 1979, p. 8).

Similarly an idea of sociological man as a role fulfiller might underpin the rationality (or irrationality *in economic terms*) of sociology. These arguments are intended only to be illustrative, to indicate the way in which fundamental differences in notions of rationality may underlie commonplace disputes.

Why do these concerns arise particularly in the study of firms and other economic organisations? The answer appears to lie principally in the complexity of these institutions. We have seen how the Williamsonian analysis is not economically determining, because of the multiplicity of 'spaces' provided by the existence of micro-monopolies even in the efficient firm. The importance of normative issues is thereby enhanced, and the true scope of economic imperialism reduced. It may be that the use which is made of these 'spaces' is governed by economic rationality and efficiency objectives, but it may not be. Interpersonal behaviour becomes important. There is no longer the possibility of always regarding the behaviour of others as parametric. We are inevitably drawn into both the rationality of games, and the rationality of aims. In these two ways the simplicity of the traditional economic rationality is exposed as inadequate, and processes, whether economic or social, become derivative, including the competition which enforces 'efficiency'.

It now becomes a matter of common interest as to which aspects of the organisation are determined by 'economic' and which by 'social' processes. When will competition be 'red in tooth and claw' as in the Williamsonian analysis? When will the rules of competition be determined by implicit agreements based on the rationality of economic man, as in North and Thomas's explanation of the evolution of economic institutions? It now seems rather improbable that the imperialism of economics can be put down merely to the inevitable process of ecology. The analogy hardly survives the need for them consciously to be acceptable to society as a whole: the evolutionary approach to ethics, periodically revived since the days of Huxley, cannot be sustained by any *simple* economic imperatives.[7] The possibility of a 'natural rationality' of course remains, but has hardly yet been demonstrated.

Concluding Comments

Is there a sense in which we can regard the economics of Williamson and the mainstream sociological analysis of institutions as completely compatible? In positive terms, as explanations of the structure of, and behaviour in, economic institutions the answer is probably 'no'. That is certainly true if we accept the tenet that there is only one descriptive truth, and that its elements must be compatible.

It is of course always possible to construct economics and sociology in ways that make them completely or largely incompatible. This paper has looked at characteristics of economics and sociology which do not appear, at least on the surface, to be fundamentally contradictory, and has examined two possible compromise treatments of the relationship between power and efficiency in organisation theory; the interpretation of power in economic terms; and the case where sociology deals with the formation of preferences, whereas economics deals with instrumental rationality on the basis of those preferences. Neither view seems to be completely acceptable. One possible alternative is that, for those areas of the investigation which are intended to be explanatory of the facts of the world, economics and sociology have competing domains of explanation based on dispute as to which assumption should be made about human behaviour for any particular problem. The issue of rationality is one deciding criterion. The 'completion of the triangle', therefore, indicates that economics in the Becker or Williamson traditions is inevitably a more restricted study than sociology: and that is why it is able to obtain the more impressive predictive results. But it is also why unrestrained economic imperialism should be resisted.

The Markets and Hierarchies approach begins with theoretical work derived not only from a reconsideration of the work of Commons but also in part from mainstream economics. It considers it in what is probably its correct domain. From this point, the approach branches out to make far-reaching claims for the limited rationality of economics. In doing so it extends beyond the area in which such assumptions prove useful and accurate characterisations of human behaviour. Economics must be prepared, in so far as it hopes to understand institutions in some holistic sense, to examine the bases and limits to efficiency more closely.[8] It can be argued that it is this endeavour that Williamson sets out upon in his recognition and elaboration of the notion of atmosphere (Williamson 1975, pp. 37–9). But an unmodified *'economics'* of atmosphere can never hope to close out the study of organisations while man continues to aspire to a more complete expression of rationality.

Notes

1. Some of the work of the Aston School betrays this confusion, but sociologists of organisations are now aware of the importance of this distinction, see Zald (1969) for example.
2. Major controversies over the meaning of 'economic development' and the role of work in welfare economics indicate that we do not always give 'psychic efficiency' full value.
3. In the absence of innovation, that is – otherwise this will merely be a tendency.
4. In unpublished work, Batstone has emphasised the importance of accounting concepts.
5. Though of course there are areas – such as the protection of innovation by patents – where this may not be the case.
6. Becker (1976) has a rather sophisticated theory of preference formation on the basis of underlying cross-cultural constants.
7. However, see Becker (1976) and Aldrich (1979) for economic and sociological defences of such positions.
8. One possibility is that the work of John R. Commons, whom Williamson quotes as the original advocate of the importance of transactions costs, could be taken up more thoroughly. Commons and the other 'American institutionalists' still provide the impetus for a school of economics in the United States, but have been virtually ignored on this side of the Atlantic. Ironically, one of Commons's main contributions was to introduce sociological content into economics, although this has been rather eroded by Williamson's particular developments of the transactions costs idea.

References

Abell, P. (1975), 'The Role of Power in Organisational Theory: Discussion Issues', paper presented to *EGOS Conference*, Paris.

Alchian, A.A. and H. Demsetz (1972), 'Production, Information Costs, and Economic Organisation', *American Economic Review*, LXII, pp. 777–95.

Aldrich, H.E. (1979), *Organizations and Environments*, Englewood Cliffs, New Jersey: Prentice-Hall.

Aldrich, H.E. and J. Pfeffer (1976), 'Environments and Organizations', *Annual Review of Sociology*, no. 2, pp. 79–105.

Armour, H.O. and D.J. Teece (1978), 'Organization Structure and Economic Performance: A Test of the Multidivisional Hypothesis', *Bell Journal of Economics*, IX, pp. 106–22.

Arrow, K.J. (1951), *Social Choice and Individual Values*, New York: Wiley.

Arrow, K.J. (1969), 'The Organization of Economic Activity', *The Analysis and Evaluation of Public Expenditure: The PPB System*, Joint Economic Committee, 91st Congress, 1st Session, pp. 59–73.

Arrow, K.J. (1973), 'Political and Economic Evaluation of Social Effects and Externalities', in M.D. Intriligator (ed.), *Frontiers of Quantitative Economics*, Amsterdam: North-Holland Publishing.

Arrow, K.J. (1974), *The Limits of Organization*, New York: Norton.

Astley, W.G., R. Axelsson, R.J. Butler, D.J. Hickson and D.C. Wilson (1980), Processual Concepts and Dialectics of Strategic Decision Making. Working paper, Organizational Analysis Research Unit, University of Bradford Management Centre, Bradford, England.

Batstone, E., I. Boraston and S. Frenkel (1977), *Shop Stewards in Action*, Oxford: Blackwell.

Bauer, M. and E. Cohen (1981), *Qui Gouverne les Groupes Industurels; Essai sur l'Exercise du Pouvoir du et dans le Groupe Industurel*, Paris: Seurl.

Becker, G.S. (1964), *Human Capital*, New York: National Bureau of Economic Research.

Becker, G.S. (1976), *The Economic Approach to Human Behaviour*, Chicago: University of Chicago Press.

Berle, A.A. and G.C. Means (1932), *The Modern Corporation and Private Property*, New York: Commerce Clearing House.

Blackburn, R.M. and M. Mann (1979), *The Working Class in the Labour Market*, London: Macmillan.

Blau, P.M. (1967), *Exchange and Power in Social Life*, New York: Wiley.

Boulding, K.E. (1968), *The Organizational Revolution: A Study in the Ethics of Economic Organization*, Chicago: Quadrangle Paperback (first edition, 1953).

Braverman, H. (1974), *Labor and Monopoly Capitalism*, New York: Monthly Review Press.

Brown, W. (1973), *Piecework Bargaining*, London: Heinemann.

Buchanan, J.M. (1968), *The Demand and Supply of Public Goods*, Chicago: Rand MacNally.

Buchanan, R. and G. Tullock (1962), *The Calculus of Consent*, Ann Arbor: University of Michigan Press.

Bundeskartellamt (1977), Bericht des Bundeskartellamtes uber seine Tatigkeit im Jahre 1977 sowie uber Lage und Entwicklung auf seinem Aufgabengebeit (50 GWB), Bundesrucksache 8/7041.

Bundeskartellamt (1979), Bericht des Bundeskartellamtes uber seine Tatigkeit im Jahre

206 Power, Efficiency and Institutions

1979 sowie uber Lage und Entwicklung auf seinem Aufgabengebeit (50 GWB), Bundesrucksache 8/2980.

Burton, R. and B. Obel (1980), 'Analysis of the M-Form Hypothesis for Contracting Technologies', *Administrative Science Quarterly*, xxx, 25, pp. 457–466.

Bythell, D. (1969), *The Handloom Weavers*, Cambridge: Cambridge University Press.

Campbell, R.W. (1978), 'New Concepts in the Study of Economic Systems', unpublished.

Carman, J.M. (1979), 'Paradigms for Marketing Theory', in *Research in Marketing*, Greenwich, Conn.: J.A.I. Press.

Castleman, B. (1978), 'How We Export Dangerous Industries', *Business and Society Review*, XXVII, pp. 7–14.

Chamberlain, E.H. (1953), *The Theory of Monopolistic Competition*, Cambridge, Mass.: Harvard University Press.

Chandler, A.D. Jr (1962), *Strategy and Structure*, Cambridge, Mass.: MIT Press.

Chandler, A.D. Jr (1977), *The Visible Hand: The Managerial Revolution in American Business*, Cambridge, Mass.: The Belknap Press of Harvard University Press.

Chandler, A.D. Jr and Herman Daems (1980), *Managerial Hierarchies*, Cambridge, Mass.: Harvard University Press.

Child, J. (1972), 'Organisation Structure, Environment and Performance: the Role of Strategic Choice', *Sociology*, 6, pp. 1–22.

Coase, R.H. (1952), 'The Nature of the Firm', *Economica N.S.*, IV, pp. 386–405, reprinted in G.J. Stigler and K.E. Boulding (eds.), 1952, *Readings in Price Theory*, Homewood, Ill.: R.D. Irwin Inc.

Coase, R.H. (1972), 'Industrial Organisation: A Proposal for Research', in V.R. Fuchs (ed.), *Policy Issues and Research Opportunities in Industrial Organisation*, New York: National Bureau of Economic Research.

Commons, J.R. (1934), *Institutional Economics*, Madison: University of Wisconsin Press.

Commons, J.R. (1950), *The Economics of Collective Action*, Madison: University of Wisconsin Press.

Crosland, C.A.R. (1959), *The Future of Socialism*, London: Jonathan Cape.

Crozier, M. (1978), *L'Acteur et le Système*. Paris: Le Seuil.

Cyert, R.M. and J.G. March (1963), *A Behavioral Theory of the Firm*, Englewood Cliffs, New Jersey: Prentice Hall.

Daems, H. (1978), *The Holding Company and Corporate Control*, Boston: Leiden.

Daems, H. (1980), 'The Rise of the Modern Industrial Enterprise: A New Perspective', in Chandler and Daems (1980, pp. 203–23).

Davis, L.E. and D.C. North (1971), *Institutional Change and American Economic Growth*, Cambridge: Cambridge University Press.

de Berris, G. and M. Bye (1977), *Relations Economiques Internationales*, Paris: Edition Dalloz.

Demsetz, H. (1968), 'The Cost of Transacting', *Quarterly Journal of Economics*, LXXXII, pp. 33–53.

Demsetz, H. (1973), 'Industry Structure, Market Rivalry and Public Policy', *Journal of Law and Economics*, XVI, pp. 1–9.

Deutsches Institut für Wirtschaftsforschung (DIW) (1975), *Input-Output-rechnung fur die BRD 1972*, Beitrage zur Strukturforschung, Heft 38, bearb. V.R. Pischner, R. Staglin u. H.Wessels.

Dill, W.R. (1958), 'Environment as an Influence on Managerial Autonomy', *Administrative Science Quarterly*, II, pp. 409–43.

Doeringer, P. and M. Piore (1971), *Internal Labor Markets and Manpower Analysis*, Lexington, Mass.: D.C. Heath.

Downs, A. (1957), *An Economic Theory of Democracy*, New York: Harper and Row.

Duesenbery, J. (1960), 'Comment' in *Demographic and Economic Change in Developed Countries*, Princeton: Princeton University Press.

Duncan, R.B. (1972), 'Characteristics of Organisational Environments and Perceived Environmental Uncertainty', *Administrative Science Quarterly*, XVII, pp. 313–27.

Durkheim, E. (1933), *The Division of Labor in Society*, New York: The Free Press.

The Economist (1976), 'The Coming Entrepreneurial Revolution: A Survey', 25 December, pp. 41–65.

Elster, J. (1979), *Ulysses and the Sirens*, Cambridge: Cambridge University Press.

Field, J.A. (1979), 'On the Explanation of Rules Using Rational Choice Models', *Journal of Economic Issues*, XIII, March, pp. 49–72.

Fitzroy, F.R. and D.C. Mueller (1977), 'Contract and the Economics of Organisation', Discussion Paper 77–25, Berlin: International Institute of Management.

Fox, A. (1974), *Beyond Contract: Work, Power and Trust Relations*, London: Faber and Faber.

Francis, A. (1980), 'Families, Firms and Finance Capital', *Sociology*, XIV, pp. 1–27.

Franko, L.G. (1972), 'The Growth, Organizational Efficiency of European Multinational Firms: Some Emerging Hypotheses', *Colloque International Aux C.N.R.S.*, 549, pp. 335–66.

Franko, L.G. (1976), *The European Multinationals*, New York: Harper and Row.

Freeman, C. (1974), *The Economics of Industrial Innovation*, Harmondsworth: Penguin Books.

Friedman, M. (1953), *Essays in Positive Economics*, Chicago: The University of Chicago Press.

Fröbel, Folker et al. (1977), *Die neue internationale Arbeitsteilung*, Hamburg: Rowohlt.

Galbraith, J. (1973), *Designing Complex Organizations*, Reading, Mass.: Addison-Wesley.

Galbraith, J.K. (1967), *The New Industrial State*, London: Hamish Hamilton.

Georgescu-Roegen (1971), *The Entropy Law and the Economic Process*, Cambridge, Mass.: Harvard University Press.

Giddens, A. (1976), *New Rules of Sociological Method*, London: Hutchinson.

Giddens, A. (1979), *Central Problems in Social Theory*, London and Basingstoke: Macmillan.

Gintis, H. (1972), 'A Radical Analysis of Welfare Economics and Individual Development', *Quarterly Journal of Economics*, LXXXV, pp. 572–99.

Gordon, D.M. (1976), 'Capitalist Efficiency and Socialist Efficiency', *The Labor Process and the Working Class*, pp. 19–39, New York: Monthly Review Press.

Gospel, H. (1977), *The Development of Management Organization in Indstrial Relations – An Historical Perspective?*, Canterbury: University of Kent, unpublished manuscript.

Hannan, M. and J. Freeman (1977), 'The Population Ecology of Organizations', *American Journal of Sociology*, LXXXII, pp. 929–64.

Hashimoto, M. and B.T. Yu (1980), 'Specific Capital, Employment Contracts and Wage Rigidity', *Bell Journal of Economics*, XI, pp. 536–49.

Hayek, F.A. (1959), *The Constitution of Liberty*, London: Routledge & Kegan Paul.

Heath, A. (1976), *Rational Choice and Social Exchange*, Cambridge: Cambridge University Press.

Herding, R. (1972), *Job Control and Union Structure*, Rotterdam: Rotterdam University Press.

Heuss, E. (1965), *Allgemeine Markttheorie*, Tubingen.

Hicks, J.R. (1935), 'Annual Survey of Economic Theory: The Role of Monopoly', *Econometrica*, III, pp. 1–20.

Hicks, J.R. (1976), 'Some Questions of Time in Economics', in A. Tang, F. Westfield and J. Worley (eds.), *Evolution, Welfare and Time in Economics*, Lexington, Mass.: D.C. Heath.

Hirschman, A. (1970), *Exit, Voice and Loyalty*, Cambridge, Mass.: Harvard University Press.

Hirschman, A. (1978), 'Exit, Voice, and the State', *World Politics*, XXXI, pp. 90–107.

Hollis, M. (1979), 'Rational Man and Social Science', in R. Harrison (ed.), *Rational Action*, Cambridge: Cambridge University Press, pp. 1–16.

Hyman, R. and I. Brough (1975), *Social Values and Industrial Relations*, Oxford: Blackwell.

Jay, A, (1973), *Corporation Man*, New York: Random House.

Karpik, L. (1972), 'Le Capitalisme Technologique', *Sociologie du Travail*, no. 1.

Kaufer, E. (1979), *Industrieokonomie*, Innsbruck, unpublished.

Khandwalla, P.N. (1972), *The Effect of the Environment on the Organizational Structure of Firms*, unpublished Ph.D. thesis, Carnegie-Mellon University.

Khandwalla, P.N. (1977), *Design of Organisations*, New York: Harcourt Brace Jovanovich.

Kirzner, I. (1973), *Competition and Entrepreneurship*, Chicago: University of Chicago Press.

Klein, B.F. (1977), *Dynamic Economics*, Cambridge, Mass.: Harvard University Press.

Korsch, Karl (1969), *Schriften zur Sozialisierung*, Cologne: EVA.

Landes, D. (1969), *The Unbound Prometheus*, Cambridge: Cambridge University Press.

Lawrence, D. and J. Lorsch (1967), *Organization and Environment*, Boston: Harvard University, Graduate School of Business Administration.

Leibenstein, H. (1976), *Beyond Economic Man*, Cambridge, Mass.: Harvard University Press.

Lindbeck, A. (1977), *The Political Economy of the New Left*, New York: Harper and Row (first edition 1971).

Lukes, S. (1974), *Power:A Radical View*, London: Macmillan.

Lukes, S. (1977), *Essays in Social Theory*, London: Macmillan.

Machlup, F. (1972), 'The Universal Bogey', in M. Peston and B. Corry (eds.), *Essays in Honour of Lord Robbins*, London: Weidenfeld and Nicolson.

Mackenzie, K.D. (1978), *Organizational Structures*, Arlington Heights, Ill.: AHM Publishing.

Macneil, I.R. (1974), 'The Many Futures of Contract', *Southern California Law Review*, XLVII, pp. 691–816.

Macneil, I.R. (1978), 'Contracts: Adjustment of Long-Term Economic Relations under Classical, Neoclassical, and Relational Contract Law', *Northwestern University Law Review*, LXXII, pp. 854–905.

Macpherson, C.B. (1973), *Democratic Theory: Essays in Retrieval*, Oxford: Oxford University Press.

Macpherson, C.B. (1977), *The Life and Times of Liberal Democracy*, Oxford: Oxford University Press.

Malmgren, H. (1961), 'Information, Expectations and the Theory of the Firm', *Quarterly Journal of Economics*, LXXV, pp. 399–421.

March, J.G. and J.P. Olsen (1976), *Ambiguity and Choice in Organizations*, Oslo: Universitiesforlaget.

March, J.G. and H.A. Simon (1958), *Organizations*, New York: Wiley.

Marcus, M. (1969), 'Profitability and Size of Firm', *Review of Economics and Statistics*, LI, pp. 104–7.

Marglin, S. (1975), 'What Do Bosses Do?', in A. Gorz (ed.), *The Division of Labour*, Hassocks: Harvester Press.

Marris, R. and D. Mueller (1980), 'The Corporation, Competition and the Invisible Hand', *Journal of Economic Literature*, XVIII, pp. 32–63.

Mauss, M. (1954), *The Gift: Forms and Functions of Exchange in Archaic Societies*, London: Cohen and West.

Meade, J.E. (1971), *The Controlled Economy*, London: George Allen & Unwin.

Mintzberg, H. (1973), *The Nature of Managerial Work*, New York: Harper and Row.

National Board for Prices and Incomes (NBPI) (1968), *Payment by Results*, Report no. 65, Cmnd 3627, and *Supplement*, Cmnd 3627–1, London: HMSO.

Nelson, D. (1975), *Management and Workers*, Madison: Wisconsin University Press.

Niskanen, W.A. (1973), *Bureaucracy: Servant or Master: Lessons from America*, London: Institute of Economic Affairs.

North, D.C. (1971), 'Structures and Performance: The Task of Economic History', *Journal of Economic Literature*, XVI, pp. 693–78.

North, D.C. and R. Thomas (1973), *The Rise of the Western World*, Cambridge: Cambridge University Press.

Novy, Klaus (1978), *Strategien der Sozialisierung: Die Diskussion der Wirtschaftsreform in der Weimarer Republik*, Frankfurt: Campus.

Oberender, P. (1973), *Industrielle Forschung und Entwicklung*, Stuttgart: Bern.

Office of Population Censuses and Surveys (OPCS) (1975), *Workplace Industrial Relations*, London: HMSO.

Olsen, M. (1968), *The Logic of Collective Action*, New York: Schocken Books.

Organization for Economic Co-operation and Development (OECD) (1979), *Facing the Future: Mastering the Probable and Managing the Unpredictable*, Paris: OECD.

Osborn, R.C. (1970), 'Concentration and the Profitability of Small Manufacturing Corporations', *Quarterly Review of Economics and Business*, LVI, pp. 15–26.

Ouchi, W.G. (1977), 'The Relationship between Organizational Structure and Organizational Control', *Administration Science Quarterly*, XXII, pp. 95–113.

Ouchi, W.G. (1978), 'The Transmission of Control Through Organizational Hierarchy', *Academy of Management Journal*, XXI, pp. 248–63.

Ouchi, W.G. (1979), 'A Conceptual Framework for the Design of Organizational Control Mechanisms', *Management Science*, XXV, pp. 833–48.

Ouchi, W.G. and A.H. Van de Ven (1980), 'Antitrust and Organizational Theory', in O.E. Williamson (ed.), *Antitrust Law and Economics*, Houston: Dame Publications.

Pfeffer, J. (1978), *Organizational Design*, Arlington Heights, Ill.: AHM Publishing.

Polanyi, K. (1957), *The Great Transformation*, Boston: Beacon Press.

Porter, M.G. (1976), *Interbrand Choice, Strategy and Bilateral Market Power*, London: Harvard University Press.

Porter, M.G. (1979), *Review of Economics and Statistics*, LXI, pp. 214–27.

Posner, R.A. (1969), 'Natural Monopoly and its Regulation', *Stanford Law Review*, XXI, pp. 548–643.

Posner, R.A. (1972), 'The Appropriate Scope of Regulation in the Cable Television Industry', *Bell Journal of Economics*, III, pp. 98–129.

Pugh, D. (1966), 'Modern Organization Theory: A Psychological and Sociological Study', *Psychological Bulletin*, October, pp. 235–51.

Pugh, D., D.J. Hickson, C.R. Hinings and C. Turner (1968), 'Dimensions of Organization Structure', *Administrative Science Quarterly*, XIII, pp. 67–90.

Richardson, G.B. (1972), 'The Organization of Industry', *The Economic Journal*, LXXXII (supplement), pp. 882–96.

Rizzo, M.J. (ed.) (1979), *Time, Uncertainty and Disequilibrium*, Lexington, Mass.: D.C. Heath.

Rose, M. (1978), *Industrial Behaviour*, Penguin.

Rumelt, R. (1974), *Strategy, Structure and Environment Performance*, Boston: Harvard University, Graduate School of Business Administration.

Sahlins, M. (1972), *Stone Age Economics*, London: Tavistock Publications.

Scherer, F.M. (1970), *Industrial Market Structure and Economic Performance*, Chicago: Rand McNally.

Scherer, F.M., A. Beckenstein, E. Kaufer and R. Murphy (1975), *The Economics of Multiplant Operation: an International Comparison Study*, Cambridge Mass.: Harvard University Press.

Schiffels, E. (1979), *Die personelle Verflechtung über den Aufsichtsrat – Eine empirische Studie in 15 ausgewahlten Wirtschaftszweigen in der BRD fur den Zeitraum 1961–1975*, Arbeitspapier Nr. 3 des Lehrstuhls für Allgemeine Betriebswirtschaftslehre I der Universität des Saarlandes, May.

Schiffels, E. (1980), *Die Zusammensetzung des Aufsichtsrates – Eine empirische Untersuchung anhand ausgewahlter Aktiengesellschaften des Verarbeitenden Gewerbes der BRD*, Dissertation 1, der Universität des Saarlandes, May.

Schumpeter, J.A. (1942), *Capitalism, Socialism and Democracy*, New York: Harper and Row.

Scott, B.R. (1970), 'Stages of Corporate Development', Harvard Business School, unpublished manuscript.

Sen, A. (1979), 'Utilitarianism and Welfarism', *Journal of Philosophy*, LXXVI, pp. 463–89.

Settle, R.F. (1976), 'Trade Effects of Occupational Health and Safety Standards', *Weltwirtschaftliches Archiv*, CXII, pp. 584–90.

Simon, H.A. (1957), *Administrative Behaviour: A Study of Decision Making Process in Administrative Organization*, New York: The Free Press.

Simon, H.A. (1962), 'The Architecture of Complexity', *Proceedings of the American Philosophical Society*, CVI, pp. 467–82.

Simon, H.A. (1978), 'Rationality and Process and Product of Thought', *American Economic Review*, LXVIII, pp. 1–16.

Smith, A. (1970), *The Wealth of Nations*, ed. by Andrew Skinner, Harmondsworth: Penguin Books (first edition 1776).

Staw, B.M. and E. Szwajkowski (1975), 'The Scarcity–Munificence Component of Organizational Environments and the Commission of Illegal Acts', *Administrative Science Quarterly*, XX, pp. 345–54.

Steer, P. and J. Cable (1978), 'Internal Organisation and Profit: An Empirical Analysis of Large UK Companies', *Journal of Industrial Economics*, XXVII, pp. 13–30.

Stigler, G.J. (1968), *The Organization of Industry*, Homewood, Ill.: R.D. Irwin.

Stiglitz, J.E. (1975), 'Incentives Risk and Information: Notes Towards a Theory of Hierarchy', *The Bell Journal of Economics*, VI, pp. 552–79.

Stonebraker, R.J. (1976), 'Corporate Profits and the Risks of Entry', *Review of Economics and Statistics*, February, LVIII, pp. 33–9.

Teece, D.J. (1979), 'Internal Organization and Economic Performance', Stanford, California, unpublished manuscript.

Thompson, J.D. (1967), *Organizations in Action*, New York: McGraw Hill.

Thonet, P.J. and O.H. Poensgen (1979), 'Managerial Control and Economic Performance in Western Germany', *Journal of Industrial Economics*, XXVIII, pp. 23–37.

Titmuss, R.M. (1970), *The Gift Relationship: From Human Blood to Social Policy*, Harmondsworth: Penguin Books.

Tonnies, F. (1957), *Gemeinschaft und Gesellschaft (Community and Society)*, translation by Charles P. Loomis, East Lansing: Michigan State University Press (first edition 1887).

Tuchfeldt, E. (1978), 'Kartelle', *Handwörterbuch der Wirtschaftswissenschaften*, Stuttgart, pp. 445–61.

United States Federal Trade Commission (1951), *Report of the Federal Trade Commission on Interlocking Directorates*, Washington: U.S. Government Printing Office.

Von Neumann J. and O. Morgenstern (1944), *The Theory of Games and Economic Behaviour*, Princeton: Princeton University Press.

Wachter, M. and O.E. Williamson (1978), 'Obligational Markets and the Mechanics of Inflation', *Bell Journal of Economics*, IX, pp. 549–71.

Weber, M. (1978), *Economy and Society*, Berkeley: University of California Press.

Weick, K.E. (1969), *The Social Psychology of Organizing*, Reading, Mass.: Addison-Wesley.

Weisbrod, B. (1979), 'Economics of Institutional Choice', unpublished manuscript.

Whymant, R. (1980), 'Workaholic Japanese Won't Take their Holidays', *The Guardian*, 13 August.

Williamson, O.E. (1964), *The Economics of Discretional Behaviour: Managerial Objectives in a Theory of the Firm*, Englewood Cliffs, New Jersey: Prentice Hall.

Williamson, O.E. (1965), 'A Dynamic Theory of Interfirm Behavior', *Quarterly Journal of Economics*, LXXIX, pp. 579–607.

Williamson, O.E. (1967), 'Hierarchical Control and Optimum Firm Size', *Journal of Political Economy*, LXXV, pp. 123–38.

Williamson, O.E. (1971), 'The Vertical Integration of Production: Market Failure Considerations', *American Economic Review*, LXI, pp. 112–23.

Williamson, O.E. (1973), 'Markets and Hierarchies: Some Elementary Considerations', *American Economic Review*, LXIII, pp. 316–25.

Williamson, O.E. (1975), *Markets and Hierarchies: Analysis and Antitrust Implications*, New York: The Free Press.

Williamson, O.E. (1976a), 'Franchise Bidding for Natural Monopolies – in General and With Respect to CATV', *Bell Journal of Economics*, VII, pp. 73–104.

Williamson, O.E. (1976b), 'The Economics of Internal Organization: Exit and Voice in Relation to Markets and Hierarchies', *American Economic Review*, *Papers and Proceedings*, LXVI, pp. 369–76.

Williamson, O.E. (1979a), 'Assessing Market Restrictions: Antitrust Ramifications of the Transaction Cost Approach', *University of Pennsylvania Law Review*, CXXVII, pp. 953–93.

Williamson, O.E. (1979b), 'Transaction-Cost Economics: The Governance of Contractual Relations', *Journal of Law and Economics*, XXII, pp. 233–262.

Williamson, O.E. (1979c), 'Public Policy on Saccharin: The Decision Process Approach and its Alternatives', unpublished manuscript.

Williamson, O.E. (1980), 'Emergence of the Visible Hand: Implications for Industrial Organization', in Chandler and Daems (1980, pp. 182–202.)

Williamson, O.E., R.B. Freeman, Dennis R. Young, Albert O. Hirschman and Richard R. Nelson (1976), 'Political Economy: Some Uses of the Exit-Voice Approach', a debate in *American Economic Review*, *Papers and Proceedings*, LXVI, pp. 361–91.

Williamson, O.E., M.L. Wachter and J.E. Harris (1975), 'Understanding the Employment Relationship: The Analysis of Idiosyncratic Exchange', *Bell Journal of Economics*, VI, pp. 250–278.

Zald, M.N. (1969), *Power in Organizations*, Nashville, Tennessee: Vanderbilt University Press.

Index

Hashimoto, M., 19, 33, 207
Hayek, F. A., 138, 207
Heath, A., 199, 207
Herding, R., 125, 207
Heuss, E., 65, 207
Hicks, J. R., 77, 188n, 207
Hickson, D. J., 205, 209
Hierarchies
 and authority, 4, 9, 93, 102, 113–15, 122, 200
 and competition, 6–11, 44–5, 175–9, 197–9
 and domination, 8–9, 82, 87–8, 93–104, 113–15
 and efficiency, 2–12, 21, 29–34, 85, 108, 110, 116, 118, 122–3, 132, 164–6, 180, 191–2, 198
 and exploitation, 9–10, 162–76
 and power, 11–12, 29, 34, 81, 86, 99, 100–103, 112–16, 134, 165–6, 169, 189–203
 and transaction costs, 2–8, 13–17, 21–4, 32, 43, 85–6, 92, 113, 118–19, 121, 124, 167–8, 198
 and systems of economic control, 17–19, 39–44, 81–158
 empirical evidence on determinants, 47–52, 55–79, 84–9, 99–103
Hinings, C. R., 209
Hirschman, A., 5, 8, 86, 88, 91, 104n, 138, 147, 149, 151–2, 159, 160, 164–6, 169, 171, 175, 207, 211
Hobbes, T., 159
Hollis, M., 202, 207
'Hora and Tempus', 141
Houssiaux, J., 104n
Human capital, 2–3, 18, 27
Hunting band, 54
Huxley, T. H., 203
Hyman, R., 118, 207

Idiosyncratic exchange, 3, 6, 11, 18, 24, 121–2, 126
India, 151
Industrial relations, 5, 12, 117
Industrial sociology, 1, 12, 117–35
Inflation, 19
Influence, 29, 73, 93–4
Information, 9, 15, 29, 44–7, 49, 51, 56, 81–3, 89–92, 95, 112, 144, 152, 162, 168
 information impactedness, 6, 45–6, 83, 109–10, 112, 121, 128, 168, 170
Inside contracting, 107–9, 111
Interdependence, 154–8
Interlocking directorates, 55, 57–64, 72, 77, 79

Internal labour market, 2, 8, 28, 117–18, 121–3, 125–6, 129–32, 134
Interstate Commerce Act of 1887 (US), 79
Intriligator, M. D., 205
IRS, 48–9
Invisible Hand, 92, 161–2

Japan, 28, 39
Jay, A., 54, 208
Job design, 27–8
Joint ventures, 55
Joyce, W., 13

Karpik, L., 104n, 108
Kaufer, E., 22, 78, 208–9
Khandwalla, P. N., 57, 208
Kirzner, I., 193, 196, 208
Klein, B. F., 193, 208
Knight, F., 193
Korsch, K., 179n, 208

Landes, D., 107, 208
Latin America, 173, 179
Lawrence, P., 29, 56, 69, 208
Learning-by-doing, 19, 107, 120
Legitimation, 9, 115, 134, 146, 152, 161, 164, 191
Leibenstein, H., 193, 208
Lindbeck, A., 187, 188n, 208
Logics of action (LA), 97–8, 101
Lorsch, J., 29, 56, 69, 208
Loyalty, 5, 86
Lukes, S., 115, 192, 196, 208

McGuinness, A., 10–11, 180–88, 193
Machiavelli, N., 190
Machlup, F., 188n, 208
Mackenzie, K. D., 29, 208
Macneil, I. R., 26, 208
Macpherson, C. B., 159, 161, 208
Malmgren, H., 24, 208
Managerial discretion, 14
Managerial ideology, 85–7
Mann, M., 131, 205
Mannheim, K., 159
Manufacturing industry, 20, 22, 24
 in Germany, 57–79
 in US, 35–8
March, J. G., 14, 16, 29, 56, 81, 144, 148, 206, 208
Marcus, M., 47, 208
Marglin, S., 9, 108, 127–8, 184–5, 188n, 208
Market failure, 15, 81, 118, 138, 180
Marketing function, 29–30, 34, 44–5, 74, 97, 100

N6